D1058291

SHAKESPEARE IN THE MOVIES

# Shakespeare
## *in the* Movies

From the Silent Era
to *Shakespeare in Love*

DOUGLAS BRODE

OXFORD
UNIVERSITY PRESS
2000

# OXFORD
**UNIVERSITY PRESS**

Oxford   New York
Athens   Auckland   Bangkok   Bogotá   Buenos Aires   Calcutta
Cape Town   Chennai   Dar es Salaam   Delhi   Florence   Hong Kong   Istanbul
Karachi   Kuala Lumpur   Madrid   Melbourne   Mexico City   Mumbai
Nairobi   Paris   São Paulo   Singapore   Taipei   Tokyo   Toronto   Warsaw

and associated companies in
Berlin   Ibadan

Published by Oxford University Press, Inc.
198 Madison Avenue, New York, New York 10016

Oxford is a registered trademark of Oxford University Press

Library of Congress Cataloging-in-Publication Data
Brode, Douglas, 1943–
Shakespeare in the movies : from the silent era to *Shakespeare in Love*
  / Douglas Brode.
p.   cm.
Includes index.
ISBN 0-19-513958-5
1. Shakespeare, William, 1564–1616—Film and video adaptations.
2. English drama—Film and video adaptations.   3. Film adaptations.
I. Title.
PR3093.B76   1999   98-56152
791.43′6—dc21

9 8 7 6 5 4 3 2 1
Printed in the United States of America
on acid-free paper

For Dr. Gerda Taranow,
who taught me to love the Bard
as much as I did the bijou

# CONTENTS

Acknowledgments     ix

INTRODUCTION     3

1. AN AUSPICIOUS OPENING     15
   *The Taming of the Shrew*

2. THE WINTER OF OUR DISCONTENT     26
   *King Richard III*

3. STAR-CROSSED LOVERS     41
   *Romeo and Juliet*

4. A FAIRY TALE FOR GROWN-UPS     60
   *A Midsummer Night's Dream*

5. THE HOLLOW CROWN     71
   *Richard II; Henry IV, Parts I and II; Henry V*

6. SOPHISTICATED COMEDY     85
   *Much Ado About Nothing; As You Like It;*
   *Twelfth Night*

7. A TIDE IN MEN'S LIVES     100
   *Julius Caesar*

8. I KNOW NOT SEEMS     114
   *Hamlet*

9. THE GREEN-EYED MONSTER     151
   *Othello, the Moor of Venice*

10. FATAL VISION     175
    *Macbeth*

11. A WOMAN OF INFINITE VARIETY                    195
     **Antony and Cleopatra**

12. SANS EVERYTHING                                203
     **King Lear**

13. YOU CAN'T GO HOME AGAIN                        218
     **The Winter's Tale** and **The Tempest**

14. PLAYING SHAKESPEARE                            233

15. AS WE GO TO PRESS                              241

    Index                                          243

# ACKNOWLEDGMENTS

With appreciation to Charlton Heston, Scott Leclau, John Liscomb, Kevin Lucas, David and Kathy Ciesielski; Royal Films International, Verona Productions, De Laurentis Cinematografica, American Film Institute, HBO Films (Animated), London Film Productions, Twentieth Century-Fox, Samuel Goldwyn Films, Fine Line Features, Commonwealth Films, Warner Bros., Columbia Pictures, Playboy Productions, Royal Shakespeare Company, Miramax Films, Twin Cities Film, M-G-M, Paramount Pictures, Republic Pictures, Mercury Films, Internacional Films Española, *Hallmark Hall of Fame*, Wisconsin Center for Film and Theater Research, United Artists, Prominent Films, Folio Films, Mogador-Mercury-Castle Hill, Rank Organization, Classic Cinemas, Lenfilm, Edwin Thanhouser, Filmways-Athene, Seven Arts.

SHAKESPEARE IN THE MOVIES

# INTRODUCTION

*Shakespeare would have made a great movie writer.*
  —Orson Welles, stage and screen director

*Shakespeare is no screen writer.*
  —Peter Hall, stage and screen director

## Shakespeare and the Movies

The above quotes, which illustrate the fact that two prominent directors of films based on Shakespearean plays can differ so drastically on the issue of Shakespeare's writing and the movies, make it clear we are wading into dark waters here. Shakespearean cinema is the only subgenre of narrative film that remains the center of an ongoing debate—not only among skeptical literary traditionalists but even those *cinéastes* who make the movies—as to whether it has a right to exist. First, though, to dispose of the traditionalists: critic John Ottenhoff, reviewing *Much Ado About Nothing* for *Christian Century* in 1993, proclaimed his prejudice outright: "My complaints about the limits of [Kenneth] Branagh's film indicate only that no performance can substitute for the richness of reading, discussing, and meditating upon a text."

With the words *no performance*, Ottenhoff dismisses stage as well as screen, expressing a dominant twentieth-century bias toward the Bard. Although academia has, for the better part of our century, been populated by like thinkers, it's important to recall that Gentle Will would strongly disagree. His plays were written to be seen, not read—at least not by anyone other than the company performing them. They were never printed in his lifetime, probably according to his wishes. The plays were meant to be enjoyed in the immediate sense, not as removed literary works to be studied, like butterflies mounted by some eager collector who presses out all the lifeblood and mummifies beauty under glass.

*3*

Orson Welles and Peter Hall, however, are another matter. Both dedicated their lives to bringing the words from the page to the stage—and screen. Hall's line of argument derives from an understanding of the essential difference between live theater and motion pictures as storytelling forms. Film professor Louis Giannetti once claimed that a blind man at a play would miss 25 percent of what was significant, the same amount lost on a deaf person watching a film. Since the advent of the movies, in nonmusical plays the word is primary; in film, however, image dominates. Or, as Hall put it, Shakespeare "is a verbal dramatist, relying on the associative and metaphorical power of words. Action is secondary. What is meant is said." However right for live theater, "this is bad screen writing. A good film script relies on contrasting visual images. What is spoken is of secondary importance."

To a degree, Hall is right, particularly when he speaks of "contrasting visual images." Legendary director and film theorist V. I. Pudovkin asserted back in 1925 that "editing is the basis of all film art." What Peter Hall fails to take into account is that Shakespeare purposefully overwrote. Set design, costuming, special effects, and the like were not always well-represented in low-budget Elizabethan theater, which made it sometimes necessary for the writer to compensate for lack of production values by vividly describing everything.

## Shakespeare Without Tears

Charlton Heston, Shakespearean stage actor as well as Hollywood superstar, made this point vividly clear (as well as the need for a nonreverential attitude, what Margaret Webster tagged "Shakespeare Without Tears") in his published journals. Heston writes, "Not every line has gold in it. If [a line] has no [poetic] treasure and doesn't advance the plot or character, it should be cut. This is sacrilege to people who read and write about Shakespeare. People who *do* Shakespeare, [however,] cut him. I'd bet my soul that Shakespeare cut Shakespeare." It's a bet he would win: References in the texts mention "two hours running time," implying that the complete script, as we know it today, was but a game plan for shortened, energetic performances.

Shakespeare's approach resembles that of a moviemaker who shoots three times as much film as he could ever use. Today's auteurs speak of "discovering" the movie in the editing room; when

Shakespeare and his producer-star Richard Burbage mounted plays, there was no such thing as a director in the modern theatrical or cinematic sense—and probably few or no rehearsals, which is unheard of in contemporary theater but the norm with movies. Burbage and Shakespeare, collaborating with everyone else in their company, apparently "discovered" the show each night—shortening or lengthening action, adding or deleting comedy, altering the tone as they performed before ever-changing audiences, which varied between respectable, middle-class types one evening and a grotesque mix of university intellects and uneducated street people the next.

This mix sounds more like audiences at mall multiplexes than those precious few who attend regional theater and desire to soak up sophistication. Today Shakespeare's name may be synonymous with Western culture, but the Bard's own audiences were interested only in a bloody good time. His plays, filled with murders, sexual transgressions, ghosts, and witches, have more in common with the latest blockbusters than anything on the art-house circuit. Critics of Shakespeare's time scoffed, dismissing him in comparison to the loftier (and better-educated) Christopher Marlowe and Ben Jonson. Shakespeare was the bravura crowd pleaser, the Elizabethan predecessor to Cecil B. DeMille and Steven Spielberg, not to William Wyler or Merchant-Ivory.

Respect for the Bard was a long time coming; support among the public, on the other hand was immediate. The mob loved Shakespeare in his time and has continued to feel that way for several centuries. On the American frontier cowboys and miners crowded the Bird Cage Theater in Tombstone, Arizona, whenever a touring Shakespeare company hit town, as portrayed in the films *My Darling Clementine* (1946) and *Tombstone* (1993). In the early part of our century, the first moviemakers, hardly a classy lot, fashioned short flicks from Shakespeare's plays for déclassé immigrants. The Bard was, at film's dawn, a big draw with the common man; how his name shortly became box-office poison will be considered in due time.

As opposed to Peter Hall, Orson Welles seized upon the fact that traditional plays are written in acts, which are the essential building block of stage drama. Likewise, the fewer changes of scenery, the better. Since the 1870s the one-set, two- or three-act play has been the norm. Turning a play into a film makes as much sense, in the words of critic Louis Kronenberger, as "cutting up a sofa to make a chair." Welles agreed: "You can't put a play on the screen. I don't believe in that." Thus, in addition to original screenplays like *Citi-*

zen *Kane*, Welles adapted novels (*The Magnificent Ambersons*, *The Lady From Shanghai*, and Kafka's *Trial*) to the screen. Never, though, did he film a play—other than Shakespeare's. As Welles understood, they aren't plays at all; rather, they are screenplays, written, ironically, three centuries before the birth of cinema.

## An Unworthy Scaffold

Like Leonardo da Vinci attempting to invent the helicopter centuries before its time, Shakespeare and his contemporaries reached into what would eventually be called cinematic territory. A film script is composed of some fifty to seventy-five brief scenes, with rapidly changing locations, and that's how the Bard constructed his works. Those five-act divisions, featured in every published volume, were added *after* Shakespeare's death, beginning with the First Folio, to faciliate reading. When Gentle Will sat down to write, his unit of construction was the cinematic scene, not the theatrical act. Structurally speaking, then, his plays seem suited to the screen; those of more theatrically oriented artists often defy cinematic treatment.

"Old Will would have loved the movies," Welles gleefully exclaimed, considering how difficult it was to portray convincingly ancient Scotland or classical Rome on the humble boards. "You can't put that on a stage," he added, "but you can film it!" Shakespeare himself dismissed his theater as "an unworthy scaffold," apologizing at the beginning of *King Henry V* for the lack of what we call theater magic. "Let us," his Chorus implores, mere ". . . ciphers to this great accompt [Britain's victory over France at Agincourt], On your imaginary forces work." He begged the audience to "Piece out our imperfections with your thoughts," since the minuscule costuming budget necessitated that "your thoughts . . . now must deck our kings."

His theater, then, was an active rather than passive experience, each viewer urged to collaborate in the creative process. The work finally comes to life in the audience's mind, which is precisely how the greatest filmmakers work. Alfred Hitchcock explained that in *Psycho*'s famed shower sequence he never showed a knife actually touching Janet Leigh's body. What transformed that horrific moment into anxiety-provoking art rather than exploitation was that the deadly penetrations took place not on-screen but in the viewer's mind. Similarly, film historian Roger Manvell noted, "The cinema can, much better than the modern theater, match the fluidity of action on the Shakespearean stage."

Not everyone would agree. In 1953, author and critic Eric Bentley, reviewing *Julius Caesar* for the *New Republic*, insisted: "The now widespread notion that Shakespeare's plays are 'filmic' is true only to the extent that they are made up of an unbroken succession of short scenes." Other than this, Bentley argued that "the actual filming of Shakespeare never fails to remind us how utterly he belongs to the stage." By "us," of course, Bentley means "me." Because his theory proceeds from a flawed premise: A specific failure on the part of a single film's director reveals a more generalized and unsolvable problem. John Gielgud as a Cassius, Bentley reasoned, "who walks through a real street loudly talking to himself can only seem demented." On the stage, ancient Rome is suggested rather than re-created, and this convention works.

Bentley confuses director Joseph Mankiewicz's handling of that moment (more accurately, Mankiewicz's failure to cinematically handle it) with the greater issue of whether the problem can be handled at all. In Laurence Olivier's *Hamlet* a solitary speech is effectively presented as a voice-over, which is the perfect cinematic equivalent of a Shakespearean soliloquy.

## All the World's a Stage

Another scribe went further still, stating that iambic pentameter (characters speaking in a stylized rather than realistic manner) rendered Shakespeare irreconcilable with the cinema. "The basic trouble with any Shakespearean film," critic Richard Mallett asserted in *Punch*, is that "the more circumstances and scenery are made lifelike and convincing, the less easy it is to accept the convention of heightened, rhetorical, rhythmical dialogue." If Mallett were right, then musical movies such as *On the Town*—in which Frank Sinatra and Gene Kelly sing their lines while dancing around a real New York—ought not to work. But here's the rub: Under Stanley Donen's inspired direction, it does.

Mallett is wrongheaded when he suggests that cinematic *mise en scène* is essentially realistic. Masterpieces of 1920s German Expressionism and the following decade's Universal horror films make clear (as do Tim Burton's *Edward Scissorhands* or David Lynch's *Wild at Heart*) that mainstream movies can stretch into surrealism. Then again, even seemingly naturalistic sets in movies by realists like Sidney Lumet (*Dog Day Afternoon*) are, if that filmmaker is to be believed, more subtly stylized than is initially obvious. Simply put, audiences accept stars who sing and dance while inhabiting the everyday world or actors who speak ordinary phrases while passing through a fabricated fairy-tale setting.

The cinema is far richer in possibility than simple minds would have it and is able to accommodate Shakespeare's heightened poetry or operatic performance if only the filmmaker is up to the task. Franco Zeffirelli, who has happily filmed Verdi and Shakespeare, proved that decades ago.

Let us grant, then, that Shakespearean cinema has a right to exist; how should any adapter rightly proceed? Of all people, traditionalist Ottenhoff (who argued against even *staging* Shakespeare!) offered the best suggestion, calling for "films that not only preserve the complexity of the Bard's words but also present a distinctive cinematic interpretation." That is, films boasting a faithfulness to Shakespeare's essence, tempered by an understanding of cinema's resources.

Nonetheless, a tension between the Bard and the bijou will never go away, at least not entirely. As critic Stanley Kauffmann noted in the *Saturday Review*: "The besetting trouble of Shakespeare on film [is] the conflict between a work that lives in its language and a medium that tries to do without language as much as it can." The glass, however, can be perceived as half full rather than half empty; attempting to bridge that gap between verbal and visual has led to highly appreciated bridges.

## A Dagger of the Mind

The director of Shakespearean cinema is akin to an Arthurian knight searching for the Holy Grail, on a quest to achieve the impossible dream by reconciling Shakespeare's immortal poetry with cinema's potent imagery. Even at its most successful, Kauffmann warned, "the result is still a bastard form—a hybrid of two antagonistic arts." Perhaps antagonistic is too strong a word; let's refer to poetry and pictures as polar, diametrically apart but not necessarily mutually exclusive.

For instance, when Macbeth spots the blade before him and wonders if it is but "a dagger of the mind," do we necessarily have to see it? The movie medium, via special effects and postproduction, is able to manage an apparition in some ways live theater cannot. Still, showing us the dagger mitigates the significant notion that what Macbeth sees is "of the mind" and therefore visible only to him. If the filmmaker does choose to show the dagger, is it then his responsibility to do so in such a way that we grasp that we're sharing Macbeth's subjective reality rather than gazing on something that is truly there? Then again, who's to say, for sure, whether the dagger is there or not? Macbeth questions, but does not deny, its existence.

If the director does show the dagger, perhaps it ought to be blurred, cinematically suggesting that mental state Macbeth describes. Finally, there is the possibility that the line Shakespeare assigns Macbeth ought to be excised entirely, if the viewer is to be treated to an image, to avoid redundancy. We need to see or hear, but not both.

As early as 1936, author and critic Mark Van Doren wrote, in the *Nation*, that the key question "is not whether the text as such is sacred. For movie purposes it certainly is *not*. The question is whether the whole of Shakespeare's effect in a given play can somehow be preserved on the screen." It's more important to be true to the spirit than the letter.

How, then, should a producer proceed? Hire a genius like Welles, a true auteur whose unique style perfectly conveys a personal vision? Such a director imposes his own perception of life on works by the Bard, resulting in remarkable films that may thematically contradict what Shakespeare intended. Or should the producer hire a skillful technician, say British director Stuart Burge, who will mount respectable adaptations? Shakespeare's text will be presented by a filmmaking approach best described as a recording device rather than film, in early theorist Rudolf Arnheim's words, as an original art form.

## Auteur! Auteur!

What, in other words, is primary here? Is the play the thing or the cinema itself? Who is the auteur? Is the dominant artist Shakespeare or his latest screen adapter? The question is easy to raise, but any answer is frustratingly elusive. Every film version of a Shakespearean play, then, is much more than just another movie, something even more than another movie derived from a work by the world's greatest poet. It is, whether or not the filmmakers are aware of the fact, a fighting document—a unique, singular, debatable, and more often than not, temporary interpretation. "Temporary" became an increasingly more significant issue during the second half of the twentieth century. In his tome *Future Shock*, Alvin Toffler defined modernism as changes occurring so quickly that we barely adjust to one before it's out of date. This forces us to drop what was relevant moments earlier and move on to the next.

Shakespearean cinema is not immune from this situation. Frank Kermode, writing in the *New York Review*, noted: "There was a time, in the history of the movies, when a man might make a version of a Shakespeare play and expect it to last for many years. That time has passed . . . because the very concept of the 'classic' performance has withered." In fact, it began withering during that all-important transitional period between 1967 and 1973, when the very notion of permanence (and, with it, an abiding respect for any ongoing tradition) all but disappeared from an ever-changing culture composed of immediately disposable pop artifacts. The classic performance of yore could be exemplified by Max Reinhardt's approach to his *Midsummer Night's Dream* (1935). The story is set in a never-never land, historically true to no time period but poetically true for all time.

Modernists travel a different route. Lord Michael Birkett, who collaborated with director Peter Hall on *A Midsummer Night's Dream* (1968), articulated why star Diana Rigg wore a minidress—a perfect fashion statement for the moment, though soon passé.

> Producers of Shakespeare used to console themselves that even if their films didn't earn much money at the time, they would somehow [gradually make the producers] rich in their old age. Being "classics," these films were bound to be shown somewhere every year and would continue to earn small residuals forever. Nowadays, it's likely to be only the most recent film version which is played, and older versions may become out of date—or rarely shown. . . . The exclusivity a filmmaker used to have over a Shakespeare subject is a thing of the past.

This explains why two versions of *Richard III* (Ian McKellen's and Al Pacino's) appeared almost simultaneously in 1996 and why the Zeffirelli–Mel Gibson *Hamlet* (1990) barely had time to become the new standard before being replaced by Kenneth Branagh's.

This raises another key question: Why the sudden proliferation of Shakespearean cinema? To answer that, we must first return to the birth of cinema. Shakespeare was all the rage with the masses who had just passed through Ellis Island, even as he had been for more than thirty decades. During this time, academia had little use for Shakespeare or, for that matter, live theater; poesy remained the domain of the ivory-tower elite. Some twenty years into the new century, academic liberals urged acceptance of plays and novels as valid literature worthy of study. By 1927, the same year sound was introduced to motion pictures, university students were studying the Bard; Shakespeare became the darling of academics, who immediately set out to tell the public at large that Will, as a literary giant, was beyond their comprehension.

Sadly, even tragically, the people listened, agreed, and turned away in droves. For the bulk of the following century, Shakespeare remained a hard sell to that very common man for whom the plays had been written. Part of the problem was that people were now forced to read him in junior high school and, suffering through the all-but-unintelligible Elizabethan English, recoiled at the thought of ever choosing to see Shakespeare in production. Ironically, that's just where the words would have been rendered clear by the body language and vocal inflection of actors.

## Deconstructing Will

How, then, does one explain today's teenagers, hardly more informed than their predecessors, lining up to see a hip-hop *Romeo and Juliet* while producers rush one Shakespearean feature into production after another? Not surprisingly, resurgent popularity with ordinary people occurred even as the academic pendulum swung back. The new order of academia sniffed that Shakespeare was politically incorrect. His plays are filled with gay-bashing gags, and he believes in the institution of marriage. As critic Jack Kroll noted in *Newsweek*: "This is an age apparently determined to debard the Bard, who has been called names like 'a black hole . . . a verbocrat' by scholars burying him under a lava flow of deconstructionism, new historicism, neo-Marxism, genderism and other ismatic attacks."

English departments at major universities, where Shakespeare had been the essential core, changed their titles to things like Textual Studies. Will was scoffed at as nothing more than another of those dead white males whose work had too long dominated the literary canon. Shakespeare would still be studied, but in a radically different context. A course examining feminist issues might include *Taming of the Shrew* or *Macbeth* as "texts," reduced to objects worthy only of scornful analysis as reactionary artifacts, revealing the conservative male's outmoded, offensive approach to women.

The perfection of the poetry, superb story structure, and well-rounded characterizations, once the basis of the academic approach, were now secondary at best. The public responded by reembracing the Bard, his plays, and, for the past century, films fashioned from them. Academia's loss is the public's gain. As ordinary people inhabiting the real world rediscovered the eternal beauty and ongoing wisdom to be found in these works, the Bard and the bijou became more inseparable than ever before.

## Toward an Aesthetic

The vision of Shakespeare's individual plays, like the more serious-minded motion pictures of today, results from two elements: the personality of the artist himself and the overriding worldview of the period during which his work was created. This meeting of man and moment culminates in an *oeuvre*, a body of work that, perceived from an overview, expresses a consistent, if gradually changing, "take" on life. Though there are basic themes to all his plays, we can also note a progression from young swain in love with the possibilities of life to mature middle-aged man to embittered bourgeois to forgiving elder statesman at last understanding and accepting his place in the universe.

We know that after arriving in London at a tender age to begin a life in the theater, Will carried considerable psychological baggage along with him. It is apparent from his writings that Shakespeare rejected extreme notions of a simple choice between good and evil in favor of a darker, more complex view of man: each of us torn by forces of brightness and darkness coexisting in a single shell, no one among us entirely pure, and redemption through purgative action always possible. That's what his greatest heroes achieve; in this regard, Shakespeare is the predecessor of our century's Alfred Hitchcock, who likewise explored the dual nature of man.

As a boy, he had probably been warned by parents and preachers of the need to reject natural impulses. Despite evidence that, on the whole, Will was a model youth, he slipped once—and once was enough. Anne Hathaway, eight years Shakespeare's senior, became pregnant, perhaps during an afternoon's dalliance with the lad. A hasty marriage was followed, six months later, by the couple's first child. Then rumors spread that the child might not be Will's; Anne might have been pregnant by another when she met and seduced him. If so, such shame may be what drove Will from Stratford to London—and, in good time, fame, fortune, and immortality. His loss in life was our gain, resulting in the greatest body of literary work ever produced.

The play, he sensed, was the thing by which he could warn young people in his audience of the mistake he had made; *Romeo and Juliet*, widely misunderstood as a paeon to romantic love, is in fact an antiromantic cautionary fable. The role-model teenagers avoid carnal consummation of their feelings until they've become loving friends and their union has been blessed by the church. Concerning Shakespeare's tendency to preach in ultraconventional terms, George Bernard Shaw complained of "the atmosphere of a rented pew." Certainly theater was, for Shakespeare, a bully pulpit: The issue of women's "frailty"—whether females can be trusted by the men who love them—is a key thread running through the comedies as well as the tragedies. It is as essential to *Much Ado About Nothing* as to *Othello*. Each play, then, is yet another variation on the theme that may have haunted Shakespeare's mind, soul, and his very being every day of his life.

Moreover, he was acutely aware of social issues. Rebellion, a dirty word to him personally, likewise appeared an unwise political option. Elizabeth I ruled England brilliantly, but without a man by her side. The Virgin Queen's genius as a ruler commanded Will's respect, but from his writings it appears that her lifestyle caused him to worry that, without a proper heir, the country might again fall into the civil wars England had endured during the War of the Roses (1455–1485). This may explain why the comedies, beginning with *The Taming of the Shrew*, urge a remarkable woman to marry; the tragedies, starting with *Julius Caesar*, deal with the disaster that follows any killing of a ruler (there were numerous attempts on the lives of Elizabeth and later James I); and the history pageant shows the horrors of an "Aengland" divided against itself.

Shakespeare did not cover the reign of every English king, only those whose stories could provide him with proper material for what he had to say. He chose only to dramatize those stories from the past that allowed him to make a comment on the present for the future good of his country. In his time, anachronistic costumes and settings were the order of the day; actors often had to provide their own costumes and appeared onstage, whatever the ostensible period, dressed as Elizabethans, adding an immediate contemporary edge to old tales. Modern directors often set those plays in diverse periods, suggesting that the tales ring true for *any* time. Or they use modern garb and rehearsal clothes, implying that Shakespeare's vision rings true for *all* time. This works because the stage is essentially an abstract medium. Film, however, is the most specific of storytelling forms, forcing moviemakers into a uniquely difficult situation.

Should *Romeo and Juliet* be set in an authentically rendered fifteenth-century Renaissance Verona, though Shakespeare obviously knew little about that era? Is it correct, as Franco Zeffirelli did, to mount a film of that play in precisely accurate historical costume but cast British stage actors, since audiences expect English accents from anything by the Bard? Is it permissible, as in the case of Baz Luhrmann's hip-hop variation, to cast popular teenage stars and set them in modern Miami while keeping the iambic pentameter intact? Should a dramatization of *Julius Caesar* be set against an accurately rendered vision of Rome, though Shakespeare's characters hear anachronistic clocks ringing?

Literary critic Maynard Mack once considered "the world of *Hamlet*," and he insisted that the imaginary place had less to do with ancient Denmark than with Elizabethan England. Shakespeare also delved into what can only be considered existential terrain: Man, as Kurt Weill put it centuries later, lost in the stars, surviving in what he dreads may be a God-abandoned universe. That holds true for each of Shakespeare's plays; all take place in a universe that, locations of individual stories aside, are part and parcel of the world according to Will. Today, then, the difficult but fascinating task of a filmmaker is to decide how that philosophical and psychological terrain can best be visualized.

# 1

# AN AUSPICIOUS OPENING
## *The Taming of the Shrew*

### Prologue: Three Early Comedies

Shakespeare started his playwrighting career with a trio of history plays (*King Henry VI*, Parts I, II, and III); he next turned to the popular genre of comedy. In quick succession, Will knocked off three agreeable minor works that still find their way into the stage repertoire: *The Comedy of Errors, Love's Labour's Lost*, and *The Two Gentlemen of Verona*. Our youthful playwright emulated the Roman comedies of Plautus, adapting that master's classical plots of mistaken identity and frustrated love to his English idiom. Despite the ongoing appeal of the plays, there have been no major Hollywood or European attempts to film any of them.

Two films borrowed elements from *The Comedy of Errors*, but neither can be called Shakespeare's. Vitagraph's silent 1908 version of *Errors* reproduced little from the Bard but his title. Audiences had to wait until 1940 when *The Boys from Syracuse*, Universal Pictures' mounting of the George Abbott–Richard Rodgers–Lorenz Hart stage show, premiered. The film starred Allan Jones and Joe Penner as master and servant who, like the Bard's Antipholus and Dromio, discover each has a double. Also starring were Martha Raye, Rosemary Lane, and Irene Hervey as the female leads. The musical is as appealingly stilted as its Broadway predecessor and, for that matter, Shakespeare's own agreeably forced farce, yet it is only loosely derived from the Bard's work.

## The Taming of the Shrew

*I come to wive it wealthily in Padua.*

—Petruchio

What's now called the "period of early comedies" concluded, in 1593, with a fourth work, *The Taming of the Shrew*, Will's most ambitious play thus far and important as his first successful attempt to employ an audience-pleasing form of entertainment for the purpose of personal expression. Shakespeare had hastily married a woman who, in the vernacular, was considered a shrew. The term did not then imply an ugly crone; rather, a handsome, if high-spirited, woman capable of great sensuality tempered by an iron will. Anne Hathaway's infamously sharp tongue may have caused Gentle Will to secretly wonder what sort of strutting male might tame her. Understandably, Will was sensitive to the existence of such situations in the pop culture of his time. Farmers sang the bawdy ballad "A Merry Geste of a Shrewd and Curst Wyfe" while delivering wares to the marketplace in Stratford's rustic streets.

After arriving in London, Shakespeare had come to admire (from afar) another "shrew" as intensely as he now admonished Anne. Queen Elizabeth had spurned a wide array of suitors, from Lord Essex to Walter Raleigh, and ruled alone. The Bard-to-be basked in the reflected glory of the great things Elizabeth had achieved for England during its renaissance. He was to remain an almost uncritical admirer of, even an apologist for, her less popular decisions. Secretly, though, Shakespeare probably shuddered over what he considered the great ruler's tragic flaw, a single failing that could ultimately undo all the good she had accomplished. Elizabeth, the Virgin Queen, would leave no clear-cut heir.

This, he knew from Holinshed's *Chronicles of England, Scotland and Ireland*, was bad—very bad. Although he was only a lowly playwright, perhaps Shakespeare employed his art as the queen's conscience, reminding her, in the guise of divertissements, that England's supreme ruler, like every good citizen, must avoid civil strife. In Elizabeth's case, she had not married during her childbearing years, nor had she named a successor. Of course, any such message had to be implied rather than stated so as not to offend the queen. Likewise, it had to amuse the general audience, ever hungry for a good time at the theater. What better approach than to endow a subgenre of comedy with a serious subtext?

A roughhewn shrew play, the text long lost and precise title unknown, had proved successful shortly before Shakespeare began writing. Simultaneous with Will's work, a similar play, *The Taming of a Shrew*, was in performance with Lord Pembroke's competing company. In his own unique and superior version, however, Shakespeare combined, for the first time, his despised wife with the beloved queen, resulting in his first great female character, Katharina.

Shakespeare was also expanding his range by devising more complex plots. Onto the straightforward story line he grafted a different fable. From George Gascoigne's *Supposes*, he lifted the tale of an appealing young nobleman (called Lucentio in Shakespeare) who changes places with his servant to woo and win a lovely lady, Bianca. To properly fuse the preexisting stories, Shakespeare devised an inspired concept: Bianca would be Katharina's demure younger sister; the sweet thing's romance would be blocked by Baptista, father to both girls, insisting the shrewish Kate be married before her much-desired sibling could.

Also hinting at his budding genius was Shakespeare's decision to add a prologue, lifted from "The Sleeper Awakened," a tale he'd found in the *Arabian Nights* anthology. Christopher Sly, a humble tinker, is discovered drunk and asleep in an alehouse by a Lord. This nobleman plays a mean trick, changing places with the lout, allowing Sly to wake and believe he's an aristocrat and that Sly's entire life as a tinker is nothing more than a single night's bad dream. The play proper is presented as an entertainment for this gullible soul, with the Elizabethan audience watching *The Taming of the Shrew* over Sly's shoulder, utilizing the theatrical device of a play within a play.

The sequence includes an early incarnation of the recurring warning against overindulgence in drink that runs through later plays, culminating in the character of Falstaff. Sophisticated ideas, fully developed during the next fifteen years, have their germination in this "induction" to *The Taming of the Shrew*. The very nature of the theatrical experience (a play within a play) as a fitting subject for popular theater presages Marshall McLuhan's notion that "the medium is the message," and various theories of deconstruction, by some four hundred years. A pre-Freudian psychological notion of interpreting dreams as reality distilled is hinted at here.

The framing device serves as perfect appetizer for the play proper. Scholar Hardin Craig summarized Shakespeare's intent: "There is method to Petruchio's madness from the start. He wishes to make Kate see herself as others see her, and for *her benefit* he transforms himself into an image of unreasonable conduct." This explains why *The Taming of the Shrew* remains popular even in our postfeminist age. In other shrew plays, the male conqueror tames a haughty woman for his own benefit through what we consider physical abuse. Shakespeare's hero hungers to make a remarkable, if temperamental, woman understand she must meet the world halfway for the greater good of herself—and everyone.

Today the key challenge in mounting *The Taming of the Shrew* is to create a tone which conveys to a modern audience that it is about achieving equality, not male dominance. Also tricky is the balance of the Lucentio-Bianca plot, penned in the sophisticated style of Italian Renaissance comedy of intrigue, with the broad, burlesque-like Kate-Petruchio main plot.

## Early Efforts

The first-known film version neatly sidestepped such issues. During the era of nickelodeons, director William Curran knocked out a twelve-minute featurette called *Taming of the Shrew* for the immigrant audience that attended early flickers. Sandwiched between vaudeville acts at New York's Stanley Theater, this turn-of-the-century minimovie concerned a pathetic would-be boxer, One Punch McTague (Eddie Gribbon), who develops a mad crush on a literary lady, Ethel (Mildred June). She attempts to civilize her Hairy Ape by introducing him to the Bard, hoping that Will's music will soothe the savage breast of McTague, a variation of the coarse hero in Frank Norris's then-popular naturalistic novel *McTeague*. As Ethel reads *Shrew*, McTague dreams that he, like Petruchio, might conquer his own Kate; the relationship of life to literature is fascinatingly present in this crude one-reeler.

America's first great director, D. W. Griffith, attempted a more authentic version in 1908, with Florence Lawrence (nicknamed the "Biograph Girl," the first true star of motion pictures) cast as Kate and Arthur Johnson as Petruchio. Griffith has been called the Shakespeare of the cinema; Kate, the self-reliant yet virginal hero, was as appropriate a heroine for Griffith as she had been to Will. Mack Sennett, Griffith's then assistant, served as second-unit director, turning Petruchio's servants into predecessors of the comic clowns and Keystone Kops he would shortly create in Southern California. That same year, Lamberto Azeglio directed an Italian version entitled *La Bisbetica Domata*, with considerably more attention paid to the establishment of a vivid *mise en scène*.

Silent versions of *The Taming of the Shrew* were shot in England and France in 1911; Barker Will, in collaboration with theatrical director F. R. Benson, recorded a stage adaptation originally performed in Stratford; Henry Desfontaines mounted a brief Gallic interpretation with Romuald Joube and Jean Herve. The biggest, and best, of the silent-screen versions was that of Italy's Ambrosio Arturo; in 1913, he starred Eleuterio Rodolfi in a then-epic twenty-two-minute retelling.

### "Kiss me, Kate!"
## *The Taming of the Shrew*
United Artists, 1929; Sam Taylor

There were no other American films of a play which would seem easily adaptable to silent slapstick. Though *The Taming of the Shrew* continued to delight audiences via Broadway revivals, Hollywood didn't approach it again until 1929, when United Artists (U.A.) simultaneously filmed silent and sound versions. The decision was economic: Since only half the country's theaters had completed their conversion to sound, U.A. hoped to ensure that this major feature (the first, and only, costarring Mary Pickford and husband Douglas Fairbanks Sr.) could be shown everywhere.

In 1966, when Pickford rereleased the classic, critic Philip K. Scheuer of the *Los Angeles Times* praised what he incorrectly believed to be exceptionally fluid filmmaking for its time. He stated: "Surprisingly they don't seem to have been confined at all by the camera and sound-booth strictures of that then-newfangled medium, the talking picture; this version of *The Taming of the Shrew* gets around so spryly that [before long] you've all but forgotten it's Shakespeare." Apparently, Scheuer was unaware that for the rerelease print producer Matty Kempo reduced the film from its original length of seventy-three minutes to sixty-six, intercutting action scenes from the silent version shot with the free and fluid camera that characterized presound cinema. The sound film had been static; the "new" version was calculated to accommodate modern audiences, unlikely to sit still for a filmed play.

Even the play, however, was less than pure Shakespeare. In the most embarrassing screen credit of all time, the sound version listed "additional dialogue by director-adapter Sam Taylor," which explains why, during the first meeting of the loving antagonists, things go something like this:

PETRUCHIO: Howdy, Kate.

KATE:     Katherine to you, mug.

Although Charlie Chaplin (who founded U.A. with friends Fairbanks, Pickford, and D. W. Griffith) is not credited, it's easy to believe he lent a helping hand in creating tone, atmosphere, and comedic sensibility. Most of Shakespeare's dialogue is replaced with knockabout comedy of the Sennett-Chaplin variety. Actors whack each other regularly, whereas the Bard's intention had been to purposefully cut back on physical abuse found in earlier shrew plays. Such physical-comedy sparring holds up on its own vulgar level and is preferable to the overwrought dialogue. Pickford and Fairbanks, like most silent-screen stars, were ill suited to sound, owing to their reliance on an exaggerated mimelike approach that had compensated for the lack of speaking voices. Sadly, they continued acting in that manner after sound was added.

At least Fairbanks, with his athletic agility, seemed right, in terms of physicality and star persona, for Petruchio. Not so Pickford, who patented an early-Hollywood, late-Victorian vision of extreme sweetness combined with quiet strength. If the public in the Roaring Twenties was ready for more complicated screen women, they did not want the "Girl With the Curl" to play such roles. Mary was anything but a shrew; playing one, she worked against the grain of her natural gifts.

The more restrained Bianca (Dorothy Jordan) subplot was allowed only one early scene, then unceremoniously dumped, paring away any hope of a complex comedy. Finally, the film appeared to suddenly stop rather than truly end when all the main characters enjoyed a round of drinks, following Petruchio's demand, "Kiss me, Kate!" In its time, this *Shrew* was accepted as an end-of-decade retrowarning; Kate's decision to domesticate, while swearing allegiance to her male as master, implied it was time for aging flappers, having enjoyed their decade-long fling, to do much the same thing. After all, the Great Depression *had* put an end to wild, wanton living. The pendulum had swung, and America turned socially conservative once more. So did Hollywood, as evidenced by this film's interpretation of Shakespeare's immortal play.

## A Long Lapse; Theatrical Interlude

If nothing else, the couple (who would shortly separate) established the play's twentieth-century identity: a perfect showcase for a husband-wife acting team, causing audiences to wonder if the two employed Shakespeare's poetry to allow their public a sneak peek into the stars' real-life relationship. *The Taming of the Shrew* became the vehicle of choice for the greatest husband-wife stage team of the thirties and forties, Alfred Lunt and Lynne Fontanne. Drawing on the knockabout quality Doug and Mary introduced while wisely sensing that the public would forever after expect such antics, the classy couple accommodated to public taste by including sight gags, a first for this duo. The stars thus introduced highbrow audiences to low-jinks comedy, in the process making vaudevillian shtick acceptable in elegant theaters nationwide. In so doing, they cemented the association of cinematic slapstick with this Shakespearean piece.

### "Some Chat With Her"
### *The Taming of The Shrew*
Verona Productions, 1967; Franco Zeffirelli

In the mid-sixties, *The Taming of the Shrew* seemed a natural for Elizabeth Taylor and Richard Burton. The two met on the set of her epic *Cleopatra*. Dick (onetime serious Shakespearean actor and B-list Hollywood star for more than a decade) was rushed in as a replacement for the departing Stephen Boyd, who sensed disaster in the air. When their infamous offscreen affair eventually culminated in wedlock (each was married to another when they met), Liz and Dick existed in a twilight zone between postscandal notoriety and born-again respectabilty. They starred in a superficial soap opera, *The Sandpiper*, as well as the serious drama *Who's Afraid of Virginia Woolf?* Burton, however, hungered to return to his roots (*Hamlet* on Broadway), while Liz was eager to try the Bard, and both wanted to do a comedy.

"In theory, it is unfair to bring actors' off-screen lives into a discussion of their on-screen performances," Moira Walsh wrote in *America*. "Nevertheless, in some cases the juxtaposition is unavoidable. When they chose this particular vehicle, the Burtons must have been wryly aware that this would happen and perhaps, still more hardheadedly, have counted on the public's morbid curiosity to add a little box-office insurance to an otherwise financially risky undertaking." As to monetary considerations, it's worth noting that Taylor and Burton produced the film themselves, contributing their considerable salaries to cover growing expenses. Not surprisingly, then, there were none of the temperamental scenes that, three years earlier, caused *Cleopatra* to go grotesquely over budget. Forsaking late-night drinking bouts, the two concentrated on making the best possible picture at the most economical price.

Wisely sensing that 1967 was a watershed year in movie history (*The Graduate, Bonnie and Clyde,* etc.), the Burtons refused to hire some Hollywood pro as director. Instead, they decided, with some element of risk involved, to allow a talented, if controversial, young stage artist to make his cinema debut. Franco Zeffirelli, a seasoned opera veteran, planned to employ his considerable gifts for lavish, ornate staging. Since he also wanted to make a naturalistic movie, his first screen effort would play as a true film rather than a recorded stage play. This dual ambition led to a midway approach between the extremes. Though Zeffirelli did not film on actual locations, instead mounting his production on four immense soundstages near Rome, he labored to create (in collaboration with designer Renzo Mongiardino) a set appropriate for a film which would combine Shakespeare's stylized dialogue with the realism expected by the film's target audience.

From the opening, the mock sixteenth-century Padua streets, depicted as deliriously winding, are crammed full of robust people, some motley in appearance, others handsomely attired. Also, braying animals, piles of vegetables (fresh or rotting), plus all sorts of wares vied for the viewer's attention. To keep the image from being a studio romanticization, Zeffirelli also included piles of garbage and a great deal of dirt. Such richly textured detail was captured on pre-exposed color film, which produced a mellow ocher glow. Thus, Zeffirelli achieved his twofold purpose: a dream vision of a real place. Burton and Taylor were attracted to Zeffirelli after realizing that his stagings were intended to return opera to the common man, the contemporary equivalent of the English unwashed that Shakespeare had comfortably played to.

"We intend to make Shakespeare as successful a screenwriter as Abby Mann," the director announced at the onset, making everyone aware of his personal vision. Over the centuries, Shakespeare had come to be perceived as the essence of what we reverently call "the classics"; Zeffirelli spearheaded the movement to cut away any such vision. His intent was to rescue the plays from their exalted reputation, making them fun again. No wonder, then, that Zeffirelli portrayed on-screen those moments that Shakespeare had (regrettably, one assumes) left offstage. In particular, the wedding of Petruchio and Kate, to which the groom casually arrives less than fashionably late.

The Petruchio of Zeffirelli and Burton turns the ceremony into something on the order of Groucho Marx in *A Night at the Opera*, a zany anarchist gleefully destroying a solemn social situation. Zeffirelli also added an extended chase, drawing on the long-established slapstick approach to *The Taming of the Shrew*, though stretching further than anyone previously dared. The boisterous sequence in which Petruchio pursues Kate for a kiss whizzes by on-screen in a matter of minutes, appearing improvised; in fact, it was carefully storyboarded, then filmed over a grueling ten days in which every detail had to be planned in advance to avoid serious injury.

Lines traditionally delivered by two actors—standing close in a drawing room—were all but thrown away (Shakespeare's dialogue, or what remains of it, can't be heard over the uproar) as the two argue in Kate's parlor. They fight their way across a farmyard (the film's only exterior set), break into a wine cellar, then retire to the barn, continuing their battle up into its loft through a handy trapdoor, she darting out the window and onto the roof, Petruchio hurrying after. When it caves in, they crash down onto a stack of wool, where Burton pins Taylor and administers their first kiss.

Yet the end results were uneven. To focus on Taylor and Burton, it was necessary to whittle down the Bianca subplot. A bigger mistake, though, was the director's decision to play this contrasting element at the same roaring pace as the main plot, resulting in an overheated movie; Shakespeare intended the subplot as a release from all the wild goings-on. Zeffirelli's approach might have fully worked were it not for a difficult situation no director, however experienced, could hope to remedy: Our own Queen Elizabeth was as wrong a choice for Kate, actingwise, as she was perfect in physical attributes.

Taylor's greatest liability has always been her nasal thin whine of a voice. Kate's words, however, must resonate more remarkably than her daring décolletage; in Taylor's case, her breasts performed beautifully, but her vocal chords proved disappointing. Elizabeth screamed, shrieked, and screeched without taking a truly strong stance against Petruchio, which would have allowed her to embody the prefeminist leanings of Shakespeare's Kate. "At best," *Vogue* complained, "Taylor can only turn the Great Shrew into a minor nag." Making her performance all the more difficult to accept was the presence of the stage-trained Burton, whose line readings were impeccable. Critics and audiences alike delighted when he gleefully eyed Kate, giving an X-rated implication to the G-rated line "Oh, how I long to have some *chat* with her!"

The film did ring true in its closing scene, when the reformed Kate dutifully explains a wife's necessary devotion to, and happy enslavement by, her husband. Zeffirelli's version was fashioned even as the modern women's movement emerged in the public consciousness; women were challenging the necessity and wisdom of subscribing to such wifely virtues. Cleverly, Zeffirelli coaxed Taylor into reading the lines with a trace of irony, suggesting Kate may now actually gain the upper hand at that moment when Petruchio believes he has finally won. In 1967 the pendulum swung once again as, due to the era's youth movement, society embraced liberal values, however temporarily. Zeffirelli included such radical ideas in his interpretation, making his version the polar opposite of Sam Taylor's.

## Variations on a Theme

Part of what allows Shakespeare to continue in popularity, even as other once-revered works become dated and fall out of favor, is that his comedies, tragedies, and histories allow for numerous interpretations. Moreover, they can be effectively adapted to current trends in entertainment and ideology. *The Taming of the Shrew* became the basis for numerous films only peripherally related to the original. The first was *Elstree Calling* (British International, 1930; Adrian Brunel/Alfred Hitchcock), an early talkie in which Kate Minola (Anna May Wong) tosses furniture at her preening male husband (Tommy Handley), halting the tirade only when Will Shakespeare (Gordon Begg) enters and intervenes.

*Kiss Me Kate*, a popular stage musical, was brought to the screen in 1953. (For details, see chapter 14, "Playing Shakespeare.") Various vehicles for the team of Katharine Hepburn and Spencer Tracy, including the beloved *Adam's Rib* (1949), draw on Shakespeare's battle of the sexes. John Ford, America's greatest director after Griffith, modeled his Maureen O'Hara–John Wayne pairings, including the period western *Rio Grande* (1950) and the contemporary comedy-drama *The Quiet Man* (1952), after *Shrew*. An even more obvious parallel occurs in *McLintock!* (1963), a relocation of Shakespeare's play to the fading frontier, with O'Hara and Wayne in fine form as the ever-battling couple. Sadly, the film was directed by Andrew V. McLaglen, the less-talented son of famed actor Victor McLaglen. Without the steady artistic hand of Ford, this film proved only intermittently effective.

Apparently, Kate and Petruchio are, thanks to Shakespeare, as permanently enshrined as symbols of battling middle-aged marrieds as Romeo and Juliet remain our reference point for young, sweet-spirited lovers; the Bard understood what author Ambrose Bierce would claim three centuries later: "Romantic love is a temporary insanity, quickly cured by marriage." Virtually any film featuring such a dueling couple can be compared to the archetypes found in *The Taming of the Shrew*; precisely how indebted the French film *Lamegre apprivoisee* (Vascos, 1955; Antonio Roman) or the Spanish feature *Mas fuerte que el amor* (Mexicali, 1959; Tullio Demicheli) are to the Bard can be debated. Clear to all is the lasting impact of Shakespeare on world culture.

# 2

# THE WINTER OF OUR DISCONTENT
## *King Richard III*

*My kingdom for a horse!*
—Richard III

Late in 1592 Shakespeare suffered under intense pressure, both professional and personal. As a writer assigned to create showcases for Richard Burbage's bombastic talent, he needed to create a character worthy of that remarkable, if less than subtle, actor. As a patriotic Englishman, he nervously witnessed growing animosity in some quarters toward the queen, culminating in attempts on her life. Haunted by England's costly War of the Roses, Will may have grown fearful that such civil strife might occur again. A predecessor of the twentieth-century philosophy that those who cannot learn from history are doomed to repeat it, he provided playgoers with a lesson in political ethics and simultaneously satisfied the needs of his superstar.

The perfect project would allow the in-embryo writer to propagandize the rightness of Elizabeth's claim to England's throne while focusing on some historical figure, charismatic if questionable, whom Richard Burbage might play. From this perspective, the Bard appears as fated to have written *Richard III* as Richard himself had been, in Shakespeare's version, destined for defeat at Bosworth Field by Henry, Earl of Richmond, shortly to be Henry VII, the first Tudor king.

The plays of Will's chief competitor, Christopher Marlowe, were then highly popular. *Tamburlaine the Great*, Marlowe's violent epic about an ancient Eastern despot, delighted the public with its vision of a Machiavellian ruler who, despite his cruelties, remains an attractive character. Burbage hungered for a similar role; in the tale of Richard (Duke of Gloucester), of the House of York, Shakespeare found material of the same mettle. The still-insecure writer emulated not only Marlowe's substance but also his in-vogue style, penning most of *Richard III* in blank verse.

Shakespeare had devoured the chroniclers of English history: Hall, Grafton, and Holinshed. In fact, they printed hearsay and gossip in the guise of unvarnished truth. Will raided their storehouses of highly embellished and narrowly interpreted anecdotes for his three-parter on Henry VI. The miniseries allowed him to warn fellow Englishmen against internal conflict by transforming old stories into cautionary fables for the present. Now he scoured the chronicles for background material on England's next significant king, who came alive in Will's imagination.

The chroniclers themselves had been influenced by *Historiae Anglicae Libri XXVI*, a 1534 tome by Polydore Vergil. The Italian writer had filtered long-ago, faraway struggles of that isle called Aengland through the conscience of his popular contemporary Machiavelli, as presented in *The Prince*. Vergil portrayed Richard as a symbol of superhuman cunning, truly a Dark Prince. Richard's ambition, having soared out of control, loosed anarchy on the land in a brief two-year (1483–85) reign marked by cruelty and chaos. Richard would, in the forthcoming production, be presented as an antagonist-as-central-character, the villain-as-hero.

The real Richard may have been guilty of some crimes history has ascribed to him. Other bits of bloodletting are now believed to have been perpetrated by his predecessor, Edward IV, or his successor, Henry VII. The most heinous murders ascribed to Gloucester (the killing of his own princely young cousins in the cold, dank Tower of London, thus eliminating any stumbling blocks to the throne) probably occurred years after Richard's death. Despite his legendary status as Richard Crookback, it's difficult to accept the myth of Richard as a hunchback, since his surviving armor suggests otherwise. More likely, young Will seized on that cruel nickname, endowing his Richard with an ugly body to symbolize his dark mind. This allowed for a vivid theatrical vision of the "wrong" that reigned supreme before the ascension of the "right" Tudors, including Queen Bess.

Once Shakespeare made his dramatic decision to further a reductive representation of Richard, it was necessary to fashion an equally simplistic protagonist. Today most historians agree that Henry VII was a mean-spirited ruler, interested only in his own well-being.

Some insist Henry was less pleasant than the much-maligned Gloucester. Nevertheless, Shakespeare presented Henry as a force of good that vanquishes the evil, which (at least, in the public imagination) was Richard.

The audience of Shakespeare's time exited the playhouse believing that despite the virtual horror show they had just relished, right had proven its might. Now, if those theatergoing citizens could only be trusted to logically follow that idea to its proper conclusion, they would make the key connection: that their own current leader was directly descended from Henry Tudor. Shakespeare's entertaining propaganda assured the populace that their beloved England did indeed exist under God's proper tutelage.

If the story was authentically English, the author's approach was imitation Roman. Like Marlowe, Shakespeare was influenced by the tragedies of Seneca, particularly their sense of a greater fate smothering individual human will. Already, though, Will was on his way to discovering his voice, emerging as the first great pre-Freudian psychological writer. Allowing his Richard to experience psychological guilt via dreams on the eve of impending defeat, the playwright transformed Gloucester from fascinating fiend into flawed human being.

Shakespeare here revealed a notable lack of the skills he would shortly master. His story emerged as convoluted, his occasional attempts at poetry were uninspired, and his characterizations were self-consciously simplistic. Yet the play became a great favorite and remains so. It's a great spook show. The central role of Richard provided not only Burbage but an endless string of actors with a worthy challenge.

## Dr. Burbage and Mr. Kean

### The Stage Tradition

As the first Richard III, Burbage established one approach to the part by presenting ugly Gloucester as strangely attractive both to other characters onstage and to people in the audience. In particular, he was irresistible to *women*. Lady Anne, initially repulsed, allows him to seduce her. Legend has it that many females in the audience swooned with sexual excitement and others screamed out their desire to be his next victim. It's easy to make a handsome villain seductive but more difficult to manipulate viewers into falling under the spell of a character who is, by his own admission, "Deform'd, unfinished."

Two centuries later, England would again be ruled by a great queen, though of a decidedly different order. Victoria emphasized the repression of evil while advocating the need for Englishmen to achieve a higher moral plane. Not surprisingly, the key actor of the nineteenth century offered a totally other Richard, as suited to the oncoming age of Victorian idealism as Burbage's sexy monster had been to Elizabethan realpolitik. Edmund Kean created an alternative that caused audiences, particularly females, to recoil in horror. Ever since, stage (and in our century, film) actors have wavered between the two traditions, presenting a terrifyingly charming Jekyll or an utterly repulsive Hyde.

## Early Experiments

William Ranous, the first stage actor to demonstrate any respect for the emerging film medium, directed and starred in an eight-minute *Richard III* for Vitagraph in 1908. Two years later, director André Calmette shot a brief film in France, followed by a British 1911 version that opened the story with the ending of *King Henry Sixth, Part III* for continuity's sake. Produced by William George Barker, directed by and starring F. R. Benson, the movie (which ran nearly thirty minutes) suffered from staginess resulting from indecision as to whether the camera ought to serve as a recording device for a stage performance or a storytelling device that conveyed the tale.

## The Hazard of the Die
### *The Life and Death of King Richard the Third*
M. P. Dudley Productions, 1912; James Keane

In 1912 a memorable silent Richard was presented while Victorian morality still held sway, doomed to disappear during the post–World War I decade of social and sexual revolution. Not surprisingly, then, *The Life and Death of King Richard the Third* (five reels, five thousand feet) relied on the Kean conception of Richard as a figure of repulsion. The film, which was long lost but rediscovered in 1996, predated D. W. Griffith's *Birth of a Nation* by three years and Cecil B. DeMille's *Squaw Man* by two; as such, it stands as the earliest example of a feature film in terms of epic scope (seventy scenes, including five large-scale battles), considerable budget (thirty thousand dollars), and a then-impressive running time of fifty-five minutes.

British-born actor Frederick Warde was no stranger to Shakespeare or American audiences. He had been trouping across the United States for half a century. (Warde accompanied Edwin Booth on that noted actor's first tour following the death of Lincoln at the hands of Booth's younger brother.) At age sixty-one, Warde tired of touring. Like most stage actors of his time, he believed that accepting work in the still-déclassé medium of motion pictures was slumming, but with his best years behind him, Warde took what he could get. When he made this film for producer M. B. Dudley, Warde had already completed a brief film of *King Lear*.

Though *Life and Death*'s credits insist this was "based on the play by William Shakespeare," director James Keane actually retained only a general interpretation of Richard (here called "Gloster") as Machiavellian, reveling in evil action. Warde winks at the moviegoing audience every time he dispatches another victim. Though the filmmakers played Richard as hunchback, they wisely chose to suggest deformity, having Warde lean uncomfortably rather than inserting a fake hump beneath his cloak.

To make the material cinematic, the Battle of Tewksbury here served as a sumptuous opener. Having defeated the House of Lancaster, Richard's brother Edward (Robert Gemp) leads his warriors into London, where he's crowned as the first king of the House of York. The film eliminates complex politics, focusing on the killings, which were only suggested by Shakespeare, here played for Grand Guignol graphicness. Henry VI is dispatched, brother Clarence (next in line) drowns in ale, and the little princes Edward and York are assassinated, as is ill King Edward. Although Shakespeare's poetry was absent even from the title cards, Shakespeare's invention of a guilty dream for Richard on the eve of Bosworth Field was retained, allowing for some patina of psychological conception. Intriguingly, director Keane played Richmond, ultimately vanquishing his own star!

The concept of mixed media (incorrectly conceived as a recent invention) was then highly popular. When *Life and Death* opened in major cities, Warde made personal appearances, reciting Shakespeare before the screening. What made Warde so beloved as a live-theater actor (his ability to play to the house) was precisely what kept him from succeeding as a film star. (He needed to bring down the performance, which was magnified several times life-size on-screen.) As

Frank Rich noted in the *New York Times*, "Warde himself thought his performance suffered from the substitution of mime for the words he loved to speak on stage." Although Warde engaged in scenery chewing, there was the occasional moment of inspiration. Todd McCarthy noted in *Variety* (1996): "(The) actor's most memorable touch has him running his fingers along his sword after running through the elderly Henry VI and then licking the blood off them." However obvious this may appear today, the moment represented a significant attempt to create clear visual correlations to Shakespeare's words.

While Keane's film deserves classic status as a time capsule, it hardly rates high marks for quality, even at its early juncture. While Keane shot *Life and Death*, Griffith was inventing the unique vocabulary of pure cinema by cutting within a scene for dramatic effect and choosing camera angles and movements to express a director's attitude. There is no such artistry in *Life and Death*, which was filmed in medium-to-long shot; the camera rarely moved except for a slight pan to keep a walking character in frame. *Life and Death* lacks creative editing (Keane cuts only to connect one sequence with the next) except for occasional close-ups of historical documents the audience must see for the sake of continuity.

As was customary at the time, scenes were tinted for emotional effect. Costumes (borrowed from Broadway productions) are lush and extravagant, though the interior sets (*Life and Death* was shot at City Island on Long Island Sound, and exteriors were completed thereafter in Westchester County) are noticeably artificial. They are sketchy backdrops and resemble the fantastical sets in George Melies's early French film experiments, only without the notable charm. This film, while invaluable for Shakespearean cinema completists, hardly rates as a masterpiece on any aesthetic level.

### "All occasions do inform against me!"
### *Richard III*
Lopert Productions, 1955; Laurence Olivier

More than forty years would pass before *Richard III* again appeared on-screen. During the post–World War II era, Lopert Productions was founded by Alexander Korda to provide high-quality British films, with Carol Reed as director (*The Third Man; Odd Man Out*). Korda approached the esteemed Laurence Olivier (who had been knighted in 1948, the youngest actor to achieve such an honor) and requested that he star in a *Richard III* film. When Reed couldn't adjust his busy schedule to accommodate this collaboration, Korda (aware of Olivier's previous successes with *Henry V* and *Hamlet*) asked Olivier to direct. A onetime veteran of England's West End theater scene, inexpensive British films, and Hollywood superproductions for David O. Selznick, Olivier had transformed himself into Orson Welles's only serious competition as the world's most notable actor-director of Shakespearean films. The commercial success of his movies (Olivier was a highbrow matinee idol) led producers to believe that Shakespeare might yet be a financially viable source for film projects.

The mid-fifties was the period when screen characters first suffered from psychological problems. Joanne Woodward won an Oscar for *The Three Faces of Eve*, while such solid stalwarts as John Wayne (John Ford's *Searchers*) and James Stewart (Alfred Hitchcock's *Vertigo*) played troubled antiheroes. Richard is a classic schizophrenic, arrogantly insisting at Bosworth Field: "Let not our babbling dreams affright our souls; Conscience is but a word cowards use." Terrified, he counters this with "O coward conscience, how dost thou afflict me! Is there a murderer here? No. Yes. I am: Then fly. What, from myself?" A selfloathing, selfloving paranoid, he kills suspected enemies, certain they are conspiring against him. Richard was as made to order for the fifties as the genially courageous Henry V had been during the war years.

Olivier's film stands as a striking example of "color noir," featuring rich hues set against the focal character's moral bleakness for ironic contrast. Richard's dark nature, crystallized in black garb, was effectively set against Technicolor renderings of bright pomp and gay ceremony. Slithering down a rope, this Richard transforms into a black widow spider; his lackeys captured in unpleasant lighting to make their faces appear green and yellow and disagreeably reptilian. Ironically, many viewers initially saw *Richard III* in black and white. The film was broadcast on TV nationwide, the same day it opened in a limited theatrical release. By paying a then-enormous $500,000, NBC and chief sponsor General Motors underwrote most production costs. They also created a possible entry in the *Guinness Book of World Records*: In a single afternoon more people saw this production than had attended performances in the three and a half centuries since *Richard III* was written. At that moment, the phrase "global village" became a reality.

Although *Richard III* featured 165 scenes involving thirty featured players, forty actors in smaller roles, and hundreds of extras for crowd scenes, it had been produced in a brief seventeen weeks, including two weeks' rehearsal time in London followed by a month of exterior shooting in Spain. In contrast, *Hamlet* had taken six months, while *Henry V* (due to wartime conditions) consumed a year. Olivier spent three weeks filming the final battle of Bosworth Field on a plain outside Madrid, insisting (like a good action hero) on performing the riding stunts himself. Olivier's desire to find a workable balance between Shakespeare's word-heavy text and the visual terrain of cinema was clear from the opening, a lavish depiction of Edward IV's coronation. The moment with which Shakespeare began the play—Richard, alone in darkness, whining about this being "the winter of our discontent"—was postponed for ten minutes. Olivier was not interested in photographing himself performing the play, rather to fully convert drama to cinema.

Which explains the many liberties taken with the original. Years later, Olivier explained: "It's a difficult play to film—involved, obscure. I felt it necessary to do more simplification than before. Though every commentator and critic through the centuries has attacked the structure, I now expect to be accused of vandalism." To speed up the action (although the director's cut does run 155 minutes, release prints were trimmed to 139), the significant role of Queen Margaret, as strong, if unpleasant, a woman as Lady Macbeth, was shorn to a virtual cameo. The mutual lamentation of the three Queens was omitted (a scene many purists consider key), along with Henry Tudor's rousingly nationalistic final speech, which resulted in a notably darker ending than Shakespeare intended.

There were notable additions. Edward IV's mistress, Jane Shore (Pamela Brown), silently glided through the film while observing all, rather than merely being alluded to, as in the play. The murder of the little princes, mentioned in Shakespeare, is graphically visualized. By far, the most controversial change occurred during the surprisingly successful wooing of Lady Anne (Claire Bloom), widow of Edward V, over the coffin of her recently dispatched husband; in the play, it had been the coffin of Henry VI. Olivier broke the single sequence into two separate scenes rather than Shakespeare's extended one.

This decision split the critics. Robert Hatch of the *Nation* complained: "Perhaps (Olivier) thought the seduction would appear less outrageous if a little time were allowed to intervene halfway through the process," allowing for the encounter of Richard with Clarence, under arrest. "In fact, it is even less tolerable, for now we must suppose that a measurable space for reflection could not show her the black disloyalty into which weakness was leading her." Philip T. Hartung of *Commonweal* insisted that "the successful wooing of Anne is more credible now that it takes place on two separate occasions rather than in one long diatribe."

Olivier's interpretation was radical enough to cause rifts not only between critics from competing journals but two writing for the same publication. John McCartney of the *New Yorker* dismissed Olivier for depicting Richard as a "creature impossible to sympathize with in any way." For McCartney, Olivier tried and failed to create a Richard in the Kean mold. In the same publication, Mollie Panter Downes praised Olivier: "[He] succeeds, if not in whitewashing Richard, at least in making him more fascinating than his victims." For Downes, Olivier successfully created a Richard in the Burbage vein.

Olivier put it this way: "The real challenge (is) to make Richard a dangerous creature, not just a hog. He was a clever and amusing man as well as a villain. That has to show, if the whole thing's not to be melodrama and hammy high jinks." Indeed, his Richard exists in the Burbage mold of villain as sex symbol, Olivier's charisma oozing through scads of hideous makeup. The wooing of Lady Anne is a case in point; however one feels about splitting the scene in two, a viewer does believe and accept her conversion from despising Richard to being spellbound by him.

Olivier shaped his material under the influence of Alfred Hitchcock, who fifteen years earlier awarded the young actor his first choice film role in *Rebecca*. For Hitch, good and evil were never opposing extremes; they always coexisted within a single human frame. That was Olivier's approach here, stirring up a modicum of Aristotelian pity and fear for the Crookback when, endangered and on foot, he shrieks: "My kingdom for a horse!" That line rings with Shakespeare's intended irony, since the crown proved hollow when the greatest power in England could not find a mount and continue the battle. Richard is reduced to Everyman—a lesson in humility learned too late.

Sir Laurence took Shakespeare's cue, making Richard bold and more admirable than before at his moment of truth. Sir William Catesby, a good soldier, marvels that the horseless leader "enacts more wonders than a man, Daring an opposite to every danger." When Catesby begs Richard to flee, the king stoically insists: "I have set my lie upon a cast, and I will stand the hazard of the die." He defiantly approaches Richmond, sword raised courageously, embracing his end. In life, he made a bad show of it; yet Richard partly exonerates himself with a noble death. Such a character demands respect without evoking sympathy, and such a character is present in Olivier's film.

## Coward Conscience
### *Richard III*
United Artists, 1995; Richard Loncraine

An entirely different interpretation was offered at the end of Richard Loncraine's 1995 version. The film, updated to the 1930s, had Richard (Ian McKellen) squatting in a jeep. Rather than hoping to fight on, the cowardly king flees after killing loyal Catesby. When Richard's vehicle becomes stuck in mud, he shrieks fearfully; a simple horse would allow him to escape. At last, he attempts to sneak away, then finally dies (like the craven heavy in an old Hollywood western), falling off a high building while pursued by the stalwart hero Richmond. Loncraine's film does not update; rather, it undermines Olivier's version—and Shakespeare's vision as well.

However controversial the 1955 *Richard III* may have seemed to scholars, Olivier's effect is traditional compared to such experiments. The atmosphere is stylized art-deco wallow, an outrageous thirties retrofashion extravaganza, not a serious adaptation of an important play. Characters cruise in sleek Bentleys; there are elegantly slinky gowns for slender girls, and men are attired in Gatsby-era tuxedos. In contrast to such divine decadence, Tony Burrough's ominous sets create an aura of modern industrialism, a bleak, workaday world paradoxically set against colorful royal lives.

Some twentieth-century conceits are clever, such as Richard viewing his own coronation in the palace's private screening room, rather like a modern ruler unconvinced of his achievement until he confronts proof positive via the media; or when his distraught wife, Anne, shoots up with heroin to dull her senses. Cleverness, however, carries only so far; the concept might have worked better as a short *Saturday Night Live* skit. Loncraine's movie was adapted from a controversial staging of *Richard III* (a Royal Shakespeare production for the National Theatre, directed by Richard Eyre). The production first made waves in London, then enjoyed success on Broadway. Despite its stage origins, though, the film is nothing if not cinematic.

Richard's opening lines do not appear for ten minutes. We first witness a pitched battle in which Richard shoots rivals in their headquarters. As a big band accompanies the victory celebration, McKellen throws away the famous soliloquy. Initially speaking a public address to surrounding celebrants, he continues in a nearby lavatory, relieving himself while, over his shoulder, confiding his true motives. Throughout, sparse remnants of Shakespeare's dialogue are delivered via brief scenes (none lasts thirty seconds) in intriguing settings, such as the film's stand-in for the Tower of London, which is the abandoned Bankside electrical generating station on the Thames. This dank, dim, dreary machine-age monolith symbolizes modern power.

If one ignores Shakespeare, this *Richard III* offers much in the way of first-tier moviemaking. Loncraine effectively creates a *mise en scène* allowing inanimate objects to contrast people and politics via perfect camera placement. As Richard verbally manipulates fellow nobility at dinner, the sequence is shot from below immense peeled shrimps, conveying that Gloucester is about to devour victims as they obliviously gobble down seafood. Loncraine's editing is borrowed from the master himself, Hitchcock. A victim's shrill scream in close-up cuts to a train (its whistle repeating the sound) entering a tunnel, allowing for brief but effective transitions of time, place, and theme. Individual shots convey symbolic as well as specific information, such as when we sense that Lady Anne is dead, since she does not react when a spider crawls across her face. Richard has already been established as a symbolic spider; we know, then, without seeing the murder, that he has killed her.

Ultimately, any *Richard III* rises or falls with the lead performance. As Godfrey Cheshire noted in *Variety*, "McKellen's Richard is less Machiavellian monster, more the craftiest of organization men, bent on pushing his power as far as the system will allow, chillingly amused at the various ruses that permit him to murder his way to the top." That clearly defines McKellen's approach. Whereas Olivier opted for Burbage's seductive monster, McKellen's grotesque makeup is more in line with Kean, a horrifying figure of disgust. If McKellen had taken this idea and run with it, he might well have come up with the perfect alternative to Olivier's. Sadly, that was not the case.

"I want to look a little like Clark Gable and a little like Vincent Price," McKellen announced. The statement, however innocuous, reveals why this accomplished actor, who does have many fine moments, ultimately disappoints. Gable is Burbage, the sexy villain; Price is Kean, the king as horror-movie heavy. Melding the two does not provide a new interpretation, only admission of failure to take a stand.

McKellen is quite devoid of the sex appeal Oliver projected, which explains why the important early scene, in which Gloucester woos and wins widowed Lady Anne (Kristin Scott Thomas), doesn't come across. To be fair to McKellen the actor, the problem also derives from adapter McKellen's cutting. Olivier abridged the text by paring away redundant passages; McKellen strips it bare. Without animal magnetism, there must be enough words to convey her conversion; missing is the connecting material that might have allowed this difficult moment to come across.

The film proceeds at a machine-gun pace; perhaps an American 1930s gangster milieu might have proved more appropriate. There's absolutely no tragic or epic weight, Richard himself more a malevolent, merry prankster than truly dangerous authority figure. The film plays like a classy period soap opera that transforms, before our eyes, into something of a different order. Initially, the humor is Shakespearean, slyly puncturing any possibility for pretentiousness. Then it changes to high-camp histrionics, going over the top in the manner of 1960s pop-kitsch culture. Richard is not killed by Henry Tudor or one of Henry's men; instead, he leaps down into a burning building. As the camera travels with him (to the tune of Al Jolson singing "I'm Sittin' on Top of the World"), he looks suspiciously like Slim Pickens in Stanley Kubricks's *Dr. Strangelove*, riding the atomic bomb down to oblivion.

The scene worked in 1964, since Kubrick employed black humor for social satire. Here there's no obvious purpose other than outrageousness and flamboyance. By this point the film has degenerated from broad spoof to outright silliness. Richard Alleva noted in *Commonweal*: "Such visual fizz constitutes the one real triumph of (a film lacking) dramatic power because it never takes on the real challenges of the play," summing up this movie as "a clever feat which skims a story that only works when [presented] in fascinating detail." Anyone who adores such a John Waters–David Lynch approach will appreciate this *Richard III* far more than those who expect cinematic artists to visually convey Shakespeare's originals.

### Deconstructing Pacino
## *Looking for Richard*
Jam Productions, 1996; Al Pacino

Al Pacino is a very different sort of performer from Ian McKellen. Both an authentic movie star and a highly regarded character actor, Pacino is blessed with both sex appeal and considerable acting skills. Which explains why he was, in his highly personal *Looking for Richard*, able to pull off the dual vision that McKellen tried, and failed, to convey. Pacino is as sexy as Clark Gable and as creepy as Vincent Price, somehow managing to project both qualities simultaneously rather than in succession. In so doing, he provided a perfect combination of Burbage and Kean.

Though his film, ostensibly a documentary, might also be covered in this book's final chapter, "Playing Shakespeare," it will be dealt with here, since so much of the play is presented within the context of the researching, rehearsal, and shooting processes that preceded the production we witness. The concept first took shape in Pacino's mind after starring as Richard III onstage. Pacino sensed he hadn't succeeded, at least not to the degree he had hoped, in conveying to modern audiences his abiding love for Shakespeare in general and this play in particular. So he assembled a motley group of literary scholars, theater professionals, and movie stars to collaborate on a home movie.

The results might alternately have been titled *Deconstructing Pacino*, revealing as much about the well-regarded star as his favorite author. As Pacino argues his theories about the play with colleagues, we learn about how he perceives the world—just as everyone's take on a favorite figure from Shakespeare is, however unconsciously, a medium of self-expression. Pacino's pilgrimage to Stratford-upon-Avon and interviews with the likes of Sir John Gielgud serve as bridges between the play's great sequences, mostly filmed at the Cloisters in New York for a sense of period. Pacino also offers discussions with street people and academics—the former offering perceptive observations on why the Bard has survived for centuries, the latter drowning the playwright in impossible platitudes and unbearable pretensions.

The closeted murder of Clarence (Alec Baldwin) and cold-blooded betrayal of Buckingham (Kevin Spacey) have never been more effectively (or chillingly) brought to the screen. The unforgettable set piece, however, is the wooing and winning of Lady Anne (Winona Ryder). Olivier handled the sequence as an actor's challenge: Could he, while appearing impossibly ugly, make us momentarily believe he might actually ply the vulnerable beauty (Claire Bloom) to his momentary desire? Pacino's approach is more profound: Now tinged with 1990s feminism via Ryder's liberated-lady image, Lady Anne is anything but a frightened, pliable, weak person. Initially, she stands strong against Pacino's Richard. When this Anne finally succumbs, it is due to some heretofore unacknowledged dark side in this seemingly nice woman. Anne, once her anger has been unleashed, clearly sees both the dangerous excitement of succumbing to sex with a man who murdered her father and husband and the kinky charms of a grotesque figure whose innate charisma allows him one triumph of will after another.

Though the sequence was shot without any of the glamorous backdrops that all but overpower the Ian McKellen version, it nonetheless works here in a way it did not in that elaborate but nonemotional version. What Pacino's film obviously lacks in production values it more than makes up for in sheer inspiration and one actor's obvious adulation for the Bard.

## Variations on a Theme

Like his later, more sophisticated *Macbeth*, *Richard III* rates as one of Shakespeare's great spook shows. No wonder, then, that Universal studios employed elements from the play for one of their chillers, after bringing Dracula, Frankenstein's monster, the Mummy, and the Werewolf of London to the screen. With *Tower of London* (1939), producer-director Rowland V. Lee mounted an effective film that first carried Gloucester (Basil Rathbone) through the historical happenings Will recounted in the three parts of *Henry VII*, so that modern audiences would not become confused by complex political situations. Maintaining the popular view of Richard as a demon, screenwriter Robert N. Lee managed (thanks to Rathbone's talent as an actor) to maintain a modicum of the humanity the Bard had added.

Rather than Richard's relationships with other members of the royal family, the Lees focused instead on the murderous incidents within the tower itself and on Richard's relationship with Mord (Boris Karloff), his chief assassin. The suave Rathbone and lumbering Karloff had already proved themselves a fine horror team in *Son of Frankenstein* earlier that year, once more forming a fascinating yin-yang of evil. In the film's best remembered sequence, they get the innocent dupe Clarence (Vincent Price) drunk, then drown him in wine while gleefully beating him.

Price's depiction of Clarence is, like his early character roles in films as diverse as *Brigham Young, The House of the Seven Gables*, and *Laura*, excellent. Sadly, Price would allow himself to be corrupted by commercialism, wallowing in popular junk rather than, like Rathbone, managing to rise above it. By the early sixties, Price had replaced both Rathbone and Karloff as the screen's scariest superstar, appearing in a succession of low-budget quickies for schlockmeister Roger Corman that included *House of Usher, The Pit and the Pendulum*, and *The Masque of the Red Death*. Though the films themselves are sumptuous and stylish, Price's performances went ever further over the top. By the time he played Richard in Corman's 1962 remake of *Tower of London*, Price's overacting was not to be believed; he made of Gloucester the very sort of simplistic demon that, years earlier, Olivier had warned against.

# 3

# STAR-CROSSED LOVERS
## Romeo and Juliet

*All are punished!*
—the Prince of Verona

By late 1594 Shakespeare was established, and his works competed in popularity with those of Robert Greene and Thomas Kyd. Still, no one compared him to the brilliant Christopher Marlowe. History plays and light comedies were all well and good, but Will had yet to attempt the most difficult genre, tragedy—the ultimate test of a playwright's mettle. Even the loftiest tragedies, including Marlowe's *Dr. Faustus*, were considered of only passing interest. Due to the plague that was sweeping London, Shakespeare temporarily abandoned theater. From 1591 to 1593 he composed culturally respectable epic poems: *Venus and Adonis* (published in 1593) and *The Rape of Lucrece* (published in 1594). Then he returned to London, ready at last to approach the tragic mode.

The thirty-year-old Shakespeare devoured Italianate novellas in search of suitable subject matter. Written 250 years earlier, they had a century before been translated into French and now, at last, English. Most likely, Will discovered the tale of *Romeo and Juliet* in a 1562 volume of English poetry by Arthur Brooke, based on a French source by Boiastuau (1559), in turn derived from a purportedly fact based *novelle* (1554) by Matteo Bandello. Forsaking the in-vogue notion of tragedy as revolving around the destiny of a great man in some position of power (the prototypical tragic hero), Shakespeare toyed with a new concept: tragic victims, a normal boy and girl destroyed by their total *lack* of power. When the play became a sensation, Shakespeare's experiment forever altered drama in the Western world.

Will found in the material, or imposed on it, his own emerging vision. On a personal level, he made over the tale of "Romeo and Giulietta" as cautionary fable. Though the source does not specify whether the two become lovers before their hasty marriage, Shakespeare's Romeo and Juliet serve as role models for teens in his audience—repressing sexual desire until receiving full church sanctity. The balcony scene is the moment when these youths undergo a metamorphosis from puppy love to mature, loving friends. "A rare example of true Constancie" is how Will described his play; perhaps, he fashioned Juliet as a foil for his own wife, Anne Hathaway, whom he may have feared was anything but constant.

Actors playing Romeo and Juliet dressed not in Italian period clothing but as contemporary English youths. As for his play's political import, when members of the Montague and Capulet clans ("two houses, both alike in dignity") preceded the leads onstage, everyone in Shakespeare's audience understood, from anachronistic costuming, that they represented the Houses of Lancaster and York. The supposedly historical Verona "feud" (historians question whether it occurred) served as stand-in for England's War of the Roses. Whatever his immediate intentions, the playwright achieved something greater. His transformation of literary lovers into universal archetypes expanded a popular, if minor, fable to a larger-than-life legend. Ever since, Romeo and Juliet have symbolized idealistic youth, their sincere emotions extinguished, if never suppressed, by the insensitive society around them.

## Early Efforts

Shortly after the birth of film, France's Georges Melies mounted a brief *Romeo and Juliet*, characterized by his in-studio approach. No trace of the film exists today. Thomas Edison produced a brief burlesque of Melies's film, which had been released in the United States, though this, too, is lost. Available, though, is Vitagraph's 1908 version; Florence Lawrence fetchingly appeared as Juliet in a crude short (ten minutes) produced by Stuart J. Blackton. Other early versions appeared in Italy (1908) and France (1910).

*Romeo and Juliet* has been filmed more often than any other play, Shakespearean or otherwise. The first ambitious version was shot on location in Verona by Gerolamo Lo Savio for Film d'Arte Italiana; such incidents as the Capulets' party and Verona street fight were lavishly staged. Later that year, Edwin and Gertrude Thanhouser produced a spectacular rendition in the United States. In 1916, Metro turned out a *Romeo and Juliet* with top male star Francis X. Bushman as Romeo, while Fox produced a competing film featuring Theda Bara, ordinarily typecast as a deadly vamp, as innocent Juliet.

Lines from the play were heard, for the first time, when John Gilbert recited the balcony scene in *The Hollywood Review of 1929,* an early sound anthology. Radiant young actress Norma Shearer appeared as Juliet. Shortly, she would emerge as a major star, thanks in equal parts to beauty, talent, and her marriage to producer Irving Thalberg, M-G-M's resident boy genius. During his brief life, this last tycoon pushed for quality projects, particularly if they might serve as starring vehicles for his inamorata. Indeed, Shearer, bitten by the Shakespeare bug, was anxious to appear in a full-length *Romeo and Juliet.* Sadly, though, the popular tide had turned; the public at large, now convinced by academics that Shakespare was above their heads, abandoned the Bard, as did the studio system, which made its money by pleasing the masses.

## All Singing, All Dancing, All Shakespeare
## *Romeo and Juliet*
M-G-M, 1936; George Cukor

For five years, Thalberg pushed for a *Romeo and Juliet* project; each time the concept was pitched, studio boss Louis B. Mayer turned thumbs down. His decision was due not only to Mayer's anticulture bias but to the Great Depression, which caused even the Tiffany of studios to cut costs and avoid risk. Still, M-G-M didn't want to be outclassed by some upstart, particularly Warner Bros., a Poverty Row outfit until Jack Warner gambled on sound, its success propelling the company into Hollywood's top echelon. Jack Warner announced plans to film Max Reinhardt's acclaimed, if controversial, stage production of *A Midsummer Night's Dream.* Not to be outdone, Mayer at last gave Thalberg the go-ahead for his dream project.

The last thing Thalberg wanted was to be accused by intellectuals (he was their darling in otherwise outré Los Angeles) of watering down the Bard. Cautiously, he embarked on a two-year period of preparation. Thalberg decided that the film's words must be entirely Shakespearean; he *would* dare incorporate lines from other plays to provide necessary transitions as well as a song from *Twelfth Night.* He also allowed an expansion of the business Shakespeare could only allude to. Tybalt, having exited following Mercutio's death, returns to the square simply because Shakespeare's "unworthy scaffold" couldn't allow Romeo to chase after him. The cinema nicely accommodates such stuff; also, Thalberg could show the busy street life of Verona, filled with knights, friars, donkey carts, salesmen, and working girls. The exquisite interiors of the Capulets' palace would include dancing staged by Agnes de Mille. Thalberg's avowed intention was to "make the production what Shakespeare would have wanted had he possessed the facilities of cinema."

To ensure that his images would ring true, Thalberg dispatched researchers to Verona. Some photographed old buildings, returning with references for art director Cedric Gibbons. Others diligently copied Renaissance paintings (Botticelli, Carpaccio, Bellini, Gozzoli) as well as surviving fifteenth century church frescoes to provide costume designer Oliver Messel with a sense of the era's clothing. Thalberg hired two experts, Prof. William Strunk Jr. of Cornell and Prof. John Tucker Murray of Harvard. Flown to Hollywood, they were given carte blanche to criticize any inaccuracies. George Cukor, already famed as "the women's director," was the one and only choice; Thalberg wanted Shearer to dominate the proceedings.

Experienced stage performers could be imported from New York, or Thalberg might go the same route as Warners, allowing his studio's popular stars to enact classic characters. Ultimately, he settled on an approach that represented the worst of both worlds. Thalberg did turn over all parts to screen players: Leslie Howard (then forty-five) as Romeo, John Barrymore as Mercutio, Basil Rathbone as Tybalt, Edna May Oliver as the Nurse, popular clown Andy Devine as Peter. Then the producer hedged, importing drama coaches from New York to school the performers. The esteemed Mrs. Frances Robinson Duff was assigned to work with Shearer, who had never stepped out on a stage. Instead of providing confidence, the approach intimidated the actors, explaining why many performances are stilted; stars adored for their naturalism were guided into awkwardly stylized theatrics.

Three months were allowed for construction of studio sets, a four-acre re-creation of Verona gradually taking shape on M-G-M's back lot. Makeup people labored to help Shearer, who had matured into a handsome woman of thirty-two, appear fifteen, which was ultimately an impossible undertaking. The shooting schedule stretched to six months so that perfectionists would be satisfied with every detail. The total cost escalated to more than $2 million, the highest ever for an M-G-M film at that time. Finally, shooting and editing were over; everyone held their collective breath, waiting to see whether critics and the public would turn thumbs up or down.

*Time* wryly noted that despite all the lavish and special treatment, *Romeo and Juliet* "remains what it has always been: The best version ever written of Hollywood's favorite theme, Boy Meets Girl." Few reviews were completely negative. The middlebrow press lavished praise, insisting that *Romeo and Juliet* raised the status of the movie medium to a higher plateau, something filmmakers had been trying to achieve since leaving the sleazy nickelodeon sideshow era behind. Critics in highbrow journals were more restrained; Otis Ferguson of the *New Republic* spoke for many when he noted: "The picture is done well, but seems little more than that—and may no more be regarded as a nuisance on the precincts of Shakespeare than hailed as Hollywood's admission ticket to the pasturelands of art."

By self-consciously working in "awe" of Will, Thalberg was the first (many would follow) to be criticized for "framing an old picture rather than executing a new one"; deferring to Shakespeare, allowing the movie medium to service him, rather than actually devising a movie from the Bard's work. In fact, though, Cukor employed his gifts as visual storyteller more fully than has been admitted; moreover, the film takes more liberties with the original, for better or worse, than anyone has acknowledged.

Credits are presented as unfolding scrolls, visually announcing a class production. That quality is enhanced when a painting provides our first on-screen image; as the camera closes in, this painting comes to life, the prologue speaking fatalistic lines about "star-crossed lovers" to Renaissance listeners. We enter high art, Hollywood fashion, and through it, Shakespeare's play. This is not, M-G-M implied, *Romeo and Juliet* readjusted for the contemporary common man; if the general public attends, they are expected to rise to the occasion. If the term "culture for the masses" hadn't already existed, it would have had to be created.

No wonder, then, that Cukor reverses Shakespeare's opening approach. In the original, servants wander into Verona's square, becoming embroiled in a long-standing argument between their masters, who later enter the meleé. This allowed Will to immediately involve those groundlings crowded close in front of his stage. The film, however, presents formal pageantry first, regal lords of both households parading with full pomp into the marketplace, bumping into one another by mistake. Only after Lords Capulet and Montague exchange unpleasant glances do servants pick up the cue, exchanging insults leading to civil unrest. In the minds of Cukor and Thalberg, there would be no groundlings in their moviegoing audience. They were right; the general public stayed away in droves.

Another alteration reassigned dialogue originally spoken by Sampson and Gregory, Capulet household servants not seen again, to Peter, the Nurse's companion. By having him instigate the fight, Cukor changed the nature of a character who later must appear lovably harmless. Peter dominates entire scenes here as he doesn't in other productions; during the fighting, it is Peter rather than key participants who remains central in the frame, comically attempting to draw his sword, stuck in its scabbard, an added bit of lighthearted business.

If Peter and the Nurse (less batty here than meddling and imperious, though still funny) are enlarged, Friar Laurence was all but eliminated by screen adapter Talbot Jennings. His first appearance, following the balcony scene, is gone, along with his basket of herbs, important in establishing him as a closet alchemist, justifying his later possession of a sleeping potion. We don't see Laurence until after the Nurse's suggestion that Juliet retire to Laurence's cell for a secret marriage. Only then does Romeo ask Laurence to marry them, which makes no sense; what if he said no? There's little feel for an ongoing friendship between Romeo and the Friar, essential to other productions. Laurence's admonition about falling out of love with Rosaline is truncated, as is his reason for agreeing to marry Romeo and Juliet, which is a desire to end their parents' strife. He's humorless rather than the traditional scene stealer.

The emphasis on spectacle is everywhere evident. The Capulets' ball, where Romeo confronts Rosaline for a brief moment before meeting Juliet, is staged in such a grand manner that one understands why M-G-M would shortly achieve fame as the primary studio for dance musicals. Even the first words of love between Romeo and Juliet are spoken as they dance.

Cukor visually introduces key characters. Juliet is initially seen petting a baby deer, symbolically suggesting her personality. She then picks up a bow and arrow, suggesting the presence of Cupid as well as her own propensity to violence, which legitimizes her later suicide. Romeo, too, is introduced through animal imagery; he's discovered in a glen, pining away for his momentary object of affection while sheep graze and a shepherd plays pipes. This establishes Romeo as part of the pastoral tradition, a young swain swooning for romantic love over aloof, unworthy Rosaline.

One traditionally troubling issue is how Romeo and Juliet share their wedding night when he is not allowed near her house. Cukor adds a sequence in which Juliet prepares a rope ladder to allow him access, making her an affirmative, clever woman rather than a giddy girl. Since the film was fashioned after heavy censorship hit Hollywood, Cukor discreetly suggests their night of bliss through montage. As the couple kiss, he cuts to lush images of rippling water, blooming flowers, and the gentler side of nature, all set against soft music. When he returns to the couple, there's no doubt as to what has transpired.

Cukor freely interprets both Mercutio and Tybalt. The former is not the eccentric purveyor of antic melancholia most directors opt for. Barrymore plays Mercutio as a renown lover; in his entrance, he woos a bevy of willing women. This is far from Shakespeare's conception but proper for Barrymore's reputation (the Great Profile) as an aging Lothario. His delivery of the Queen Mab speech, traditionally a drunken intellectual's improvisation, here becomes a regular guy's witty spiel. When he turns serious, Mercutio appears as a Roman Stoic; during his death scene, Barrymore convinces all around him that he has suffered only a mere "scratch," then slips away to die privately. Rathbone's Tybalt seems less Prince of Cats and Machiavellian perpetrator of mischief than stuffy and pompous, a strutting, humorless foil for Mercutio's preferred courtier.

This film's Tybalt, having insulted Romeo, only to be told the lad wants no trouble, accepts that statement and is ready to leave. Mercutio, however, restrains him, not to keep Romeo from having to duel by valiantly offering himself; rather, to instigate trouble where none exists. This shifts the source of bloodshed from Tybalt to Mercutio, making the Prince of Cats more sympathetic than usual while rendering Romeo's subsequent killing of Tybalt an unnerving, out-of-control act (here Mercutio merely gets what he was asking for) rather than Shakespeare's righteous revenge.

Cukor includes the oft-eliminated apothecary scene as well as Laurence's messenger to Romeo locked away with a plague victim. The final sword fight between Romeo and Paris, the participants dwarfed under immense arches, presages the famed Errol Flynn–Basil Rathbone duel in Michael Curtiz's *Adventures of Robin Hood* two years later. Juliet's death is more believable here than in other productions, Cukor introducing the device and her determination early on. When Romeo is banished, she discovers his forgotten dagger; we view, from her point of view, an extreme close-up implying the object's imminent importance. Juliet holds it close, then utters her line: "If all else fail, myself have power to die." Normally, this sounds like a naive girl's romantic boast; since Shearer says those words while clutching the dagger, it makes perfect sense for her to employ it at the end.

As the Prince speaks his final words of admonishment during the burial that ends the feud, he transforms into the Chorus, reciting Shakespeare's moral ("All are punished!") as actors dissolve into the figures of the previously glimpsed painting; we end where we began, reminded this is art first, entertainment second. Too arty, in fact, for the public; coupled with the failure of Warner's *Midsummer Night's Dream* a year earlier, the major studios backed off the Bard for more than a decade.

### Such Sweet Sorrow
## *Romeo and Juliet*

Verona Productions, 1954; Renato Castellani

The next significant cinematic *Romeo and Juliet* conveyed the state of the art, and drastically altered the industry, during a decidedly different decade. In the early 1950s assembly-line filmmaking—reality re-created on studio back lots—diminished. Postwar audiences, particularly returning veterans, had seen too much of the world to continue accepting Hollywood fabrications of it. Following a wave of popular imported films, the studios began shooting on location. Movies had to be made in color, or people would stay home and watch black-and-white entertainment on television, which, with the moviegoing audience growing ever younger, increasingly kept older Americans at home.

James Dean's on-screen image, first in *East of Eden* and then *Rebel Without a Cause*, reflected the youth audience's own rebellious attitudes toward parental figures who couldn't comprehend teenage idealism. At the time of his death, Dean was scheduled to appear in films of Nelson Algren's *Walk on the Wild Side* and Tennessee Williams's *Summer and Smoke.* He would be replaced in both projects by Britain's Laurence Harvey; it made sense, then, that Harvey was the actor of choice for a mid-fifties *Romeo and Juliet.*

The 1954 *Romeo and Juliet* was hailed as the first to feature actors who approximated the characters' ages. Harvey was twenty-five at the time; costar Susan Shentall, nineteen. Also acclaimed was the breathtaking color photography and stunningly capturing Italian locales. This was the dream project of Renato Castellani, who made his reputation directing *Two Cents Worth of Hope*, a transitional film between the fading postwar neorealist style and emerging films about troubled teens. After attending a revival of Cukor's *Romeo and Juliet*, Castellani exited the theater in anguish over the spectacle of middle-aged actors incarnating teenagers on faux fifteenth-century sets. Then the concept hit him: Since he was searching for a project, why not *Romeo and Juliet*? The Italian director found a financial backer in England's J. Arthur Rank, veteran of Olivier's three Shakespearean adaptations, leading to one of the many international coproductions so popular then.

Robert Krasker, who sumptuously shot *Henry V* for Olivier, was engaged as cinematographer. Closely collaborating with Castellani, Krasker captured diverse locations as breathtaking tableaus, each purposefully shot in the distinct style of some Renaissance master whose approach was appropriate for the content of any individual shot, such as Vermeer's astounding light-and-shadow effects, Filippo Lippi's uncanny feel for embellished detail, Carpaccio's intellectualized concept of color, Pisanello's compositional eloquence, Lorenzo Monaco's lyricism, and for shots that linger on Shentall's beauty, Veneziano's adoration of the female form.

Castellani early on abandoned his initial concept of shooting entirely in Verona for authenticity. Some spots alluded to in Shakespeare's play remained intact; others, sadly, did not. The director was seized with a new inspiration: Travel across Italy, find various places untouched by time, shoot the film with a broader notion of "on location." All in all, ten Italian cities provided well-preserved locales.

What emerged was a quintessential distillation of High Renaissance style, offering an entire era as immortalized in its art and architecture. Such an approach could be called self-consciously decorative. As Walter Goodman pointed out in the *New Republic*, "The play is *not* the thing . . . his best tool [is] the camera, his goal the visual image."

Castellani represented a new post-Olivier wave, not only employing the camera to translate a play into pure cinema but subverting Shakespeare's texts to the tenets of moviemaking as well. The effect was of seeing Shakespeare, not unlike some beautiful butterfly preserved under glass, tastefully immortalized for all time, with the life force pressed out. So Castellani felt free to drastically cut the original. Missing were memorable lines in the balcony scene, almost all the low-comedy relief (particularly Peter and the Nurse), as well as the Queen Mab dream speech, Mercutio himself reduced from Hamlet-like pre-existential voice to bit player. With the apothecary gone, Romeo stabbed himself rather than accomplish the deed with poison.

Likewise, the director liberally added material, including a scene that explains why Friar John fails to deliver an all-important message to banished Romeo. "We had come to see a play," Robert Hatch wryly commented in the *Nation*. "Perhaps we should not complain that we were shown a sumptuous travelogue." The film, lauded in Italy (winning the Golden Eagle of St. Mark, Grand Prize at the Venice Film Festival, where the audience delighted in gorgeous panoramas of their country) was scorned in England. British theater critics savagely attacked not only the sparsity of dialogue but also the throwaway approach taken toward surviving lines. Is Castellani's *Romeo and Juliet* a masterpiece or a mess?

In its defense, the director perceived himself not as interpreter of Shakespeare, akin to a live-theater director, but as an auteur: the primary artist, freely adapting the play to his own medium, much as Shakespeare felt free to transform a preexisting Italian *novelle* into an Elizabethan play—taking from the tale what he needed, shaping it as he saw fit, and discarding all else. Castellani did to Shakespeare what Verdi had done when borrowing the plot of *Othello* to create his opera *Otello*. He created a unique and viable work. Moira Walsh of *America* defended the *Romeo and Juliet* film as "a work of art which is unified, genuinely cinematic and, even more than [Olivier's] *Henry V*, bears the mark of a single creative talent at work."

Conversely, those who attack it contend that Shakespeare is not some minor storyteller but the greatest playwright ever. Shakespeare's sources, rough and crude, begged for a great artist to improve on them. Shakespeare's play is a finished work, deserving the respect due a masterpiece. The filmmaker, working in an essentially dramatic medium (retaining Shakespeare's words, as Verdi did not), has a responsibility to respect the original's integrity. "Castellani's *Romeo and Juliet* is a fine film poem," *Time* admitted, lamenting: "Unfortunately, it is *not* Shakespeare's poem!" Castellani's film is difficult to judge. As cinema, it's terrific; as an adaptation of a great play, it's terrible.

Unfortunate as well was the acting. Shentall was a secretarial student spotted by the director in a London pub, picked for her "pale sweet skin and honey-blonde hair," but she never rose to the role's demands. Shentall appeared right for the part (if one believes Juliet should be a blonde) but delivered her lines in an uninspired manner. Young Harvey, already an accomplished stage and screen actor, unwisely played down Romeo's passion. He concentrated instead on a soft, poetic performance that muted his striking similarity to James Dean and probably hurt the film's possible impact in America as well.

**Fortune's Fool**
## *Romeo and Juliet*
BHE/Verona Productions, 1968; Franco Zeffirelli

Why not retain what was best about Castellani's experiment—young performers, authentic locations, and vivid color—while keeping such elements in proper perspective, rather than letting them overwhelm the text? That was Franco Zeffirelli's thought when, after completing *The Taming of the Shrew*, he resolved to try *Romeo and Juliet* next. Zeffirelli wisely determined that his would be a Shakespearean film about young love, retold for the "love children," drawing on the generation-gap mentality that developed during the mid-sixties revolutionary fervor over civil rights and the Vietnam War.

This was the age of the British Invasion in music and fashion, so an English cast was now fully acceptable to American audiences. Zeffirelli understood his target audience. "The teenagers of the play should be a lot like kids today," he insisted. "They don't want to get involved in their parents' hates and wars. Romeo was a sensitive, naive pacifist, and Juliet strong, wise for a fourteen-year old. That is why I chose inexperienced actors. I don't expect a *performance* from Olivia [Hussey] or Lenny [Whiting]. I want them to use their own experience to illustrate Shakespeare's characters."

The director claimed to have chosen Hussey for her "classical beauty—mesmerizing eyes (and) coarse strength." What he most liked about Whiting was "a gentle melancholy, the idealistic face Romeo ought to have." Actually, both were trained and experienced. The youngest member of Britain's National Theater, which supplied many actors for this production, Whiting had played the Artful Dodger in the Dickens-based musical *Oliver!* Hussey studied for four years at London's Italia Conti Drama School, then starred opposite Vanessa Redgrave in the West End production of *The Prime of Miss Jean Brodie*. Still, at age fifteen, the half-Argentinian, half-English girl was the youngest Juliet on record in a professional performance.

The approach worked; *Romeo and Juliet* proved a huge success, particularly with the young. "The scenes may be in ancient *palazzi*," Maurice Rapf observed in *Life*, "but, filmed with untheatrical documentary lighting, they seem less far removed from us in time. We see with mild shock of recognition that old folks represent an existing social order against which hot-blooded, individualist youth must rebel to make a better world—even on pain of death." Viewed thirty years later, the film was, like Shakespeare's play, less a youth-versus-adult diatribe than Rapf insists. When Romeo and friends crash the Capulet party, Juliet's parents accept him, adhering to the prince's dictum against civil unrest; young Tybalt (Michael York), catalyst of the tragedy, is the one who refuses to submit. Shakespeare, a conservative, would not state that untested youth is morally superior to the adults; Zeffirelli, who would later identify himself as an outspoken conservative, followed suit.

Zeffirelli learned from reviewers who had found fault with his *Taming of the Shrew*, and he adapted on-target crticism into his emerging technique. With *Romeo and Juliet*, he established an approach for cinematic Shakespeare that has been accepted as the norm ever since. Realizing it was wrong to create vivid images inspired by the words while retaining dialogue rendered redundant by the camera, Zeffirelli and collaborating screenwriters Franco Brusati and Masolino D'Amico pared down the play in a consistent manner. Shakespeare's lengthy descriptions were intended as compensation for his own inability to show such stuff; the Elizabethan audience needed to first hear in order to then see in their mind's eye. Such passages now best serve as stage directions.

No more effective example exists than the sequence in which Mercutio (John McEnery) and Tybalt accidentally meet, becoming involved in a duel to the death. Shakespeare described at length the atmosphere in Verona so that his audience could properly envision the mood. Zeffirelli took his cue from the text: "In these hot days, is the mad blood stirring." As Anthony West noted in *Vogue,* Zeffirelli "draws from (this phrase) the vision of an almost visible heat pressing down on the dry, close, nerve-wrackingly airless little town, turning the last screw of the lethal boredom which will make men seek to kill each other to relieve their exasperation at having nothing better to do." The following duel is, then, "all viewed through a faint haze of dust and summer heat," as Mollie Panter-Downes described it in the *New Yorker.*

Like Castellani, Zeffirelli realized that contemporary Verona did not offer enough possibilities, therefore, he filmed individual shots in diverse areas, from Tuscany to Umbria. The scenes he staged involving street gangs were played (in spite of accurate period costumes) as modern kids with bad attitudes. They were also highly influenced by *West Side Story* (1961), which abandoned Shakespeare's language but retained his vision for a *Romeo and Juliet* redux set on New York's mean streets. In addition to a suggestion of modernity through movement, Zeffirelli also opted for a unique interpretation of the Tybalt-Mercutio duel, logically deriving from contemporary gangs. Rather than play the scene as Shakespeare intended, where the youths meet with bloody conflict in mind, Zeffirelli chose to show bravado gone bad. His kids bait each other, half-kiddingly, believing things will remain under control; they use their swords, like switchblades, to tease.

Tybalt and Mercutio here become, according to Robert Hatch of the *Nation,* "a couple of neighborhood warlords, vaunting their courage with grandstand high jinks, trying for a victory by humiliation, and giving no strong impression of a taste to kill." Each tries to outmacho the other without actually drawing blood. When Mercutio is wounded even as Romeo tries to halt the dangerous wisecracking, Tybalt appears stunned to realize he's inflicted a lethal wound, skulking off guiltily. This increases sympathy for Tybalt, who is now less a minor Machiavellian and more a victim of circumstances.

When Mercutio calls out curses on Capulet and Montague alike ("a plague on both your houses!"), another twist emerges. Instead of mourning Mercutio even before he falls, his friends believe this to be one more joke. Mercutio has been portrayed as a modern nihilist rather than a Renaissance sophisticate. So his fellows laugh at the wise guy's bad puns ("tomorrow, you shall find me a grave man"), gasping in horror upon realizing that, like the boy who cried wolf, Mercutio was serious. Although this may not be what Shakespeare envisioned, it does not negate the author's vision.

For Shakespeare, the heart and soul of *Romeo and Juliet* was a vision of two morally fine people who want to do the right thing. Their tragedy is that they find themselves in a no-win situation: Remaining true to their families or to their prince proves mutually exclusive. They are damned if they do and damned if they don't. Their attempt to marry in the eyes of God represents a doomed desire to follow the rules when the rules are right. What we see is not revolution for the hell of it; rather, rebellion in the service of greater good. "See," the Prince says with a sigh, "how Heaven finds ways to kill your hate with love."

Shakespeare expressed the families' reconciliation in words. Zeffirelli replaces them with a powerful image; members of both households, in separate mourning lines, converge to carry the caskets together. Only a variation on primitive sacrifice of innocent victims can replace civil sickness with health, dispersing anarchy through restored order. This was the essence of tragedy for the ancients; Shakespeare and Zeffirelli repeat that tragic conception in Renaissance and contemporary terms. In the end, the sick city experiences the necessary catharsis.

A complex Moresque dance was added for the Capulets' ball, expressing the relationships between various partygoers through onscreen movement. The gathered multitude become perfectly realized human beings in brief snatches of dazzling imagery. Also added here was Nino Rota's "Love Theme From *Romeo and Juliet*." The song is halfway between a period ballad and a hippie-era tune and connects historical trappings with modern attitudes.

Just as Castellani offered his version of why Friar John failed to deliver the message, so does Zeffirelli. Whereas Castellani's slowed down the action, Zeffirelli brilliantly hit on a briefer but more effective approach. John doggedly treks toward Mantua, unaware that the rider swiftly passing him is Balthasar, who wrongly believes Juliet is dead and hurries to inform his master. As Romeo rides back to join Juliet in death, he passes John at precisely that moment when the oblivious friar waters his donkey, his back to the roadway. John swivels around even as Romeo passes unseen, wordlessly suggesting the machinery of fate at work, an idea Shakespeare verbally made clear in Romeo's epiphany: "Some [horrific] consequence, yet hanging in the stars" will result from his innocent party-crashing action.

Zeffirelli's decision to drop the duel with Paris at Juliet's tomb speeds up the slowing action while keeping Romeo sympathetic by not having him kill such a decent fellow. The decision to eliminate

Rosaline was, however, questionable. For us to accept the developing "true love" of Romeo for Juliet, it is necessary to earlier witness his romantic infatuation with Rosaline. This immature Romeo, a teenager in love with the idea of being in love, gradually gives way to the mature Romeo, truly and totally in love with a human being. We cannot appreciate the lofty place he arcs to if we haven't glimpsed the ordinary point at which he began.

One intriguing element of the Castellani and Zeffirelli films is the manner in which both directors attempt to communicate Shakespeare's mixed feelings about Friar Laurence. Shakespeare's Laurence is a decent man; he believes in the need for order, hoping to end the feud while ensuring that the teens do not engage in premarital sex. However, he uses his cell as a place to experiment with forbidden arts.

In Zeffirelli, Laurence is first glimpsed in nature, picking herbs, a devilish glint in his eye. Later, in his cell, Laurence is framed by surrounding alchemy equipment, suggesting that he is unknowingly trapped by his own ungodly experiments. In Castellani, our introduction is a shot of Laurence's rectory, the camera closing in on a bird's nest over the entrance, implying that nature has unwisely been allowed to intrude into this pocket of civilization. His room is upstairs, with wide windows, opening onto the natural world outside; he himself is more open to nature than a religious man should be. After devising the scheme with Juliet, she leaves; suddenly, a white rabbit hops in through the window, sitting—unafraid—before Laurence. He smiles and pets the creature; the symbolic significance of rabbits to ancient Wiccans as a symbol of unrepressed reproduction suggests his devilish side.

## I Defy Thee, Gen-X Stars
### *William Shakespeare's Romeo and Juliet*
Twentieth Century–Fox, 1995; Baz Luhrmann

Australia's Baz Luhrmann, veteran of music videos and the dance-musical *Strictly Ballroom*, hoped to outdo even Zeffirelli in making *Romeo and Juliet* "relevant" to youth. He sensed that in 1996 the story must be given an up-to-the-minute ambience. Having studied Zeffirelli's version and retaining most of its carefully cut script, Luhrmann updated the setting (though not the dialogue) to a gangbanger milieu: Verona Beach, Florida. (Despite the Miami look, the film was shot in Mexico City, with additional work in Veracruz.) Luhrmann took the gang interpretation suggested by Zeffirelli and—for better or worse—fully realized it.

Montagues and Capulets are competing mobs, shooting it out with oversized automatic weapons (which they refer to as "swords"), cruising in hot, customized cars while wearing designer clothes. The action scenes were reminiscent of recent John Woo and classic Sam Peckinpah; other sequences played like extended MTV rock videos. Accoutrements included pearl-handled pistols, black leather, silver-heeled boots, and a lingerie collection worthy of Madonna. As Peter Travers commented in *Rolling Stone*, the intention was to "make *Romeo and Juliet* accessible to the elusive Gen-X audience without leaving the play bowdlerized and broken." Hip-hop music played loudly and incessantly, and hot young stars Leonardo DiCaprio and Claire Danes enacted the leading roles. Teenagers, to the surprise of some, turned out in droves and the result was a box-office success.

Not everyone agreed that this was a marvelous idea. Luhrmann's version isn't "just an abridgment," Richard Alleva noted in *Commonweal*. "It's a specimen of clip art. Luhrmann has extracted from each scene those few lines that give enough information for the plot to function, plus a few more too beautiful or too famous to be jettisoned. His is a real 'movie movie,' its dialogue just another component of the soundtrack along with gunfire, screeching brakes, and the slapping of surf onto the beach." Critics debated whether the impressionable young audience witnessed an altered and diluted version, thus being misinformed and ill served by the film, or whether the essence of Shakespeare shone through, whatever the surface enticements. Though this might not be the stuff a purist's dreams are made of, it couldn't be denied that modern youth *did* turn out for Shakespeare, no mean feat in itself.

Some of the modernizations work well. Having the chorus spoken as a TV newscast at the beginning and end seems right. So, too, does Friar Laurence's lost message (via a courier service) to Romeo in Mantua (here a desert trailer park) that believably gets misdelivered. The apothecary scene (cut from Zeffirelli and most versions) is effectively restored as a drug deal. Other touches, though, are too much of a stretch, even for those willing to accept anachronism. The police chief's banishing Romeo for a street killing rather than sending him to jail is patently absurd. Likewise, the image of Romeo returning, with police helicopters in hot pursuit, and slipping into the church but *not* being followed in by the SWAT team that spotted him.

Luhrmann's approach can be dismissed, as it was by one critic, as "Shakespearean snack food." It can also be appreciated as an important attempt to bring Shakespeare out of the elitist enclave of high culture, proving even in the MTV era of the oncoming millenium that the Bard's vision rings true.

Surprisingly, Luhrmann emphasizes the one aspect of Shakespeare such a hip young filmmaker might have been expected to excise: the religious element, which is more significant here (and true to the Bard's intent) than any previous version. From the opening shot, Luhrmann imitates Martin Scorsese's *Mean Streets* technique of bringing the camera up high, assuming a God's-eye view, then shooting over statues of Christ to imply that the people below are so involved with their gritty reality, they fail to glance up at the still-existing spiritual presence. Though they inhabit what they perceive to be a God-abandoned universe, He is very much with us, if less than pleased by widespread amorality.

Romeo and Juliet constantly emphasize the "divinity" of their love; Luhrmann films them surrounded by religious icons. When a momentarily out of control Romeo kills Tybalt, he regains composure and throws himself down in front of a statue of Jesus, begging forgiveness. The heroes are portrayed as young born-agains, their rebellion less against adult authority figures (who have small roles) than the non-spiritual world everyone else accepts. No matter how revolutionary the hip-hop approach may appear, this plays as the most *reactionary* of all *Romeo and Juliet* movies, and is true to Shakespeare, who wanted to communicate the concept that wild youth acts troublesome only when they have been denied sources of old-fashioned spirituality.

Perhaps most surprising is that DiCaprio and Danes were disappointing, decent enough when playing the highs and lows of emotion, faring less well when required to actually speak Shakespearean dialogue and make it ring true. Paul Sorvino, a veteran gangster-genre star (*GoodFellas; The Firm*), played Fulgencio Capulet as typical Mafia-movie patriarch, while Brian Dennehy, as Ted Montague, incarnated an equally clichéd white-Establishment crime boss. More enjoyable were Miriam Margolis, making Juliet's Nurse a comical Hispanic rather than cockney Elizabethan, and Pete Postlethwaite, whose Father Laurence caught the character's charming ambiguity.

In Luhrmann's directorial choices there is one truly great moment: the playing of the couple's final scene. Romeo discovers

Juliet in an apparent state of death and reaches for his poison; ordinarily, Juliet wakes moments *after* he dies. Here, though, we notice Claire Dane's Juliet beginning to wake *before* Romeo takes the poison. The timing is simply devastating; every time her hands move or her eyes flicker open, Romeo happens to be glancing in the opposite direction. Such impact is impossible onstage, where sudden editing to extreme close-ups does not exist. Never before has a *Romeo and Juliet* film elicited such audience involvement; it is almost impossible *not* to scream out for her to move more quickly and for him to go slow. When Romeo turns his back and takes the poison, she sits up, smiling, reaching to him, unaware of what he's done. Romeo turns, in the process of dying, and comes to grips with how very much alive she is, how terribly close they came to defying all odds against them.

How sad, then, that Luhrmann immediately undercuts the remarkable beauty of what he's achieved. In the film's most sordid image, Juliet blows her brains out with a pistol, which is photographed from a bizarre angle to heighten the revolting grotesquerie. The director has moved, in a moment, from perfect cinematic tragedy to the garish-kitsch excesses of modern melodrama. Such extremes characterize the ultimate effect of his film. No wonder *Variety*'s Todd McCarthy wrote: "As irritating and glib as some of it may be, there is indisputably a strong vision here that has been worked out in considerable detail."

## Variations on a Theme

Shakespeare's genius, even at this early point in his career, allowed him to transform (however unconsciously) a unique pair of young lovers into universal symbols; the Bard elevated two Italian teens (their actual existence dubious at best) into archetypes whose problem is understood even by the multitude that has never read or seen the play. In America, the famed feud between the Hatfields and the McCoys led to the legend that a boy and girl from the fighting families fell in love but were destroyed by the hostility; certainly the 1949 film *Roseanna McCoy* with Joan Evans and Farley Granger romanticized the real-life hillbillies into charming, well-scrubbed youths worthy of Shakespeare.

To this day, any tale of teen romance, menaced by a hostile world, is referred to as a variation on *Romeo and Juliet;* James Dean's couplings with Julie Harris (*East of Eden*) and Natalie Wood (*Rebel*

*Without a Cause*) were perceived, in their time, as 1950s variations on the theme. Onstage in the mid-1950s and on-screen in 1961, composers Stephen Sondheim and Leonard Bernstein collaborated with choreographer Jerome Robbins to musically reset *Romeo and Juliet* in New York's mean streets, with white and Puerto Rican gangs in conflict over turf (*West Side Story*).

Over the years, versions have been filmed in Spain (*Julieta Y Romeo*, 1940), Egypt (*Shulhadaa el gharam*, 1942), Mexico (*Romeo y Julieta*, 1943), India (*Anjuman*, 1948), France (*Les Amants de Verone*, 1949), Russia (*Romeo and Juliet*, 1954), Czechoslovakia (*Romeo, Julie a tma*, 1959), Italy (*Romeu Giuletta e romeo*, 1964), Canada (*Rome-O and Julie 8*, 1979), Brazil (*Romeu Y Ulieta*, 1982), and the United States (*China Girl*, 1987). The feuding families can become competing rural ranchers or big-city bootleggers, but the young people always remain essentially the same.

When, in 1961, writer-director Peter Ustinov decided to puncture the decade-old Cold War with humor, he concocted *Romanoff and Juliet*, in which Sandra Dee, as the daughter of an American ambassador, falls in love with John Gavin, son of the ambassador's Soviet counterpart.

During the peace-and-love era, shortly before Zeffirelli's version reached theater screens, young people were flocking to see Warren Beatty and Faye Dunaway in *Bonnie and Clyde* (1967) and Dustin Hoffman and Katharine Ross in *The Graduate* (1967), concerning pairs of edgy outlaws and disenfranchised rich kids at odds with a corrupt Establishment. Though Shakespeare's intent appears to have been considerably less radical than such contemporary counterparts, the play's legend has acquired a life all its own; lest we forget, a 1964 rock-and-roll song by the Reflections featured the refrain "Just like Romeo and Juliet . . . " That era's greasers understood what that meant as surely as do the Gen Xers who lined up for the hip-hop version with Leonardo DiCaprio and Claire Danes.

# 4

# A FAIRY TALE FOR GROWN-UPS
## *A Midsummer Night's Dream*

*What fools these mortals be!*
—Puck

By 1594 Shakespeare was the public's favorite playwright, but could this country-born crowd pleaser create a sophisticated show, engaging the interest of a more discriminating audience? An important source of income for the Lord Chamberlain's Men was earned by providing entertainment at noble weddings. A lighthearted comic satire, including a wedding ritual not unlike the one actually performed earlier that day, would serve as a perfect conclusion to a night of celebration, one attended by the queen herself. So Will concocted *A Midsummer Night's Dream* for a marriage ceremony, either that of the third earl of Bedford to Lucy Harrington (December 12, 1594) or the earl of Derby to Elizabeth Vere, daughter of the earl of Oxford (January 26, 1595).

Like the balls of skillful jugglers he had witnessed at rural fairs, the Bard would keep four separate stories in perfect syncopation. The framing device was drawn from classical mythology. The conquest of Hippolyta, queen of the Amazons, by Theseus of Athens, had been translated from Plutarch by Sir Thomas North, and also featured in Chaucer's *Canterbury Tales*. Through this tale of royal submission and wedding, Shakespeare could slyly slip in a suggestion to honored guest Elizabeth; the actor playing Hippolyta would, after all, be dressed in a costume anachronistically resembling Bess's own garb.

A tale of young nobles, similar to those in attendance, focused on mismatched couples. Intelligent Hermia is promised by her father,

Egeus, to arrogant Lysander. He in turn is fawned over by gawky Helena, while shy Demetrius pines for Hermia. Here Shakespeare drew on plots from Italian novels, endowing a stereotypical story with his own strong sense of moral purpose. In defying her father, Hermia is not unlike Juliet. Also Juliet, like Hermia, steadfastly remains chaste, even while sleeping beside her beloved; the woman's rebellion is directed at wrongheaded authority, not conventional values.

To represent the full social spectrum, Shakespeare created a set of lower-class characters in Bottom the weaver and his companions, who slip into the forest to rehearse *Pyramus and Thisby*, a tragic play not unlike *Romeo and Juliet*. They are called "rude mechanicals," because these are men who work with their hands and are caricatures of groundlings who might catch the play at some future date. Finally, Will added the fairy plot: Oberon, king of the fairies, tries to tame his own beautiful shrew of a wife, Titania.

All four plots are connected thematically via the recurring device of difficult pairings—not surprising considering the author's own. Earlier comedies, like *The Taming of the Shrew*, had been strictly social; real people in a real world. *A Midsummer Night's Dream* presented his first Green World, where everday folk desert civilization for some natural place and where they're in constant danger of reverting to a bestial level. Bottom actually turns into an ass, the physical symbol of what thematically threatens everyone. This is done by the hand of Puck, who is a mischievous sprite rather than a dangerous Satan. Always the pre-Freudian psychologist, Shakespeare refuses to explain whether the dreams of fairies are real or imaginary. Right you are if you think you are; if the characters believe their dream, it's real for them.

## "Scene shifters, rejoice!"

### The Stage Tradition

The enchantments, which were probably only suggested in Will's own time, were improved upon as the state of theatrical art became ever more elaborate. In 1692, *A Midsummer Night's Dream* was turned into an opera (with music by Henry Purcell), *The Fairy Queen*, and enough Shakespeare was eliminated to make room for a Chinese chorus and six dancing monkeys. An 1816 version (music by Henry Bishop) proved pyrotechnically remarkable, in sight and sound, causing purist William Hazlitt to complain: "Oh, ye scene-shifters, ye scene painters, ye machinists and dreamakers, ye men in the orchestra, rejoice! This is your triumph; not ours"—and assuredly not the Bard's. By the turn of the century Will's words took a backseat to special effects; this was the general approach at the birth of cinema, a storytelling form that naturally lent itself to such spectacle.

## Early Films

The movie medium, as French auteur George Melies proved, allowed for a fuller realization of the fantastical than live theater. Surprisingly, then, *A Midsummer Night's Dream* was one of the few Shakespearean plays this magician turned moviemaker never attempted. The first-known movie (all of eight minutes in length) was produced in Brooklyn in 1909 by Vitagraph. Charles Kent directed Dolores Costello and her sister Helene, both as fairies. Kent opted for on-location shooting in Central Park, including the famed Bethesda fountain. Such grounding in reality made the special effects, including Puck's wild flights, all the more breathtaking to the immigrant audience, who, like Shakespeare's own groundlings, delighted in such stuff.

That same year, France's Le Lion films offered a loose adaptation, *Le song d'une nuit d'ete, d'apres Shakespeare,* featuring Tudor Hall. Italy's Paulo Azzuri had a go at the play in 1913, resulting in a twenty-minute charmer that, like Vitagraph's, was shot entirely outdoors. For its time, Azzuri's film rates as sophisticated in terms of convincing acting and creative camera work. Also in 1913, Germany's Stellan Rye directed a sensuous version, emphasizing the sexual entanglements. Titled *Ein Sommernachtstraum,* the brief flicker was shot in the sumptuously grandiose style Max Reinhardt had established for live-theater productions.

Presaging high camp in the 1960s, Reinhardt's gleefully over the top approach was also obvious in another German version (with the same title) produced in 1925, running fifty minutes. Noted actor Werner Krauss (*The Cabinet of Dr. Caligari; Othello*), played Bottom. Director Hans Neumann so emphasized the sexual element that German censors pronounced the film off-limits for children. This made the film a commercial success with curious adults. The more sophisticated among them noted that in addition to graphic nudity, this movie also boasted a greater helping of Reinhardt-style spectacle than Rye's previous version. Some wondered out loud why Reinhardt himself hadn't been hired to make the movie. That situation would shortly be rectified in, of all places, Hollywood.

# "Ill Met by Moonlight"
## *A Midsummer Night's Dream*

Warner Bros., 1935; Max Reinhardt

Though his name is forgotten by all but devoted theater buffs today, Reinhardt was the Orson Welles of his time: flamboyant, fascinating, and controversial. He mounted live productions of Shakespeare with razzle-dazzle to spare. The public was overwhelmed by take-your-breath-away effects, though academics wondered whether all the theater magic overshadowed the Bard's poetry and purpose. Reinhardt's stage production of *A Midsummer Night's Dream* was a phenomenal hit in Vienna and he was persuaded to bring the company to America to stage the show at the Hollywood Bowl.

Among those in attendance was Jack Warner, the brother in charge of determining which films Warner Bros. would produce. Mostly, he opted for lucrative topical crime dramas and backstage musicals. There was, however, the matter of prestige brought by the Oscars, which gave M-G-M the premier position due to adaptations of literary works such as Charles Dickens's *Tale of Two Cities* (1935) and *David Copperfield* (1935). From the moment Reinhardt's production began, all Warner could think about was what a wonderful motion picture this fanciful production might make. Moreover, the Warner technicians could assist Reinhardt in expanding his vision, creating remarkable images, like characters dissolving into thin air. *A Midsummer Night's Dream* became Jack's dream project, but shortly after, an escalating budget and commercial failure would qualify it as a nightmare.

Years earlier, Reinhardt scoffed at cinema as an inferior second cousin to live theater. He had reversed that position, announcing, "The motion pcture is the most wonderful medium for the presentation of drama and spectacle the world has ever known. The screen has leaped further ahead in the last few years than the stage has evolved in centuries." Reinhardt signed on, only to learn that Warner would not consider importing stage players from New York; he instead allowed his beloved stock company to try their hands at Shakespeare. These popular stars had varied talent but were cast nonetheless. Demetrius was played by Dick Powell, Hermia by Olivia de Havilland, Puck by Mickey Rooney, Flute by Joe E. Brown, and Oberon by Victor Jory. James Cagney, the king of the lot, was allowed to pick any role; he decided on Bottom, sensing that the ultimate challenge for a great actor is to play a bad actor.

Warner hoped (in vain) that such famous names would attract the public despite a sudden turnabout of Shakespeare's status with the mainstream. As Reinhardt struggled to create an acting style able to bridge the gap between ultramodern performers and stylized poetic dialogue, Jack Warner decided that the stage veteran (who had never before helmed a motion picture) needed help and assigned studio director William Dieterle. It proved a happy pairing; Dieterle was an old friend of Reinhardt's from Germany, where the master had awarded Dieterle his first acting job.

Now an experienced hand, Dieterle could take responsibility for technical elements, leaving the sixty-two-year-old Reinhardt free to concentrate on matters of image and interpretation. Never once did Reinhardt concern himself with finances. Although Warner originally committed a then-whopping $1 million (the highest in the studio's history to that date), Max quickly drove the cost up another half million during his ninety-day shoot, not taking into account months of preproduction or the task of later editing eighty-five miles of film down to one hundred thirty-two minutes. For the forest, Reinhardt ordered sixty-seven truckloads of trees and shrubs delivered to the largest soundstage in movie history up to that point, 350 feet long by 175 feet wide, which was larger than a football field. The moment Reinhardt focused his intense theatrical lighting system (forty arcs and 720 five thousand-watt lights) on the set, his foliage wilted. Technicians rushed in to cover the plants with luminous paint, thus serendipitously adding to the magical quality of Tinseltown's first Green World.

Owls, ravens, and turtle doves were brought in to complete the textural density of an alternative universe. As the production continued, it took on ever more prestige—and expense. Felix Mendelssohn's famed music, inspired by the play, was adapted for inclusion by Erich Wolfgang Korngold, the studio's resident musical genius. Also inserted: a Bronislawa Nijinska ballet, transforming the project into something far beyond Shakespeare. What organically emerged might be considered an apotheosis of culture or a grotesque, embarrassing example of kitsch, with a combination of talents most critics insisted were ill met by moonlight.

When public response proved nil, Warner hurriedly trimmed away thirty minutes (mostly from ballet sequences) for future showings. (Long-missing footage has since been restored.) Critics expressed mixed emotions; *Time* praised the breathtaking set designs and cinematography but complained about the "monotonous howlings" of ten-year-old Rooney and the "over-energetic jabberings" of Cagney. A movie that mixes and matches faux-Grecian sets with Brooklynese accents does appear at odds with itself. Those rare heartland viewers who showed up at local bijous for a taste of the Bard were astounded at the then-radical image of a black male sprite seducing a lilly-white virgin. Joseph Breen's Hollywood censors raised their eyebrows, closely considering whether this was art or eroticism.

In fact, Jack Warner, during those early days of Will Hays's Production Code, was anxious enough about the comical kissing between top macho star Cagney and Brown's cross-dressing companion in the play within a play to suggest adding a wife for Bottom, defusing any possible confusion about the character's sexual identity. Max steadfastly refused, insisting that Shakespeare's text remain intact, at least that part of it he himself didn't truncate. With trepidation, Warner relented, realizing this was his riskiest project. As film historians Kenneth Rothwell and Annabelle Melzer would note in retrospect: "The 'Americanization' of Shakespeare by way of German Expressionism was what this film was all about—a cultural Declaration of Independence against the widely held prejudice that only British actors can play Shakespeare. Hollywood was saying Shakespeare is for the entire English-speaking world, not just the English."

Reinhardt's appreciation of anachronistic theater was obvious from the opening. Theseus (Ian Hunter) and Hippolyta (Verree Teasdale) appear in the expected ancient-world garb; guards likewise sport helmets and armor. When the camera cuts to the cheering crowd, however, middle-class characters, particularly women, are dressed in Elizabethan English finery. Likewise, the rude mechanicals are the British working class of Shakespeare's time, more likely to head for Sherwood Forest than a wood outside Athens. This adds to the fairy-tale-for-adults quality, a story taking place once upon a none-too-specific time, and far, far away, in a marvelous realm of myth and legend rather than history.

However one feels about individual performances or the cutting of lines in favor of music and movement, no one can deny that the imagery catches the viewer's eye, jolts the mind, and lingers in the memory. The biggest problem was the staging of the play within a play. It is anticlimactic, following the rightful pairing off of young lovers. Onstage, the lengthy farce that follows can be made to work, since in Shakespeare's time the *real-life*, royal-wedding audience watched Bottom and company over the shoulders of the *theatrical* royal-wedding audience, breaking down barriers between theater and actuality. When the play is filmed, such theater magic evaporates.

## Antique Fables and Fairy Toys
### Sen Noci Svatojanske
Ceskoslovensky Film, 1959; Jiri Trnka

That problem was faced and solved in 1959 by Jiri Trnka. In his seventy-four-minute animated version, the Czechoslovakian puppet maker added a sequence that justifies the presence of the play within the play in a film. Scuttling the stage tradition that presents *Pyramus and Thisby* as an exaggerated comedy, its sole purpose to entertain the double audience, Trnka transformed the rude mechanicals's show in mid-performance. Bottom, up to that point a dreadful actor, is dynamic rather than static; here, for the first time, events of the previous night have changed him as a person, widening his scope and view. Undertandably, then, Bottom is altered as an artist as well. His initial overacting gradually gives way to a more restrained performance; initial laughter from gathered nobles likewise dies down.

For Trnka, like Shakespeare, Bottom was far from mere comic relief. He served as the author's self-deprecatingly humorous autobiographical figure. Shakespeare and Trnka shared the dubious status of being country bumpkins who had the audacity to try to become ambitious artists; since both rose to the heights of their respective crafts, it made sense that Bottom, who was their on-screen representative, would as well.

Puck, clearly Shakespeare's other favorite among the characters, likewise stirred Trnka's imagination. Though portrayed by a doll, Trnka's Puck is complex: delightfully devilish, yet charmingly innocent. This Puck is less a fantasy figure than real-life boy endowed with superpowers, his childish psyche running out of control as he indulgingly exercises unrestrained power that he isn't mature enough to deal with.

Trnka spent two years on the project, adapting the miniature art of his homeland to the wide-screen process, thereby making the film viable in the American market. This necessitated deserting his beloved Agfacolor, which lent a warm, fairy-tale glow to such previous endeavors as *The Emperor's Nightingale*. Instead, he shot with

Eastmancolor, rendering everything more realistic, which was not the tone Trnka wanted for his fairy tale. He and composer Vaclav Trojan conceived of their piece as "a spectacular fairy ballet"—less an adaptation of Shakespeare, performed by puppets, than a translation of Shakespeare's stage play into a different artistic medium: puppet animation.

Trnka worked not in the tradition of previous Shakespearean cinema, but rather in the vein of Verdi, fashioning an opera from *Othello*, or Prokofiev, with his ballet created in honor of *Romeo and Juliet*. Trnka's conception was to cut away most of the dialogue, expressing every idea and emotion through mimelike movement, retaining only those words needed to make transitions comprehensible. This necessitated creating the most sophisticated puppets ever seen, since they had to convey complex ranges of expression. Rather than presenting the illusion of movement, as he had done in the past, Trnka insisted that every motion convey character: Courtiers walk in ways that suggest their cool, ceremonious attitude; young lovers express youthful passion with each turn; rude mechanicals convey genial vulgarity through visual gestures rather than verbal gags; sprites imply the alternative reality of a sensuous dream with every flick of a hand.

For the first time in his career, Trnka fashioned puppets from plastic rather than wood so that they would be more malleable. Other directors had recently complained, in the words of one, that wide screen was "good for nothing except filming snakes." This, of course, only attests to the inability of such filmmakers to creatively adapt to the ever-changing cinematic form. Functionally employing wide screen, Trnka simultaneously played three scenes on-screen which, in Shakespeare, follow one another in sequence, creating a virtual three-ring circus on the screen. At other moments, Trnka sensed the need for intimacy, creating a "frame within the frame" by arranging angles so that trees, buildings, or other objects block off the left and right sides of the screen.

Tragically, all of Trnka's imaginative work was undercut when the film's English-language distributors, concerned the result would be a hard sell, persuaded Richard Burton and members of the Old Vic to dub in voices. Even with this unnecessary addition, the film remains one of the finest examples of Shakespearean cinema; the greater tragedy is that at the time of this writing it remains unavailable.

## We Shadows Have Offended
### *A Midsummer Night's Dream*
Royal Shakespeare, 1968; Peter Hall

The sparkle and lightness Trnka discovered in *A Midsummer Night's Dream*, then vividly brought to the screen, is nowhere found in Peter Hall's 1968 film, nor was it meant to be. "It is not a pretty, balletic affair," Hall later insisted, "but erotic, physical, down to earth." Having staged the play three times during the past decade, Hall became fascinated with the controversial theories of Polish critic Jan Kott. His revisionist notion held that *A Midsummer Night's Dream*, properly understood, was not a fairy tale for grown-ups but a dark, disturbing play which psychosexually investigated the Id despite being written more than three centuries before Freud. Though there's some element of truth to that, such thinking can easily become reductive and banish the beauty and complexity of the piece when seized on too narrowly.

Though produced for British TV, this version was filmed rather than videotaped. It also received limited theatrical release, which brings it within the parameters of this study. Hall was attacked for extreme use of close-ups but insisted this had been an aesthetic choice: "Shakespeare had to deal with close-packed theaters, a huge audience compressed in a small space and stationed all 'round the actors, really on top of them. He wrote so actors could literally talk to them, not boom away over their heads. The closeness of the camera [then] is no embarrassment. It is, in fact, a support. It insists on thoughtful speech!"

Yet the close-up, however effective on the small screen, soon grows tiresome during a larger-than-life theatrical projection. Television and filmmaking are separate forms; the product of directors who believe the two are interchangeable appears as naive as those who, a century ago, wrongly believed that film was an electronic extension of live theater. Hall's "film" fails to work as theater, television, or cinema—or, for that matter, as Shakespeare.

Following Kott's lead, Hall seized on a speech by Titania (often cut from lush productions owing to apparent incongruity) in which the queen of the fairies insists this particular summer seems like winter, with endless rain, constant mist, and much mud. Hall chose to shoot in Warwickshire during September and early October, purposefully working under the worst weather conditions imaginable.

He avoided Mendelssohn's nineteenth-century romantic music as well as the lovely Pre-Raphaelite vision of an enchanted kingdom. Indeed, the only "greens" on view here are sickly sea greens for faces of sprites, who wear drab, earthy, leaden-looking clothing—when they are dressed at all.

"This is not a film *from* a stage production or a film *based* on the play," Hall insisted. "It attempts to bend the medium of film to reveal the full quality of the text." To establish his total reconception of the play as a film, rather than recording his preexisting production, Hall avoided the studio. Despite an ostensible Athenian setting, he perceived the play not as Mediterranean but Northern, moving cast and crew to Compton Verney. A seventeenth-century home and surrounding grounds served as a natural setting. Adding to that sensibility, Hall's cinematographer, Peter Suschitzky, filmed with a handheld camera, adding a documentary flavor. Then, fearful of becoming *too* realistic (thereby rendering Shakespeare's stylized poetic dialogue ridiculous), Hall dubbed in all sound and voices later, eliminating natural noise in favor of a tightly controlled track.

Theseus (Derek Godfrey) was played as a serious British manor lord rather than a gleeful pagan warrior. The young men (David Warner's Lysander, Michael Jayston's Demetrius) were Renaissance courtiers not unlike those who might appear before Elizabeth herself. The sprites (Ian Holm as Puck, Judi Dench as Titania, Ian Richardson as Oberon) emerged as horrific Halloween creatures rather than classic creations of Greek myth.

Many of the fairies appeared nude; this was, recall, the age of Aquarius and *Hair!* Furthering that modern sensibility, Hermia (Helen Mirren) and Helena (Diana Rigg) were bedecked in Carnaby Street miniskirts. Hall used a minimum of editing owing to his belief that "Shakespeare works in paragraphs rather than sentences," deriving his montage from the text's intrinsic rhythm. So scenes drag on in single-camera setup as they would not in a film by, say, Franco Zeffirelli. Certainly Hall succeeded in making this as unpleasant a viewing experience as possible, "challenging" audiences with an alternative perception. Ultimately, though, the work seems a distortion; remove the pleasurability from Shakespearean comedy and you remove the audience's reason for attending.

This is a film of heightened ugliness, which—in its defense—makes it as frightfully representative of the late sixties as Warner's was, with its crystallization of high culture, of the mid-thirties. "There could not be a greater contrast between this version and that of Reinhardt," Roger Manvell noted, the earlier film reflecting "the romantic, spectacular tradition at its height." Whatever one thinks of Hall's *A Midsummer Night's Dream*, Shakespearean cinema completists should catch it if only for purposes of comparison with Reinhardt's polar opposite.

## A Variation on the Theme

Woody Allen's 1982 film, *A Midsummer Night's Sex Comedy*, was inspired by Shakespeare's *Midsummer Night's Dream* (as well as Ingmar Bergman's *Smiles of a Summer Night* and Jean Renoir's *Day in the Country*), allowing for a multiple homage to Allen's favorite sophisticated comedies. A departure for a filmmaker who ordinarily shoots in Manhattan, *Sex Comedy* sets the problems of three attractive couples to music by Mendelssohn rather than Gershwin, the norm for Allen.

*A Midsummer Night's Sex Comedy* is set in 1906 in a Green World that looks suspiciously like rural Connecticut. More than once, couples are mismatched, as in the Bard's play. There's even an element of the supernatural: A miraculous globe allows the sensuous six to peek into an alternative dimension of sprites, coexisting with the real world, much as Titania, Oberon, and Puck did. Though the dialogue is contemporary (and anachronistic for the supposed time period), Allen labors sincerely (if not always successfully) to bring Shakespeare's pastoral spirit to the screen. We always sense the paradox of a filmmaker who admits to hating the country but awkwardly works in a genre that celebrates both the beauty and danger of nature.

# 5

# THE HOLLOW CROWN
## *Richard II; Henry IV, Parts I and II; Henry V*

*This scepter'd isle, this other Eden, this England.*
—John of Gaunt

Following the diversions of *A Midsummer Night's Dream*, Shakespeare was ready to tackle the history play again with newly enhanced playwrighting powers. In *Henry VI* and *Richard III*, he had chronicled the conclusion of England's War of the Roses, employed in the present as a cautionary fable for the future. Now the Bard provided a prequel, depicting the beginning of that long, costly conflict. The result was his spectacular tetralogy about decades of dueling between the houses of Lancaster and York. Both houses were "alike in dignity," but their personal ambition made them oblivious to the greater good, and they all but destroyed the "royal throne of kings," to which both families aspired.

In 1595, Shakespeare returned to Holinshed and the chroniclers, also drawing from a recent, popular epic poem by Samuel Daniel, *A History of the Civil Wars Between York and Lancaster*. Freely inventing from these sources, he fashioned *The Tragedy of King Richard II*, which stretches beyond historical epic into the realm of full-blown tragedy in a way *Richard III* had not. Despite the title, the truly tragic figure isn't the foolish fop of a king, Richard of York, but his chief rival for the throne (and eventual supplantor), Henry Bolingbroke, duke of Hereford, of the House of Lancaster.

*Richard II* is weak, effeminate, corrupt, and sentimental. He possesses none of the necessary kingly qualities, but he does rule by divine right. Among the honorable men he offends is Bolingbroke, who is banished on Richard's whim; compounding this mistake, the king wrongfully seizes lands belonging to Bolingbroke's father, John of Gaunt. Bolingbroke is wise, strong, capable, fair-minded, and a natural leader. He possesses every quality required by a king, but he isn't in line for the throne, and therein rests the central concept of the play.

Is it ever proper to dethrone a king, however incompetent, if he is not outwardly evil? It's all but impossible for the audience, then or today, *not* to root for the usurper. To make matters more complex, Bolingbroke is morally gray. He agrees to lead the rebels (a term which, however positive in our time, was anathema to Shakespeare's generation) only for "the general good," to save what his father describes as "demiparadise." At moments, though, Bolingbroke appears more ambitious than he would care to admit or perhaps is aware of on a conscious level.

Bolingbroke, both saviour and usurper, serves as predecessor to the modern antihero. He is doomed if he does and doomed if he doesn't. After dethroning Richard and declaring himself Henry IV, the new king is overheard by his followers grumbling that his reign would go easier if only Richard, imprisoned, were out of the picture. When those friends slip off to do the deed, however, Henry rushes to Richard's aid but arrives too late. Did he knowingly speak Richard's death warrant, then have second thoughts? Did he have no idea that his words might be taken literally? Shakespeare leaves the situation ambiguous. Henry experiences both relief and guilt at Richard's death and pledges a pilgrimage to the Holy Land which he'll continually put off.

If, at the end, Bolingbroke seems less the emerging hero, so Richard conversely grows in stature. "I wasted time," he says with a sigh, "and now time doth waste me." The line conveys self-awareness, if tragically tardy, coupled with an admission of kingly responsibilities. Richard has grown, too late to save his life or crown but not too late to redeem him in the audience's eyes. As Richard expires, we like him more than we thought possible; when Henry offers feeble excuses for his rude, if understandable, act of rebellion, we're disappointed in a man we once uncritically admired.

## "Down I Come, Like glistering Phaethon"
## *Richard II*
The Stage Tradition, TV, and the Film That Never Was

*Richard II* is one of the few Shakespearean plays that have never been filmed, even during the silent era, when producers drew heavily upon the Bard's work. This is not so surprising, according to actor Maurice Evans, who stated that the trick to making Richard work necessitates taking "a [questionable] person, with all his faults, then play him so the audience becomes sympathetic in the second act and bleeds for him in the last one." Evans twice portrayed Richard on the New York stage, on Broadway in 1937, then again in 1951 at City Center. Having become associated with the role, it came as no surprise when, in 1953, he announced plans to mount a film. As a result of Olivier's popular English epics and M-G-M's commercially successful *Julius Caesar* (1953) producers were once more willing to bet their investment money on the Bard.

Filippo del Giudice, who produced Olivier's *Henry V* and *Hamlet*, agreed to do the same for *Richard II*, which was budgeted at a hefty $1.5 million. Margaret Webster, a top professional in her field, was engaged as the editor for a film that would never see the light of day. Instead, Evans ended up playing Richard II on a live *Hallmark Hall of Fame* TV production. Television is, in fact, more appropriate for this play. There are no big battles to fill a cinematic canvas and no central character, hero or villain, to dominate a huge screen via a larger-than-life performance. As critics have noted, *Richard II* is an "intimate play"; TV, with its natural reliance on the close-up, is more suited to it.

Which helps explain why critics of the time felt that this production failed—though one year earlier Evans's TV *Hamlet* had been hailed. That show was specifically planned for the unique nature of the medium, emphasizing soliloquies in close-ups and paring away spectacle. Unfortunately, with *Richard II*, Evans held to the concept for his aborted movie. Little wonder Jack Gould of the *New York Times* complained: "The tragedy of the playboy ruler was lost amid a bewildering preoccupation with setings, props, and effects. Too often the camera and not the play was the thing."

The bloated production, which was awkwardly jammed onto a small screen, proved that television as a storytelling form was complimentary of, rather than similar to, movies. As Marshall McLuhan later noted, the medium is the message; therefore, the content of a particular play should dictate whether it is adapted for film or TV, and such decisions should not be made arbitrarily.

## The Death of Chivalry
### *Falstaff* or *The Chimes at Midnight*
Internacional films Espagnol, 1965; Orson Welles

Although never filmed in the silent or early sound eras, the two parts of *Henry IV* and the subsequent *Henry V* all but beg for a large scale. The focal figure isn't the title character but his oldest son, Hal. A wastrel frequenting the London inns, Hal causes consternation in his father, who wonders what will become of his beloved Britain when this "unthrifty" youth ascends to the throne. "The old king is a murderer," Orson Welles once flatly stated, who "has usurped the throne." Shakespeare actually conceived of Bolingbroke as a decent, if dubious, man who did not ambitiously seek greatness; rather, he had greatness thrust upon him. Henry IV ploddingly does the best he can, all the while knowing he is not truly "legitimate"— though Hal will be.

Welles first expressed interest in tying various chronicle plays into a single epic while mounting the Mercury Theater stage production *Five Kings* in 1938. The show was a failure, but without that early experiment Welles might never have brought so glorious a work as *Falstaff* (a.k.a. *The Chimes at Midnight*) to life on-screen. Begrudgingly admitting that five kings were two too many, Welles settled for a brief glance at one (Richard II), followed by portraits of the next two (Henry IV and V). Welles tightened the *Henry* plays incorporating the finale of *Richard II* at the beginning, the opening of *Henry V* at the end, plus several lines from *The Merry Wives of Windsor*, which features Sir John Falstaff and friends but in a less serious situation. *Falstaff*, like the plays, is composed of three parallel stories: the unhappy reign and painfully slow demise of Henry IV, ever eager to do right by England; the initial decadence of Prince Hal, whose wild behavior may be God's punishment for Henry IV's treatment of Richard; and the boisterous, bawdy comic misadventures of Falstaff, Hal's delightfully dangerous foster father, who was tagged

"Lord of Misrule" by C. L. Barber in his book *The Fortunes of Falstaff*. (A fictional character, Falstaff may have been modeled on the actual Sir John Oldcastle.)

*The Chimes at Midnight* is the greatest of all Shakespearean films and boasts a unity of pace and simplicity of purpose lacking in Will's rambling tetralogy. Welles's approach to the narrative rates as an improvement rather than a bowdlerization, but thematically what he accomplished is at best controversial. "The Falstaff story," Welles insisted, "is the best of Shakespeare—not the best *play*, but the best *story*." Though that may be true, the words reveal more about the man speaking than the work spoken of. The film's power to fascinate derives largely from the degree to which Welles employed Shakespeare to serve his own ends rather than lending his considerable gifts in the service of the Bard.

It is significant that Shakespeare wrote these plays relatively early, between 1595 and 1599, before the period of the great tragedies. The playwright associates with Hal, and the prince's rite of passage is a literary projection of Will's own difficult journey toward maturity. Welles directed *Falstaff* toward his career's close; although he would continue acting for another two decades, this was his swan song as an auteur. The stage tetralogy ends with a grand early-spring sense of life's happy renewal, but the movie closes with a melancholy late-autumn aura of pervasive death and decay.

Though Welles followed Shakespeare's story line, he altered the focus. Welles made Falstaff (whom he would play) the central character. He would portray Falstaff as the clown as tragic hero rather than as humorous relief and a foil to the Henrys. Filmed during the mid-sixties, mostly in Barcelona and Madrid, *Falstaff* fits the tenor of those times. Welles's vision of the rift between Henry IV (Sir John Gielgud) and Hal (Keith Baxter) is formed by the generation-gap conflict, with Falstaff as an aged hippie guru, part Timothy Leary ("sack" substituting for LSD) and part merry prankster Ken Kesey, while the tavern itself is depicted as a virtual commune, an Elizabethan Alice's Restaurant. Battle scenes, brilliantly realized in unglamorous black and white, were aimed squarely at the youth audience during that era of divisive war in Vietnam.

"He [Falstaff] is the most completely *good* man in all of literature," Welles said. Welles discovered in his source what he wanted to find, and the subject matter allowed him to express himself at that point in his life both personally and professionally. For Will,

Falstaff represented a throwback to Vice figures of medieval morality plays, albeit transformed into a three-dimensional character; to
Welles, Falstaff is a fine fellow and the rotund symbol of everything
that's best in the world. Welles does not "act" the role, as he had
done with Macbeth or Othello, because Welles *is* Falstaff, with Sir
John's experiences paralleling Welles's own brilliant but brittle
career. There is "no distance between Welles and Falstaff," Joseph
McBride noted in his Orson Welles biography— which is key to the
film's greatness as an original work as well as its serious limitation
as cinematic Shakespeare.

When Shakespeare wrote Falstaff's early words to Hal, "Banish fat
Jack, banish all the world," the literary artist stood at a distance
from his character, giving an old blowhard a desperate line of self-
defense. When Welles recites that line, the artist is at one with Jack,
expressing this as simple, unvarnished truth. This was "quite a free
adaptation," as Welles biographer James Naremore put it. "It's really
quite a different drama," Welles freely admitted. In Welles's defense,
we should note that he gave his film its own name. By distancing it
from the source, Welles made clear this should be viewed (and
judged) as a new work by himself, inspired by an old one by Shakespeare. "*Chimes* is a somber comedy," Welles continued, "the story
of the betrayal of a friendship." Shakespeare would have been
astounded by the first part of that statement; for him, the tetralogy
was a history cycle with comedy relief.

The Bard would have agreed with the latter, though, if with a significant distinction: For Will the betrayal is perpetrated on Hal by
Falstaff; in Welles's vision it's the other way around. Shakespeare's
tetralogy is about the difficult birth of a golden age, the world's
"greatest garden"; for Welles, the golden age had already passed. So
the current action of it is filled with nostalgia for a bygone past,
entirely preferable to the present. This fits not only Welles's point of
view during this bleak period of his life but throughout his *oeuvre*,
since *Citizen Kane* and *The Magnificent Ambersons* concern themselves with just such situations.

In *Falstaff*, as in the plays, we encounter dual worlds: the cold,
ordered universe of the palace, the warm, chaotic realm of the
tavern. Long shots display the castle (representing Henry IV) atop
the hill. The tavern (representing Falstaff) is below, and Hal is constantly moving back and forth between the two. Shakespeare would
have approved of such a *mise en scène*: castle and king on high, Falstaff down low—physically and, by implication, morally. By travers-

ing the two, Hal combines the best of both without the worst of either. Thus, as king, he will be warm yet orderly, an ideal prince.

John Gielgud was well chosen for "the old king," not only because of his brilliant acting but due to his noticeably thin build; he exists as a foil to Welles's fat Falstaff in physique as well as philosophy. Gielgud's Henry IV, soliloquizing on his inability to enjoy the sleep that commoners take for granted ("Uneasy is the head that wears a crown"), reawakens that key theme. So does Hal, upon becoming king, when he insists that he has actually "dreamed" his entire life up to that point. He was "asleep" as to his responsibilities and duties and is now awake for the first time. Falstaff is a part of that prince's dream and must necesarily recede as the new king at last opens his eyes.

When Henry IV dies and Hal is named king, Falstaff gleefully shouts, "Take any man's horses; the laws of England are at my command." For Shakespeare, this was a horrific notion. If Falstaff were to rejoin Hal, England would fall into chaos, once more an unweeded garden. So when Hal ascends and sends Falstaff away, Shakespeare presents Hal's transformation into a perfect prince, the polar opposite of Richard III. Welles, however, lifted the opening scene from *Henry V*, grafting it onto his movie's end, thereby providing a pessimistic ending, which details Falstaff's sad death. Clearly, Welles and Will are, as artists, much like Beatrice and Benedick from *Much Ado About Nothing*: Always there's a "merry war" between them.

Hal's imminent imperialism (the invasion of France) is something Shakespeare heartily approved of. Welles does not; by having Keith Baxter's Henry V step into the banners and all but disappear among them, with his eyes suddenly sad, Welles visually implies that the new king will be swallowed up by his role as world conqueror. To present what Shakespeare actually intended, though, Welles would more correctly have had Hal walk toward us, smiling broadly, banners waving wildly in the background. Welles was always less interested in filming Shakespeare, however, than using the source material as a jumping-off point for an original work by Orson Welles.

In the most Catholic sense of the term, Shakespeare wrote a redemption saga: Hal redeems himself by turning away from Falstaff. "Presume not," Hal tells his corpulent former companion, "that I am the thing I was." Yet Hal's "noble change" in Shakespeare is the prince's ignoble change in Welles—though, again to be fair to the filmmaker, it's worth noting that audiences from the Elizabethans to moderns have always fallen in love with Falstaff. The

Bard created something of a Frankenstein's monster; what was intended as a symbol of what we all should abhor was beloved by everyone. That explains why Will provided a promise at the end of *Henry IV, Part II* to bring Falstaff back in the next play; though this promise would be broken, the full cast of lovably decadent tavern louts returned in *The Merry Wives of Windsor*, which has never been the subject of a major English-language film. What a shame Welles did not have funds to keep his supporting cast on hand and film that wonderfully bawdy comedy on the Spanish locations, where he'd just completed what may well be the greatest single film ever derived from Shakespeare—if far from a film that remains true to Shakespeare's vision.

## Neither Fish nor Fowl

### A Variation on the Theme

There are two ways in which Shakespeare can successfully be updated for our time. One is to go the route of *West Side Story*, retaining plot and themes and eliminating poetic dialogue in favor of modern street lingo. The other is to keep the poetry despite anachronistic placement on modern mean streets. The audience adjusts to this formal, unrealistic element as they do to song and dance in *West Side Story*. The commercial success of 1995's *Romeo and Juliet* stands as a case in point. Doomed to failure, though, is a mixing and matching of modern speech with Shakespeare's poetry; just as the audience adjusts to the one, they're forced to move back to the other. Yet that neither-fish-nor-fowl middle ground was the route taken in 1991's *My Own Private Idaho* by Gus Van Sandt, an eccentric filmmaker known for offbeat hits (*Drugstore Cowboy*) and embarrassing misses (the *Psycho* remake).

*My Own Private Idaho* is an odd combination of interesting elements that never jell into a cohesive whole. Borrowing from the tetralogy (particularly *Henry IV, Part I*), Van Sandt presents Keanu Reeves as his Prince Hal. The son of Portland's mayor, he opts for a life on the streets in the company of an old Falstaffian dropout. Though this plot has possibilities, Van Sandt too often lets the Shakespearean parallels falter in favor of an intense, unpleasant focus on the sordid sex lives of male prostitutes in the Pacific Northwest. Even admittedly gay critics and audiences were split as to the results. The story line moves so far from the Bard's that when various characters (including River Phoenix as a hustler-Hotspur) suddenly start spouting poetry, the effect is ludicrous.

## Band of Brothers
### *Henry V*

Two Cities Films, 1945; Laurence Olivier
Samuel Goldwyn Company, 1989; Kenneth Branagh

At *Falstaff's* end, our brief glimpse of Henry V implies that we see a "finished" man, however young. Hal, having completed his rites of passage during the preceding misadventures, has now achieved maturity and appears in control of the crown, England, and himself. The two film versions of *Henry V* (Laurence Olivier's in 1944 and Kenneth Branagh's in 1989), however, take radically different attitudes toward the first difficult years of Henry's kingship, which was the formative period Shakespeare focused on.

Olivier's interpretation of Henry is essentially static. He has achieved full heroic status before the film begins and he self-assuredly solves each new problem as it arises, supremely confident that he is more than up to the effort. Branagh's Henry instead affects a pose of proper kingly behavior, seeming secure to others. Inwardly, he remains a complex, confused man with severe doubts about his abilities. Even though he has abandoned his wild early ways, this dynamic Henry V will fully believe in himself only after proving his worth in debate and combat, "arcing" during the course of the film.

Olivier and Branagh assumed polar approaches, to tone and theme as well as character, partly due to their different social-historical contexts. Olivier's was wartime England. Britain needed patriotic propaganda. A spectacular film, recalling past greatness and the ability to overcome against all odds, would aid the war cause. Winston Churchill suggested to Olivier that a *Henry V* film would be much appreciated.

Shakespeare offers *Henry V* as an ideal, in comparison to *Richard III*, the earlier vision of total evil. He shows that in *Henry V* (1599) he has matured as an author, no longer simplifying situations; rather, humanizing characters by showing the dark sides of bright heroes and decent elements in villains. Thus, in *Henry V*, Shakespeare includes the scene in which boyhood friend Scroop, caught in a traitorous scheme, is coldly sent to his death. Also, Henry's harsh words before the gates of the French town Harfleur ("your naked infants piled upon spikes") as to their coming fate if surrender is not prompt shows another side to his character. Finally, Henry hangs old Bardolph, most lovable of the Falstaff gang, with regret but without hesitation, when the companion of Henry's youth is caught stealing from a church—a double violation of Henry's dictum against pillaging and the sanctity of any religious place.

Churchill expressed concern about all three scenes, and Olivier pared them away. These omissions make Olivier's Henry a more than perfect role model, inspiring total loyalty from his countrymen. He is what Churchill requested: the fantasy hero figure England needed during its darkest hour. Olivier had fashioned the right film and Henry for that moment in time.

Not surprisingly, then, Olivier's portrayal of the battle at Agincourt is played as a Cecil B. DeMille spectacle. Broad vistas allow for panoramic views of brightly colored, magnificently armored knights fighting valiantly under a clear blue sky. Throughout, Olivier keeps his image in long-shot range, emphasizing the epic element of Shakespeare's play while eliminating the psychological. This, however, was the very aspect Branagh would, half a century later, seize upon. Of the play itself, Branagh insisted: "I feel it has been unjustly treated as a jingoistic hymn to England."

Moreover, Branagh believed Henry had more in common with alienated, neurotic Hamlet than Olivier's English Siegfried suggested. Like Sir Laurence, Branagh made his film-directing debut with his *Henry V*. The Belfast-born Reading-raised Anglo-Irish actor was twenty-seven years old when he set to work on his movie and was eight years younger than Olivier at the time of his auspicious directing debut. At that time, Branagh had recently left the Royal Shakespeare Company to form (with actor David Parfitt) the Renaissance Theater Company. Their concept was to mount populist, antielitist productions, rendering the plays easily accessible to the general public. They wanted Shakespeare for the common man, a contemporary equivalent of the original Elizabethan audience.

Branagh and executive producer Stephen Evans raised, from a variety of financial sources, nearly $10 million for their first film. A master manipulator, Branagh convinced some of England's most respected Shakespearean performers (Ian Holm, Judy Dench, and Paul Scofield) to play supporting parts. Branagh was so cinematically inexperienced that on the first day of shooting at Shepperton Studios he surprised everyone by admitting he didn't realize it was his job to shout, "Action!"

Nevertheless, he had carefully storyboarded the visual scheme, then brought the picture in on time (seven weeks) and under budget. Not everyone felt comfortable with some young upstart daring to compete with the abiding memory and lofty reputation of Olivier's *Henry V.* "The greatest act of hubris since Prometheus absconded with the rights to divine fire," huffed one outraged London critic; but as Branagh stated, "I passionately believe that all of Shakespere's plays need to be constantly reinterpreted," adding: "If a previous *Henry V* had existed, it certainly wouldn't have stopped Olivier." Though he greatly admired Olivier, Branagh understood that his own vision of the Bard's work in general and *Henry V* in particular was radically different from that of his idol.

Branagh replaced Olivier's declamatory theatrical delivery of great speeches with a naturalistic rendering. "Whereas Olivier's Henry was a knight in shining armor," Branagh explained before his film's release, "I feel the play is about a journey toward maturity." His Henry learns by doing, unsure whether any of his decisions will work out for the best, trusting in his own instincts for a positive outcome. If Olivier's film was shaped by the time during which it was created, that holds equally true for Branagh's. Completed in 1989, this *Henry V* was influenced by abiding international memories of the Vietnam fiasco and the patent absurdity of the recent Falklands war.

Olivier (though a commoner by birth) had played the role as aristocrat, a lofty hero to his faceless troops, an inspirational leader transforming simple clay into a fighting force. Conversely, Branagh's men are carefully particularized as individuals; *their* leader draws his inspiration from *them.* Although Olivier did include the "band of brothers" speech moments before the final battle, these words are all but thrown away, insignificant in his film's context. We are more taken by his charismatic appearance and mellifluous voice than his words. In Branagh's version, the words themselves rather than the man speaking are what we remember. Branagh's Henry is identical in appearance to his soldiers.

Indeed, he *is* them! When Olivier's Henry, face covered by cape and shawl, attempted to mix with his men on the eve of Agincourt, it appeared a clever trick perpetrated by a blueblood learning what his troops thought of him. When Branagh's Henry does the same thing, the impact is something else entirely. He tries and, sadly, fails to once more be at one with the old tavern crowd. This Henry still possesses the common touch but is removed by responsibilities of office. In Olivier's version, Henry's youthful experiences are barely mentioned, since they were the momentary madness of immaturity and are now irrelevant. In Branagh's version, the ghosts of the past haunt Henry, which necessitated flashbacks to the old days at Mistress Quickly's tavern. These scenes, lifted from *Henry IV, Part II*, are lit in the style of Rembrandt, with the richly colored past absolutely glowing, as opposed to the grim present, which is captured in unglamorous natural lighting.

Even as the portrait of kingship is decidedly different, so, too, is Branagh's reenactment of Agincourt. Here the horrific fighting takes place in the midst of a muddy field, under dark skies and in a somber atmosphere. The emphasis is on the brutality of hand-to-hand, medieval-style warfare. This perfectly expresses Branagh's late-eighties realistic sensibility (he admitted to watching Oliver Stone's *Platoon* before filming), as compared to Olivier's romantic portrayal of combat. Olivier's Agincourt was imbued with the "good war" sensibility of World War II, while Branagh reached back to the grimness of World War I with men squatting in the muck and squalor of soaked slit trenches, captured by the camera in intimate close-to-medium ranges. In each case, the director's technical choices communicate his point of view.

Branagh's character derives his strength from an absolute trust that God is on his side, implicit but not emphasized in the Olivier version. Henry's prayer to the Lord (in which he humbly asks forgiveness for Henry IV's transgressions, pleading that the sins of the father not be visited upon this son) is as central to Branagh's vision as it was peripheral in Olivier's. If we do believe these English will ultimately win, it can only be because of divine intervention, for their leader demonstrates no notable quality other than absolute faith. No wonder Branagh had musical director Pat Doyle include "*Non nobis domine*" ("*Not* unto *us*, O Lord, but unto *thy* name give glory"), sung by Henry's troops, during the postvictory march. Conversely, the stirring orchestral score William Walton provided for Olivier suggested that Henry won the triumph due to his innate skills—which, in fact, the real Henry did.

Nowhere, though, is the directorial difference between Branagh and Olivier so clear as in their choice of framing devices. Olivier's artistic contrivance is rightly one of the best-loved moments in all Shakespearean cinema, where the camera pans over a detailed re-creation of Elizabethan London and gradually moves in on the Globe Theater as a performance is about to begin. An audience composed of a few aristocrats and university students, middle-class citizens, and groundlings crowding in front eagerly await the show. A Chorus (Leslie Banks) begs everyone to forgive their "unworthy scaffold" and employ each viewer's "imaginary forces" to fill in what the company is unable to provide. As our star makes his entrance (Laurence Olivier playing Richard Burbage playing Henry V, on a stage within the cinematic image, a play within a film) the camera closes in. We are now at one with the Elizabethan audience.

When this simple stage gradually transforms into a grand reenactment of history, the moviegoing audience understands that this is a visualization of the transformation the play's viewers are imagining in their minds. Olivier is making over the simple staged suggestion of history to the spectacular vision Shakespeare hoped to inspire them to see.

Branagh's film begins in the movie studio where his *Henry V* was filmed. The Chorus (Derek Jacobi) strikes a match, illuminating the encroaching darkness. He is the only personage in modern dress. This Chorus is clearly familiar with modern conveniences and throws an electric light switch. As he opens huge doors to an adjoining room, the camera passes by to witness a minimalist re-creation of the past. Here the camera eye closes in on history. When the Chorus reappears, his modern dress reminds us that this figure is a surrogate for the moviegoing audience; he *is* us, peeking in on an old play, confirming that it passes the test of time.

Olivier's Chorus served as a bridge between the gathered Elizabethans (we "moderns" moving back in time with the play rather than having it brought forward for us). Olivier's approach was the generally accepted 1940s technique of construction; that is, creating a reality for the viewer of that time to enter and exist within. Branagh's is 1990s deconstruction, always reminding us of the essential artificiality of any drama, stage or film. "Branagh makes us understand that his medium is film alone," Stanley Kauffmann noted in the *Saturday Review*, "and that cinematic means, rather than transmutations of theater, will be his matter"—his medium *and* his message.

Branagh's Henry, though necessarily harsh, is nonetheless sensitive in a way Olivier's blissful once-and-future hero-king is not. Critic Sally Beauman noted that Olivier "removed from the hero's mind almost every doubt"; Branagh put them all back in. Indeed, if

Branagh hadn't wanted to convey his own interpretation, there would have been no justification for making his movie, since Olivier's was perfect, in terms of its avowed intention, and could not be improved on. An alternative, however, is something else, enriching the cinematic tradition of Shakespeare, and that is precisely what Kenneth Branagh provided.

# 6

## SOPHISTICATED COMEDY
### *Much Ado About Nothing; As You Like It; Twelfth Night*

> *Beauty is a witch against whose charms*
> *faith melteth into blood.*
>
> —Claudio, *Much Ado About Nothing*

By the mid-1590s, Shakespeare's main concern was with the English history pageant. Occasionally, though, he still took artistic respite with a comedy. However charming and clever (*Merry Wives of Windsor; All's Well That Ends Well*) or dark and disturbing (*Merchant of Venice; Measure for Measure*) the tone and temper might be, the diverse comedies share signature themes with more seemingly serious plays. Indeed, they often threaten to turn into tragedies and qualify as comedy less for their humor (since there are great gags in the tragedies and histories, too) than for the fact that they conclude with upbeat endings, most often life-affirming weddings rather than the funereal nihilism of the tragedies. Three comedies of this period, all turned into major movies, are here treated in the order Will most likely wrote them.

### The Geography of Intrigue
### *Much Ado About Nothing*
Renaissance Films, 1993; Kenneth Branagh

*Much Ado About Nothing* allowed Shakespeare to revise, on a more sophisticated level, the twin love stories from *The Taming of the*

*Shrew,* demonstrating how far he had advanced, in a few short years, as a writer. Now he was in supreme command of poetic dialogue, plot structure, and in-depth characterization.

In Matteo Bandello's collection of Italian tales (first published in Lucca in 1554), Will discovered the story of two innocent young lovers torn apart by a villain's malicious plot to convince the boy that his chaste beloved secretly invites men to her boudoir. From Edmund Spenser's popular poetic paeon to Queen Bess, *The Faerie Queene* (1590), he borrowed the device of a maid dressed in her mistress's clothing to make the faux indiscretion appear real. Then the Bard's unique gift kicked in, creating from scratch the couple that gives this play its distinction: Beatrice and Benedick—Petruchio and Kate on a more sophisticated level. To please the groundlings, he added Dogberry and his Watch. In the denouement, these country rubes save the day, to the delight of lower-class audiences, even as their betters fail to see through the shoddy conspiracy.

There are no metaphysical elements here (*Much Ado About Nothing* is a social rather than Green World comedy), but there is a pivotal Prince who is good, if flawed. Prince Pedro's bastard brother, Don John, is the Machiavelli whose dubious ancestry defines him, in Elizabethan terms, as "unnatural." This may be a dramatic reviving of Shakespeare's possible fears as to his own children's questionable parentage. Both good and bad princes manipulate people: Don Pedro, to arrange a happy marriage between bickering Beatrice and Benedick; and Don John, to destroy the arranged marriage of naive Hero and Claudio. In each situation, the "plot," whether benign or evil, results in life as theater; the characters in the play "performing" as "actors."

In 1988, while still relatively unknown, Kenneth Branagh had appeared in a stage production directed by Dame Judi Dench. During the opening sequence, Branagh winced while watching the show unfold as high art, imagining *Much Ado About Nothing* as popular entertainment. That's what it had been in Elizabethan times, intended for the enjoyment of ordinary people rather than as elitist escapism. As someone who grew up in a blue-collar neighborhood, Branagh knew full well that our modern equivalent of Shakespeare's playhouse is the commercial Hollywood movie. So as several soldiers politely marched onstage, suggesting Don Pedro's troops returning to Messina, Branagh fantasized the scene redone *Magnificent Seven* style, with rugged riders hurrying over a hill. When the women prepare to meet them, Branagh pictured the ladies seminude, as in soft-core porn.

During Beatrice and Benedick's exchange of witticisms, Branagh recalled beloved verbal bouts between Katharine Hepburn and Spencer Tracy. Dogberry and the Watch spouting malapropisms brought to mind the Keystone Kops by way of the Three Stooges. And when the song "Cry No More, Ladies" appeared, Branagh chuckled about how charming it might be if presented as a nickelodeon sing-along, with bouncing ball over the words so that audiences could join in.

When, five years later, Branagh had the opportunity to mount a film version, he opted for all of the above. Which explains why he forsook British stage performers, casting American stars: Denzel Washington as Don Pedro, Keanu Reeves as Don John, Michael Keaton as the idiot savant Dogberry, and Robert Sean Leonard as the handsome, if callow, Claudio. "I always liked the ballsiness of American film acting," Branagh admitted. "The full-blooded abandon. This play seemed to require it." As for classically trained actors, the Irish-born director scoffed at their "incomprehensible booming and fruity-voiced declamation."

American stars were "free of any actory mannerisms and the baggage of strutting and bellowing that accompanies the least effective Shakespearean performances. . . . We wanted audiences to react to the story as if it were in the here and now and important to them. We did not want them to feel they were in some cultural church." As to Denzel Washington, a black actor in an Anglo role, Branagh opted for color-blind casting. Washington was the contemporary actor who struck him as most royal, so that was that.

To achieve a balance between respect for Shakespeare's world-class words and naturalistic acting, Branagh did keep two assistants on hand during the lengthy rehearsal process. Russell Jackson, of the Shakespeare Institute in Stratford-upon-Avon, took the responsibility of making all cast members (particularly the Americans) consciously aware of when they were speaking prose or poetry, emphasizing the different demands of each. Hugh Crutwell, former director of the Royal Academy of Dramatic Art in London, assisted every actor in developing a "back story" to round out the characters into three-dimensional people rather than presenting waxwork figures in an old play.

Taking his cue from Shakespeare's anachronistic approach, Branagh avoided setting his film at any one moment in history. He opted for an indefinite-past golden age, as we might imagine while listening to a storyteller relate a tale from "once upon a time." The "period," if one can call it that, falls somewhere between Shakespeare's own 1600 and 1900, when the modern age began and magic disappeared from the world. Women's clothing appears seventeenth century; the heroic men's tailored uniforms, eighteenth century; and the black leather breeches worn by villains, nineteenth century S & M garb. If the *mise en scène* suggests a collage from past periods, the tone is decidedly modern. As heroes and ladies lounge about in the midday sun, the interracial as well as international crowd of attractive people appear to have stepped out of a Ralph Lauren advertisement. In scouting locations, production designer Tim Harvey fell in love with the idyllic quality of Italy's central region, particularly the lush, seductive landscapes surrounding Villa Vignamaggio in Greve, where, in 1503, Lisa Gherardini Giaconda (the model for the *Mona Lisa*) lived. The on-screen result was, in Branagh's own words, a place of "primitive passion where people live in the sun, eat, drink, and have sex."

In *Time*, Richard Corliss noted that that vision was achieved. Branagh made the play "so fresh and moved it so fast that audiences will forget it's Shakespeare." While emphasizing the possibilities for pleasure, Branagh was careful to include weightier themes, perfectly combining respect for Shakespeare's vision with an audience's hunger for entertainment. His *Much Ado About Nothing* is the filmic equivalent of that mid-nineties bestseller *Men Are From Mars, Women Are From Venus*; true to the Bard, Branagh suggests that the earthy, sensuous wisdom of women is far preferable to the macho posturings of men, which he mercilessly ridicules—particularly in the guise of his own character, Benedick.

This film is cinematic in more significant ways than the pictorial jazzing up of man-woman confrontations. The dancing is not only fast and furious, but what is more significant, it is central to the director's vision of community. Branagh also opts for subtler visual symbols. When Beatrice and Benedick, at last united in the love each has so long denied, swear eternal allegiance, the director-adapter shifts this scene to a hidden chapel, built specifically for the film, where they speak beneath a cross, conveying Shakespeare's insistence on the need for his heroic couples to restrain and contain passion within conventions at once social and religious. By confining the entire affair to a single villa, Branagh emphasized what critic David Denby of *New York* referred to as "the geography of intrigue" and highlighted the spying so dear to Will's heart; indeed, in Elizabethan times, the play was popularly referred to as "Much Ado about *Noting*."

Denby also noted that Emma Thompson's delivery of Beatrice's "O that I were a man!" speech came "as close to a feminist reading of the play as [possible] without altering the meaning of the text." Most critics reserved their warmest praise for Thompson. Stanley Kauffmann of the *New Republic* gushed: "I'll try to restrain myself. She has elegance. She has the finest command of inflection and style. She has spirit and soul. She is the first film actress since Katharine Hepburn to make intelligence sexy."

If there was a flaw, most reviewers agreed with Anne Barton of *The New York Review of Books* when she lamented Branagh's decision to "transform Michael Keaton, as Dogberry, into a menacing, sadistic, and profoundly unamusing thug." Branagh eliminated Dogberry's most significant speech in which he reveals himself as "a man who has suffered losses," once wealthy but now reduced to protecting the wealth of others, which he does to the best of his humble abilities. Others found the darkness of Keaton's approach a nice foil to the brightness of all the other goings-on. Keaton, as an Elizabethan Beetlejuice, prowls the alleys just outside this timeless realm where, as in *Romeo and Juliet* and other more serious plays, romantic love must—if a relationship is to survive—be transformed into true friendship.

**Love at First Sight**
## *As You Like It*
Inter-Allied-Film, 1936; Paul Cinner

Shakespeare drew stories from varied source material, adapting freely; here he closely followed the structure of a popular poetic novel from about ten years earlier. Thomas Lodge's posthumously published *Rosalynde* began with an opening statement that the reader should finish this *"booke"* only *"if you like it."* Will took the title, the female lead, and the pastoral plot and romantic entanglements from Lodge. He added another element, the English outlaw ballad, which enjoyed revived popularity in the 1590s. The Lord Admiral's company, a key competitor, had great success with a Robin Hood play. So Burbage persuaded Shakespare to add Merrie Men the next time he whipped up a Green World confection.

Will had already written comedy with strong romance; now it was time to try a pure example of the romance genre. He addressed the very issue of love, in all forms, from platonic devotion to over-whelming physical attraction, along the way touching on every pos-sible in-between emotion. By contrasting the selfless love of Old Adam for his master, the outcast-aristocrat Orlando, with the intense but passing romantic yearnings of the superficial shepherdess Phebe ("Who ever loved that loved not at first sight?"), the Bard could explore the varying, even contrasting, concepts we unwisely group under the misleading catchphrase *love.*

Always anxious to stretch his creative talents, Shakespeare was intrigued by the concept of the pastoral, which is any portrayal of a simple life lived near nature and shown as preferable to a sophisti-cated one in civilization. Such stories date back to Greece's The-ocritus and Rome's Vergil; more recently, England's Edmund Spenser (*The Shepheard's Calender*) and Sir Philip Sidney (*Arcadia*) Angli-cized this tradition. Such works idealized the shepherds, presented as engaged in gentle love play and rarely working—a far cry from real-ity. Shakespeare combined this escapist concept with his own inter-est in characters who flee a corrupt court, a plot he had handled in *A Midsummer Night's Dream.*

Will reimagined Lodge's story for a broader audience, allowing shepherds and servants to serve as audience surrogates for groundlings. The poetic dialogue would be Shakespeare's own, more rough and ready than Lodge's courtlier approach. Jaques, a solitary melancholy among the banished Duke's company, is a character added to Lodge's story via the inspiration of Shakespeare. Jaques serves as a bridge between Mercutio and Hamlet; he is the sardonic wit as supporting player, speaking the play's greatest soliloquy, the Seven Ages of Man, which insists that each of us, naively believing we live a unique life, repeat a simple pattern that leads solely to the grave.

Jaques's speech embodies Shakespeare's vision during his darkest hour, a necessary foil for the general good spirits, offsetting them without spoiling the happy mood. Shakespeare also added Touch-stone, the Court Clown, adjusting his big-city attitudes to country life. His Rosalind resembles Beatrice of *Much Ado About Nothing*—bright, witty, and independent. Yet Beatrice's wit could turn nasty, revealing sadomasochistic torment; Rosalind, no less aware of the world's pitfalls, remains bright, buoyant, and clever, though never cutting. Akin to Olivia in the upcoming *Twelfth Night*, she is strong-willed and sharp-witted. Yet Olivia falls apart when she falls in love; Rosalind, though capable of loving deeply, never loses self-control. Like Viola, she disguises herself as a boy (Ganymede) and befriends a nobleman without letting him take control of her fate. Rosalind is, simply, Shakespeare's ideal woman, combining the best qualities of his other heroines without suffering their limitations.

On the American stage, Katharine Hepburn brought her unique presence to the role, creating the quintessential Rosalind for our twentieth century; on film, she would masquerade as a boy in George Cukor's *Sylvia Scarlett* (1935). Unfortunately, Kate did not play the part in Paul Czinner's 1936 motion picture. Czinner mounted his ambitious $1 million film as combination valentine–vanity project for his wife, German actress Elisabeth Bergner. The casting was disastrous. *Newsweek* noted that she "voices her passion in German gutturals," also pointing out "her temperamental inability to stop wriggling." According to film historian Roger Manvell, Bergner "had a screen personality diametrically opposed to that of Rosalind. Rosalind is a forthright woman, capable, provocative and determined beneath her surface diffidence and charm. Bergner's screen [presence] has an ageless, kittenish quality." Bergner is dizzyingly coquettish, all wrong for Rosalind.

The pity is, if one can manage to overlook Bergner's impossible performance, this British production has much to admire. *As You Like It* marked Olivier's first screen appearance in Shakespeare; his Orlando, masculine yet sensitive, is in itself enough to make the movie worth watching. Leon Quartermaine's reading of Jaque's "man is a poor player, strutting" briefly onto the world's stage is exquisite, happily preserved for all time on celluloid.

Clearly, everyone involved hoped to achieve something special in the way of a fusion between Shakespeare and the cinema. Sir James Barrie, who had created a preadolescent Arden of his own in *Peter Pan*, fashioned the treatment, which screenwriter R. J. Cullen and Karl Mayer expanded into a scenario, cutting Shakespeare without adding anything else. "I would like you to believe we have made the film with love and with reverence," Bergner stated. "We have had slightly to cut the longer speeches, but every word that we have left out has only been after argument, quarreling, and occasional tears." She understated the trimming because one-third of the play is gone. Missing are several significant speeches, including Jaques's boast that through verbal expression of his dark intellect he might "cleanse the foul body of the infected world" and his cynical undercutting of all the happy marriages at the end: "There is, sure, another flood toward, and these couples are coming to the ark." Still, the film's rewards far outweigh its limitations.

Czinner consistently employs animal imagery to express Shakespeare's themes. For the opening, featuring Orlando and his beloved servant, the camera slowly moves over realistic foliage, capturing natural characters with a simple barnyard backdrop, including pigs and chickens. Cinematographers Hal Rosson and Jack Cardiff create, through drab black-and-white images, the appropriately realistic sense of hard farm life. We are then prepared when Oliver, Orlando's cruel brother, intrudes and slaps our hero across the face. The camera cuts to the court of usurper Duke Frederick, where the blindingly sterile white of brightly lit palace buildings conveys the emotional coldness found here. Swans swim by proudly, while ostriches arrogantly stroll about as Rosalind and the duke's fair-minded daughter, Celia (Sophie Stewart), are encountered. We have met two sets of characters belonging to two different worlds; shortly, they will all slip off to the magical realm of Arden.

First, though, they meet at the wrestling match, allowing Czinner to reveal considerable gifts at cinematic storytelling. There's nothing stagey about the way he portrays this event; beginning with a long shot showing the court in attendance, moving to medium takes on Orlando wrestling with Charles (Lionel Braham), then to close-ups on Rosalind and Celia's reactions, the sequence is removed from any theater origins.

The forest looks self-consciously unreal, which is the very point. Of the true Duke, Charles the wrestler discloses: "He is in the forest, and a many merry men with him; there they live like the old Robin Hood of England . . . and fleet the time carelessly, as they did in the golden world." The play is about man's unending desire to leave the everyday world behind and seek an ideal existence, regaining the glory of the good old days or, rather, what we want to believe were better times, easy to do now that they are gone. Arden is Shakespeare's Shangri-la. Such a spirit is present, thanks to a set design, constructed in shades of gray, allowing us to see an Arden as removed from dark farm or bright court as they were from one another. Lazare Meersom's ability to bring alternative worlds to vivid life on-screen had earlier been displayed in the Gallic classic *Carnival in Flanders*. We encounter a wood teeming with differing classes: aristocracy, minor nobility, middle class, peasants, country bumpkins, even the confirmed noncomformists Jaques and Touchstone, who join the heterogeneous group while maintaining their distinct individualities. In essence, Shakespeare's diverse audience saw onstage an artistic mirror image of themselves.

Meersom managed the proper effect by creating, on a studio soundstage, an Arden at once fantastical yet believable. Naive critics, like John Marks of *Sight and Sound*, foolishly complained of the "fake flora and genuine fauna prodded in the wings." This is precisely as it should be: half real, half imaginary. As in the play, there is evidence of Shakespeare's desire to stop short of romanticizing nature as an ideal, where everyone and everything can happily coexist. True to the bard's suggestions, Czinner effectively visualizes a snake in this demi-Eden, crawling over the sleeping body of Oliver; as Orlando peers on, the snake slithers away, only to be replaced by an even more dangerous lion. Will is too much the realist to believe that nature is entirely benign, and Czinner rightly brings the playwright's vision to the screen intact.

Touchstone woos pretty Audrey, even as she milks a cow—the single workaday element in an otherwise enchanted wood. As he does, rabbits dance about, suggesting the reproductive force which, apart from romance or friendship, draws clown to wench. A dissolve montage allows for a neat transition from Orlando's poem to the image of his carving a heart on a tree. Czinner conveys Shakespeare's notion of romantic love as a form of madness, especially in comparison to deep friendship. The introduction of a gender-bending element (Rosalind, disguised as a boy, who entices new "pal" Orlando to pretend to be wooing "him," and pretending "he" is Rosalind, who, unknown to Orlando, he/she really is) plays as light comedy while mimicking Shakespeare's life-as-a-theater theme. When Rosalind eventually throws off her disguise, we know they will live happily ever after, enjoying the best of both worlds: Romantic attraction coupled with deep friendship, both necessary, to Shakespeare, if the relationship is to last.

When all the key characters finally face off with one another, Czinner pans, then swish-pans, between them. The technique implies that while these people stand close to one another, they really don't know much about friends and lovers, the camera work makes them appear so near to, and yet so far from, one another. A terrible case of miscasting has always kept this otherwise fine film in eclipse.

## An Ill-Favored Thing
### *As You Like It*
Squirrel-Sands Films, 1992; Christine Edzard

Modern dress can work well for Shakespeare on screen or stage, though only if performed with full understanding of, and proper respect for, the intent of any individual play. That was not the case, at least for most English critics, with this self-consciously bizarre approach to one of the most charming comedies ever written. Here, Orlando (James Fox) is banished from contemporary London, a concept which might have played if only he subsequently fell in in love with Rosalind (Emma Croft) in a fitting up-to-the-minute equivalent of Arden. Instead, Orlando goes from bad to worse, stepping into an unrelentingly grim slum where, in place of shepherds and swains, the young duke encounters the homeless, living in cardboard boxes. "It sounds as ugly as it looks," Lawrence Halliwell noted, "with some wretched speaking of the verse." Nigel Andrews, in London's *Financial Times*, likewise complained: "We feel like victims of a mobile theater experiment, moving our camp stools from one daft venue to the next as we follow a bunch of under-rehearsed actors belting it out into the void." As always, there were those who defend anything remotely avant-garde. Adam Mars-Jones of the *Independent*, though critical, proved kinder owing to such an aesthetic: "In this misguided and also perversely endearing version, Christine Edzard ultimately proves the Bard's resilience, but she proves it the hard way." Such a comment suggests this film was far more amenable to those who enjoy the offbeat and experimental, rather than a high-quality traditional approach to what was intended, in truth, as an appealingly conventional play. Only Ilona Halberstadt, of *Sight and Sound*—the British film magazine long famed for cheering-on any attempt at outrageous cinema—offered a rave: "Edzard restores to filmed Shakespeare the means and immediacy of cinema, daring to present, as the theater has been doing since the nineteenth century, Shakespearean text in a modern context." Though live theater has indeed been doing just that, any single modern-context performance on stage or screen ought to be praised or damned not for the approach, but for the degree of success achieved within its context. Due to generally negative reactions, this motion picture has not, as we go to print, been officially screened in the United States.

# Speak For Yourself, Cesario
## *Twelfth Night*
Renaissance Films, 1996; Trevor Nunn

Shakespeare ended his middle period with *Twelfth Night*, an effortless blending of the preceding plays's most appealing qualities. From *Much Ado About Nothing*, he salvaged the domestic household as it would have functioned during the late Renaissance. He also added "serious comedy," via the unrequited love Orsino, Duke of mythical Illyria, harbors for Olivia, who has sworn not to marry following her beloved brother's death. From *As You Like It*, Will revived his crowd-pleasing concept of a young woman disguising herself as a man; Viola, separated from her twin brother, Sebastian, during a sea storm, assumes masculine attire to protect herself. As Cesario, she befriends Duke Orsino, who sends her to woo Olivia for him. Olivia promptly falls in love with this handsome "boy," who is herself intoxicated with Orsino.

Half social comedy and half Green World divertissement, *Twelfth Night* was written late in 1599 for a special manor performance. The play is derived from diverse preexisting materials, such as *Gi 'Inganni*, a popular Italian farce from a half century earlier, where the device of male and female identical twins, constantly mistaken for one another, was used. Other characters were drawn from anthologies, chronicles, and other authors' English plays, here combined in an entirely original manner.

Owing to the sophisticated tone, *Twelfth Night* makes few accommodations for a groundling audience, so rude mechanicals were notably absent. Yet a comedy must provide laughs, so there is Feste, a Touchstone-like clown. Each plot allowed the Bard to examine some recurring interest. Continual confusion of brother with sister replays the appearance-reality motif in a lighter mood. The manner in which the mischievous Toby Belch makes everyone believe supercilious Malvolio is insane raises Shakespeare's inquiry into the nature of madness. Characters "bewitched" by the beauty of others implies the fickleness of romantic love, compared to the lasting emotion of friendship. Viola and Olivia represent variations on the liberated, yet chaste, ideal woman. Ambition appears when Malvolio attempts to rise above his station, while life as theater runs through every plot, tying all elements into an organized whole.

Vitagraph's J. Stuart Blackton produced a one-reeler in 1910. Florence Turner, as Viola, emerged from the Great South Bay onto a Long Island beach at Bayshore, which subbed for enchanted Illyria. *Twelfth Night*, which remained a perennial theatrical favorite, was not brought to the screen again until 1947, when a Spanish musicalized version, *Noche de Reyes*, was directed by Lucia Luis, starring Fernando Rey. Russian director Yakow Fried adapted the story in 1955, via an elaborate production, for Lenfilm; *Dvenadtsataia noch* featured Katya Luchko in dual roles as Viola and Sebastian, with Anna Larlonova as Olivia. Though considerably less known than the Soviet adaptations of Shakespearean tragedy, this is an equally fine interpretation. Despite the obvious loss of the Bard's dialogue, Fried (who likewise devised the screenplay) managed to sustain the proper tone of sophisticated romantic comedy, undercut by the broad, vulgar clowning of Sir Toby Belch (M. Yanshin), Andrew Aguecheek (G. Vipin), and the Clown (B. Freindlich). "It is culture shock to hear an Elizabethan ballad sung as though the vocalist were a strolling troubadour at the local Russian Tea Room," Kenneth Rothwell and Annabelle Melzer noted in *Shakespeare on Screen*, hastening to add: "What the film lacks in faithfulness to the Elizabethan World Picture, it more than compensates for with rollicking energy and honest enthusiasm for the subject."

Critics agreed that the film, which arrived on American shores at the height of cold-war animosity, neatly cut across cultural barriers, speaking to the essential humanity of all people despite careful cutting that reduced the running time to a mere ninety minutes. Fried effectively opened up the play by moving key scenes outdoors, taking advantage of the striking Soviet seacoast, while filming those sequences that had to be set indoors on the most decadently elegant settings left in postrevolutionary Russia.

Also, he filmed in Sovocolor to avoid the bleak starkness associated with that country's black-and-white Shakespearean tragedies. "Most of his principals," A. H. Weiler pointed out in the *New York Times*, "temper (their) fervor with an appreciation of Shakespeare's snarled romances. . . . Although they are Russians and their language gives *Twelfth Night* an exotic flavor, they play the comedy in the lusty spirit of the Bard." At a time when nuclear war seemed inevitable, Russians and Americans managed to happily make a temporary truce via a mutual respect for Will.

Other than a tasteful *Hallmark Hall of Fame* NBC televised performance in 1957 starring Maurice Evans and Rosemary Harris,

Hollywood film producers avoided this piece. The only American producer who dared do a version was Hugh Hefner. In 1988, he commissioned a soft-core porn version for the Playboy Channel. By the mid-nineties, however, gay liberation had come out of the closet, all but overtaking popular culture; a film of *Twelfth Night*, with its Elizabethan gender bending, was a great idea waiting to happen. So theatrical director Trevor Nunn (whose only previous films were *Hedda* and *Lady Jane*) and movie producer David Parfitt (Kenneth Branagh's collaborator on *Much Ado About Nothing*) mounted a handsome version, released in America by Fine Line.

Parfitt and Nunn shot *Twelfth Night* entirely in Cornwall, making extensive use of the picturesque coast. They completed all exterior filming during the autumn months, for a gorgeous array of fall colors as well as an overpowering melancholia conveyed by perpetually gray skies. This look is striking; whether it's what Shakespeare had in mind for his festive play is debatable.

In its all-important first third, *Twelfth Night* is slow-going—particularly compared to Branagh's *Much Ado About Nothing*. A greater problem, though, is one that has plagued stage productions for centuries: The comic bits involving gross Toby Belch (Mel Smith), pretentious Andrew Aguecheek (Richard E. Grant), and silly maid Maria (Imelda Staunton), however ripe for humor, seldom strike anyone as funny when visualized, live or on film. Belch tends to come off as a Falstaff without the charm that makes Sir John's horrible habits tolerable; the nastiness of the plot against Malvolio violates the celebratory comedic climate, moving into a predecessor of the comedy of cruelty.

That problem is compounded here by the casting of Nigel Hawthorne as Malvolio. He rescues the character from the cliché Malvolio's name suggests (i.e., bad fiddle or one who is out of tune). By making the man less vicious and considerably sympathetic, however, Hawthorne causes the plot against Malvolio to appear all the more disasteful. At the play's end, dislikable young Malvolio stalks away, viciously cursing everyone; here a humbled old gent packs his bags and quietly leaves, making us feel sorry for a sad, decent man with no place to go. Earlier, though, Hawthorne does provide the film's high point. Convinced Olivia is mad for him, he dares enter her boudoir wearing a grotesque outfit, grinning at imminent seduction; *Twelfth Night* reaches a farcical pitch which, sadly, it never again achieves. A bigger problem is Ben Kingsley as Feste. There is nothing festive or clownish about him; he's played as a variation on

Jaques, that deeply disturbed malcontent. Audiences approaching this film with no previous knowledge would never guess Feste is a man of motley; instead of delivering his lines in an ironic manner, bald-pated, darkly cloaked Kingsley spits them out as curses. The function of Feste is negated, which makes the film bleaker than it ought to be.

Helena Bonham Carter is a marvelous Olivia—an intelligent, deep person rather than the silly, distracted woman she's often depicted as. Thus, when she goes head over heals crazy with love, the effect is all the funnier. Numerous touches ring true, such as having Sebastian arrive in the land with a copy of *Baedeker's Illyria* under his arm, a contemporary nod to Shakespeare's anachronisms. Also impressive and appreciated is Nunn's decision to underplay rather than overdo gender bending, which is more appealing by not being pushed for topical purposes. The scene in which Viola (disguised as Cesario) and Orsino almost kiss, under the spell of a romantic song, is a marvelous statement about love that's true enough to cross all lines.

Ultimately, though, this film comes across as a Kenneth Branagh movie without the Branagh magic. Costuming was clearly derived from Branagh's approach; the characters are outfitted in an assortment of late-nineteenth-century uniforms and gowns. Nunn did not employ those American actors who added such notable energy to Branagh's films, however, thereby moving Nunn's work into the art-house cinema realm (that "movie-movie" Branagh cautiously avoids). Still, there is much that is charming here, particularly Imogen Stubbs as the disguised Viola, heatedly pursued by Helena Bonham Carter's obsessed Olivia.

Nunn went to great lengths to emphasize that this was a movie, not a stage play, including an elaborate depiction of the shipwreck, after which Shakspeare's Viola crawls out of the sea. The locations are vivid; still, Richard Alleva of *Commonweal* held that the very qualities that make *Twelfth Night* such a magical piece on the stage negate its possiblities for film. The willing suspension of disbelief, necessary for us to accept that everyone believes Viola is a boy, works better when the lighting, costuming, set design, and performance style are all artificial, legitimizing the artificiality of the premise. "But what happens when you put the actors in nature and point a camera at their only moderately made up faces?" Alleva asked; the contrivance at the heart of this piece cannot stand such a strong dose of reality.

"Shooting on location," Alleva insisted, "no matter how stylish the production values, entails a certain inalienable naturalism which is at odds with the fairy-tale doings of *Twelfth Night.*" In fact, Alleva is only half-correct, since *Twelfth Night* is only half fairy tale. Illyria exists, like the play itself, midway between the real world of Renaissance Messina and the enchanted world of the forest of Arden. A production of pure fantasy like *A Midsummer Night's Dream*, if shot in a real forest, would prove disastrous; *Much Ado About Nothing*, a social comedy in which reality is never violated, is perfectly suited to shooting at an actual villa. Since *Twelfth Night* is half and half, real settings strike us neither as disastrous nor delightful, rather as acceptable if less than satisfying.

This *Twelfth Night* never invokes the kind of all-out audience response (particularly raucous laughter) that Branagh's *Much Ado About Nothing* elicits. To be fair, that could be due to the fact that here Shakespeare opted for sophisticated humor rather than belly laughs.

# 7

# A TIDE IN MEN'S LIVES
## *Julius Caesar*

*This was the noblest Roman of them all.*
—Antony, on Brutus's death

In *The Parallel Lives*, written circa A.D. 100 in Rome, the Greek intellect Plutarch fused his twin fascinations with history and philosophy. Fact-based tales were shaped and embellished to convey clear moral lessons. In 1559, Jacques Amyot translated Plutarch into French; Sir Thomas North, a multilingual sophisticate, adapted the work into idiomatic English in his *Lives of the Noble Grecians and Romans*. This version was published in 1595; Shakespeare, ever on the lookout for potential material, picked up a copy. Having completed his cycle of history plays but before beginning the period of great tragedies (1602–1608), the Bard offered a transitional piece. To do so, Will returned to the key theme of his historical tetralogy: the moral issue of killing a king.

By employing the story of Julius Caesar, the Bard could address an intriguingly complex variation: what do you do with a ruler who manages the country well, yet is ambitious enough to want more than even he has any right to? Caesar had created an empire, as had Elizabeth; like her, he had grown controversial, inspiring loyalty from the masses and enmity among a vocal minority. The Bard desired to communicate, in the guise of a bloody-good entertainment, how disastrous such an assassination was for any country. Anachronistically performed at the Globe, *Julius Caesar* would simultaneously take place in the past and present. Caesar would be dressed not in a toga but as an English king; "Roman" senators would don garb befitting British nobility. Though Will remained essentially true to Plutarch's conception, he freely shaded characters and events for his own purpose.

Although Caesar is the title character, he is hardly the leading one. Brutus and Cassius, as they flowed from Shakespeare's quill, emerged not merely as coconspirators but dramatic foils. Brutus is the idealist who kills Caesar to save the republic when Caesar's ambition threatens its limited democracy. Cassius is a cynic, embittered by his own inability to achieve greatness and hungry to taste power. The Machiavellian Cassius works his wiles on Brutus. This aspect of the plot is influenced as much by the medieval morality play and *The Prince* as Plutarch, since Shakespeare shaped a Brutus who, Faust-like, sells his soul to Cassius's devil in the flesh. Brutus emerges as a tragic hero; his appealing naïveté ironically brings him down.

Which explains why Shakespeare's Antony could, at the end, gaze down at the body of Brutus, the man who murdered his beloved mentor, proclaiming, "This was the noblest Roman of them all," and meaning it. Shakespeare also invented the play's most memorable moment, Antony's funeral address over Caesar's body, which appears neither in Plutarch nor any earlier stage renderings. No matter that Antony's words were created by an Englishman fifteen hundred years after the fact. For the following four centuries, politicians the world over would crib from that speech, adapting strategies for manipulating the masses to their own ends. The abstract truths this play offers about the world of politics and distinct·types of people who inhabit it transcend specifics of Rome, 44 B.C., due to Shakespeare's ability to dramatize universal situations through a specific setting; the tale rang true for Elizabethans and does for us today. Which explains why *Julius Caesar* works well when performed in modern dress or rehearsal clothes.

## Early Efforts

The first film version of *Julius Caesar* (1907) was not an abbreviated adaptation but a five-minute portrayal of Shakespeare sitting in a garret and penning the piece as characters leap to life from his imagination. The director was France's Georges Melies; one year later, American producers Stuart J. Blackton and Sigmund Lubin fashioned competing one-reel (ten-minute) shorts, focusing on the play's exploitive elements, particularly the murder in the senate. Also in

1908, Giovanni Pastrone, who would initiate the Italian spectacle genre with *Cabiria* (1914), mounted his own one-reel *Caesar;* another variation on the story, *Brutus*, was produced in Italy in 1910 by Enrico Guazzoni, with expanded settings and fuller narrative. American Charles Urban may have attempted an early color *Caesar* in 1911; that same year, G. W. Jones filmed a stage play directed by Frank Benson at the Stratford Memorial Theatre in England.

## An Idealization of Revenge
### *Julius Caesar*
Avon Productions, 1952; David Bradley

Independent filmmaker David Bradley shot a full-length *Julius Caesar* in and around the vicinity of Northwestern University. The black-and-white ninety-minute "feature" (total budget, $15,000) tread a delicate balance between advanced amateur and Poverty Row professional, earning high marks from critics for sheer audacity, if not technical quality. As Bosley Crowther of the *New York Times* delicately put it, "This company of earnest collegians has given a firm pictorial character to the sombre and severe old drama of intrigue and political violence." Otis L. Guernsey Jr. of the *New York Herald Tribune* politely added that "it has the strength of a fresh, intense and ambitious piece of work" while also noting the "rough handling of the spoken poetry," which was delivered, by aspiring young actors, with "brute force rather than with a gentle touch of understanding," leading to "a general weakness in the acting."

With one notable exception. Former drama student Charlton Heston, who had earlier created costumes for Bradley's *Macbeth* and starred in his silent *Peer Gynt*, portrayed Antony. This was a role Heston, now a New York professional working in the live golden age of televion, would have relished performing in Franklin Schaffner's *Studio One* CBS production (March 6, 1949); he had been awarded the small part of Cinna. Catching his former collaborator's scene-stealing work, Bradley rang up Heston, insisting he should have been Antony, a concept Heston did not disagree with. Bradley then offered to pay him fifty dollars a week if the budding star would return to Chicago. (The camerman was the film's only other salaried person.) Heston did, shortly revealing the combination of charisma and talent that would soon vault him to the top echelon of movie stars. Guernsey observed that "Antony's funeral oration, delivered to an angry crowd portrayed by students, is the best-staged scene in the film, with the changing temper of the mob clearly represented and with Heston photographed mostly from below and looking like an idealization of revenge."

Harold Tasker played Caesar, Grosvenor Glenn was Cassius, with Bradley himself assuming the role of Brutus. The movie was shot so as to take advantage of the city's Roman architecture; an abandoned football stadium made do for the Colosseum, Caesar was murdered in the Mason Temple (which, conveniently enough, had been modeled on the actual Roman Senate), while Antony delivered his funeral oration on the steps of the Field Museum. Too often, though, the nearly nonexistent budget called attention to itself: A single tent stood in for an army encampment, two shields were supposed to imply a Roman battle line, and a close-up of a fire was all Bradley had to convey the violent revolution that swept Rome after Caesar's assassination.

However much one wants to support the fine intentions of high-minded local filmmaking, the film's considerable defects outweigh its noble ambitions. Like Heston, Bradley was afterward offered a Hollywood contract; the director's later work proved surprisingly unexceptional considering such exciting alternative-cinema origins. (For more on David Bradley's career, see also the chapter on *Macbeth*.)

## More Stars Than in the Heavens
### *Julius Caesar*

M-G-M, 1953; Joseph Mankiewicz

Modern dress had been basic to Orson Welles's approach when the *enfant terrible* mounted a Mercury Theatre interpretation in 1937, emphasizing parallels between Caesar's overwhelming ambition and the contemporary rise of fascism. Tagged the Black Shirt version, this staging was produced by Welles's longtime collaborator John Houseman, who devoted his life to Shakespeare's work. Fifteen years later, Houseman convinced Hollywood to bring the Bard back to the screen.

M-G-M, ever status conscious, proved susceptible to Houseman's dogged determination. An all-star cast might attract the public, particularly if the era's most exciting young actor, clamoring for roles that would expand his range, was top-billed. Marlon Brando (then a veteran of only three films) would play Antony, firmly distancing himself from Stanley Kowalski, the unpleasant, modern brute he had portrayed in *A Streetcar Named Desire*. Though intrigued by characters from the ancient world, Brando had refused to perform in *The Egyptian* and upcoming *The Prodigal*, which were mindless cardboard spectacles in color and wide screen. The Bard was another matter; *Julius Caesar* would allow Brando to work not only in a classical setting but with a great script. Brando was heartened to learn that Joseph L. Mankiewicz, recently associated with the multi-Oscar-winning *All About Eve*, would direct. Mankiewicz and Houseman would garb their characters in togas to satisfy the M-G-M brass. However, they would avoid allowing their film to degenerate into superficial spectacle, instead emphasizing universal human and political drama. Mankiewicz said, "It's a good, rip-snorting piece of blood and thunder, coupled with eternally new and true-for-today characters."

That was enough for Brando, who was delighted to also learn that the film would be shot in black and white. At this time, "big" pictures, particularly historical epics, were invariably in color; black and white was reserved for ultramodern "little" films like *Marty*. Houseman insisted, "We kept it in black and white because there are certain parallels between this play and modern times. People associate dictators with newsreel shots of them haranguing the crowds. Mussolini on the balcony, that sort of thing. With color, you lose that reality; the show becomes a mere spectacle." The level of spectacle was indeed reduced, if with ironic results. "They have succeeded, perhaps beyond their hopes," Parker Tyler noted in *Theater Arts*, but "the result is a film without heroic proportions." Houseman and Mankiewicz had accentuated the Bard's artistry while playing down the cinema's rich potential for expanding Shakespeare's showmanship.

Their production emerged as respectable, polite, and noncontroversial, resembling upper-middle-brow *Hallmark Hall of Fame* TV presentations. "The picture is more a competent Shakespearean production which happens to be on the screen than it is a creative piece of filmmaking," Moira Walsh noted in *America*. Indeed, Mankiewicz strictly avoided reaction shots, instead keeping his camera tight on the speaker of any soliloquy. Such an approach is theatrical rather than cinematic; a director ought to cut away the moment any character begins speaking to fully exploit the camera's remarkable ability for nonsynchronous sound, letting us hear one thing while seeing another. More significant, this *Julius Caesar* lacked what critic Parker Tyler referred to as a "lucid idea"—some organizing principle, on the order of Olivier's "a man who could not make up his mind" approach to *Hamlet*, which, however debatable, endowed Olivier's film with its sense of a central purpose.

The film lacked modern topicality, but one way to ensure modernity, despite period trappings, would have been to take the film's cue from Brando and acquire an ultracontemporary cast of talented Americans, with Montgomery Clift a natural for Brutus. The audience would quickly adjust to Romans with idiomatic American voices, which was essential to the film's meaning. On the other hand, if a more classical reading was the goal, James Mason was perfect for Brutus, and Richard Burton was the logical Antony. Simply, the combination of Brando and Mason was wrong; Mason's exquisite elocution made Brando's Method mannerisms appear absurd.

The problem, however, stretched beyond the incompatability of Brando and Mason; Louis Calhern (Caesar) was a veteran of M-G-M superproductions; John Gielgud (Cassius) was primarily a stage actor; Mason, though British, was a bona-fide film star; and Edmond O'Brien (Casca) was a veteran of film noirs. Even the women clashed; Greer Garson (Calpurnia) was a holdover from the golden age of studio fabrications; Deborah Kerr (Portia) was one of the emerging realistic actors. The result was a hodgepodge of talents that did not belong together in the same picture.

Despite his supposed genius, Marlon Brando appeared intimidated by Shakespeare and came across as stiff, seemingly frozen with fear that he might make a wrong move. Nowhere is this problem so evident as in Antony's funeral address. Antony must begin softly, sensing he is at odds with the crowd, then slowly but surely seduce them, his voice growing ever more self-assured as listeners waver, finally building, crescendo like, toward a fever pitch, sending them off to kill. Brando offers a one-note recitation, the entire speech tense, angry, shrill; there's no variety to his half-dozen deliveries of "honorable men."

The film does have its champions, among them Bennet Cerf, who hailed it as "one of the most impressive—and exciting—movies I've ever seen." To be sure, this *Julius Caesar* is not without merit. One effectively cinematic moment occurs when Brutus, alone in his home, ponders possible action. Mankiewicz visually shows us the character's sense of entrapment, filming him through branches of a tree, which appear ready to close in on him. Another striking scene takes place immediately after the oration. As the crowd roars out of control, Brando's Antony turns his head halfway toward the camera, smiling wickedly. Shakespeare's "Cry, havoc!" speech is omitted, since Brando's face says it all; for once, a picture truly is worth a thousand words.

Shortly thereafter, Antony approaches a bust of Caesar and turns it around to face him, transforming the statue into a mirror; we know, without needing to be told in words, that he has grown ambitious. Another impressive touch is the retention of, even reemphasis on, a key issue: the give-and-take between free will and fate. The film's finest sequence is the early discussion between Brutus (James Mason) and Cassius (John Gielgud), which allows two masterful performers to work their magic. Mason mostly reacts, with understated but expressive facial gestures, to Gielgud's stunning recitation of key phrases, including: "Men are sometimes masters of their fates" and "The fault lies not in our stars, dear Brutus, but in ourselves." Yet it would be wrong to quote such lines as expressions of Shakespeare's point of view; Cassius is a devil in the flesh. By allowing himself to be won over, Brutus seals his fate, which he will indeed learn is controlled by forces greater than he can contradict.

Likewise, Louis Calhern's Caesar, superstitious from the start, ignores the Soothsayer's warning of the Ides of March and his wife's dream, first admitting: "What can be avoided, Whose end is purposed by the mighty gods?" then arrogantly adding: "Yet Caesar shall go forth." What most effectively comes across is Shakespeare's own state of mind at the time he wrote *Julius Caesar*: an artist trying to reconcile his own conflicting attitudes about destiny and self-determination. Unfortunately, Houseman and Mankiewicz were too often in awe of Shakespeare. At the beginning, they show hordes of Romans entering the Coliseum but keep us outside with Brutus and Cassius. Only later do we hear (via Casca) of Antony's participation in the games, Caesar's epileptic fit, and the sly manner in which Caesar and Antony manipulated the adoring public. Since this is a movie, we ought to see more and hear less.

Fortunately, Mankiewicz and Houseman did stage the battle at Philippi in which the forces of Antony and Octavius defeat those of Brutus and Cassius. Although filmed in Bronson Canyon, close to

Hollywood Boulevard, we are momentarily sucked into the realm of spectacle. Antony's ambushers hurl javelins and spears, then rush in, swords ready, for the kill. As the battle becomes hand to hand, however, there's a fade to black that disappoints the audience, eager for a big fight scene. The filmmakers' stated desire to avoid popularizing Shakespeare in such a manner seems wrongheaded, for the Bard was a popular entertainer first and serious artist second; he would, if he could, have staged that fight.

Instead of a scene showing Titinius's desperate ride, we see Pindarus on a hill, shouting down descriptions to Casius. This pulls the audience out of a moviegoing experience by reminding them that this is, in fact, a filmed play. "I suspect that if Shakespeare had been the scriptwriter on this project," Philip T. Hartung argued in the *Commonweal*, "he would have taken *more* liberties with his original play than did producer John Houseman."

Several other important moments were missing, including the poet Cinna's words (though mentioned, he is never seen) and the brief argument between Antony and Octavius moments before the battle. One effective element is Mankiewicz's handling of the women's roles. Young Portia (Deborah Kerr) comes across as an early feminist, begging her husband to treat her as an equal (rather than as a trophy wife); had Brutus shared his plan, commonsensical Portia would have argued against it. By the same token, Calpurnia (Greer Garson), though an Establishment retrowoman, offers her husband sage advice; had he listened, Caesar would have survived. Though the play features scant scenes for women, the primary role of women in Shakespeare's vision is fully conveyed.

Another plus is the final third of the film, often considered the play's weakest part, as the sense of anxiety dissipates following Caesar's death. Here, though, Antony—so ambiguous early on—reveals, in scenes with Octavius and Lepidus, his essentially nasty personality, allowing us to grasp that he is more Machiavellian than Cassius. A crosscut to the tent of Cassius and Brutus shows them, on the eve of ruination, coming close together as friends, Cassius leaving much of his cynicism behind. It is a measure of Shakespeare's irony-in-artistry that he could make us dislike Antony (whom we were originally predisposed to admire) at the moment he achieves power and, conversely, like Cassius (whom we despised at first sight) precisely when he loses it.

However much we may have wished, early on, for Antony to revenge Caesar, when he at last accomplishes this goal, we are left with a hollow feeling; absolute power has corrupted Antony absolutely. He will be an effective leader, though a ruthless one. A truly great prince must, like Henry V, project humility and humanity as well as hauteur; Antony, like Cassius before him, has developed a lean and hungry look, setting up his highly ambiguous character in Shakespeare's sequel, *Antony and Cleopatra*.

### Savage Spectacle
## *Julius Caesar*
Commonwealth United, 1970; Stuart Burge

Ever since getting a taste of the Antony role while still a recent college graduate, Charlton Heston had been hungering to play the part in a big-scale film. After achieving superstardom following DeMille's *Ten Commandments*, and then receiving the Best Actor Oscar for William Wyler's *Ben-Hur*, Heston let it be known that he would accept a considerable cut in salary if anyone was willing to mount an alternative interpretation of M-G-M's highly regarded (some would say overpraised) film. During the early sixties, Orson Welles (who had directed and costarred with Heston in the film-noir classic *Touch of Evil*) called one night, enthusiastically explaining that CBS wanted him to direct a filmed *Julius Caesar* for a network broadcast. Richard Burton was supposedly set to do Brutus, although negotiations with the network broke down and the project was eventually discarded.

Heston's offer to take a salary cut remained open. As it happened, a young Canadian producer, Peter Snell, needed to sign a major name before assembling his first feature film. The moment an A-list actor agreed to play Antony (for $100,000, a fraction of his normal paycheck), Snell had little trouble raising a modest $1.6 million to shoot *Julius Caesar* on a tight budget. Heston's name also made it easy to attract other talent. John Gielgud had done Brutus onstage, Cassius on film, and was happy to now play the title character. Orson Welles, a onetime stage Brutus, was anxious to do that role. There was only one problem. The character of Brutus, young and innocent, wasn't right for a middle-aged, overweight man; "He's too fat!" exclaimed Gielgud, though admitting that Orson would have been a wonderful choice, actingwise. Welles might have made a fine Cassius, though his portliness would have rendered Caesar's pronouncement "Would he were fatter" ridiculous. Caesar was already taken; but Casca would be acceptable, even though it was a minor role. Throughout preproduction, Welles was touted as being on board; when shooting began, he was notably absent.

Sadly, Snell never offered Welles the director's chair; had he, this *Julius Caesar* (whatever the outcome) would have caught the attention of the world's *cinéastes*. Apparently aware of Welles's legendary excesses, Snell decided to go a safer route, hiring a journeyman professional with TV experience. Stuart Burge had never mounted a motion picture but was eager to try after having recorded the Olivier *Othello* on film. Moreover, Burge had helmed a BBC production of *Julius Caesar*, acclaimed for its total lack of staginess. So the work inched slowly toward fruition. Snell and Heston agreed to shoot in 1967, though cameras didn't roll for two years.

During that time, cast members came and went. Diana Rigg and Judy Parfitt would be Portia and Calpurnia, Richard Chamberlain would play Octavius. Owing to the international flavor, Snell wanted Omar Sharif for Brutus; when that didn't happen, American actor Jason Robards, despite misgivings, assumed the role. He had never before attempted Shakespeare; worse, he was unfamiliar with the play, never having seen it; worse still, he was in a deep depression and was drinking heavily over the unpleasant ending of his marriage to Lauren Bacall. The casting decision would prove a mistake. Problems began when Robards arrived in London for a two-week rehearsal period and immediately let it be known he didn't care for Burge's approach.

Deciding to improvise in front of the camera so that his work would be "fresh" when shooting started in Spain, Robards ceased showing up for rehearsal and started hitting the pub circuit. No wonder, then, that he appears to be acting in a different film than everyone else. In the first half, when others play their parts quietly and naturally, Robards's work resembles a satiric send-up of bad Shakespearean acting: all elocution, no emotion, with the words slowly spoken in a numbing monotone. After the assassination, when the cast gradually tightens its style to suggest the play's classic stature, Robards goes the other way and rants and raves in a realistic style.

There are other flaws. The budget didn't allow for the spectacle necessary to bring ancient Rome to life. Yet the Heston name created viewer expectations of another grand spectacle on the order of

*El Cid.* Medium-range (rather than long) establishing shots seemed an obvious attempt to conceal the lack of a worthy set design. Rather than historical Roman togas, the costuming by Julia Tevelyan Oman was instead modeled on a baroque vision of classical Rome, as later imagined by eighteenth-century painters. Heston described the costumes as "anachronistic, ugly, and impossible to wear."

Howard Thompson of the *New York Times* tagged the film as "flat and juiceless as a dead haddock." Despite its own limitations, M-G-M's 1953 version towers over Burge's version. However, there are qualities that shouldn't be overlooked, individual elements that, in some instances, outclass their counterparts in the Mankiewicz film. Chief among them is Gielgud's performance. Sir John makes Caesar marvelously ambiguous, alternately sly and foolish. We here believe that this man could early on see through Cassius's false show of friendship, yet be vulnerable enough to flattery that he could be lured to the forum against all logic. Louis Calhern offered a simplistically pompous Caesar, while Gielgud creates a wise and weary man, proud of his accomplishments rather than ego driven all out of compass. When he dies, we are moved in a way we were not in the earlier film.

The assassination scene is staged more realistically and believably here. In the 1953 film, the killing, once it begins, does not noticeably change in tone. Caesar stands among senators who fall upon him en masse. Since the assassination proceeds from Caesar's refusal to bend on a noble's banishment ("I am as constant as the north star"), it makes sense to have Caesar initially seated, across from the body of senators, who recline in a gallery. This allows us to believe that what Caesar initially perceives as a normal debate could quickly transform into a confrontation, then escalate into brutal violence. The marvelous looks that pass over Gielgud's eyes reveal his changing reaction to, and growing fear of, the men before him. When attacked first by Casca (Robert Vaughn), then others in turn, Caesar rises, stumbling about aimlessly as he is further mangled. When he spots Brutus (whose back remains turned to the doomed man), Gielgud's eyes light up, wordlessly conveying Caesar's certainty that he'll find solace. But when he grabs Brutus's arm, Caesar notices a knife, then watches in disbelief as the blade punctures his stomach. Gielgud's reading of the legendary "Et tu, Brute?" allows the line, for once, to play as the perfect conclusion to what occurred rather than a remote quote from antiquity.

Another scene, approached in an original manner, features the cynical Antony, the crafty Octavius, and the good soldier Lepidus deciding (after their coup) who is to live and who is to die. Heston offered the ingenious idea of having the men discuss their hit list while hedonistically reclining in a Roman bath attended by nubile slave girls rather than stiffly sitting around the conventional table. This produced a sense of "chilling detachment" via an ironic contrast between men enjoying superficial creature comforts while casually dismissing comrades. It's "a meeting of Mafia capos," according to Heston in his 1995 autobiography *In the Arena*, "with Antony as godfather."

No actor could erase the memory of Gielgud's Cassius (which in itself makes the M-G-M film worthwhile); still, Richard Johnson offers an alternative that is unique yet satisfying, playing down the Machiavellian interpretation that Gielgud emphasized. Gielgud's Cassius was haughty, self-important, and epicene, while Johnson's Cassius comes across as ruggedly masculine, a man made bitter by experience and harboring legitimate complaints. Gielgud's Cassius, angrily questioning why he hadn't achieved Caesar's status, seems superficial and self-pitying. Johnson rails against the unfairness of life because he is one of those qualified people who get lost in the shuffle.

The production emphasizes how Cassius's every decision, such as standing against Brutus's ill-guided notion of sparing Antony or the awful decision to let Antony speak, is right on the money. Toward the end, Burge includes a sequence Mankiewicz trimmed away in which Brutus, misguided as ever, sends word to Cassius to reinforce him at Phillippi. Cassius knows that it is ill advised to risk all the troops in a single fight. Yet his love of Brutus, whom he initially hoped to exploit, has now expanded and is quite genuine. He has arced completely and can only sadly shrug, then ride into the valley of death. The dignity of this self-sacrifice, missing from Mankiewicz's film, alters the audience's reaction, so that, at least in part, because of Robards's incompetence, this *Julius Caesar* threatens to become "The Tragedy of Noble Cassius."

Also included is the full role of Octavius, played by Chamberlain as an effeminate Hotspur. Whereas the 1953 production all but eliminated Octavius, Burge's version comes closer to Shakespeare's. Octavius and Antony at first appear well matched; by the end, they bridle at one another because Octavius is a little boy, jealous of

Antony's natural leadership abilities. This parallels the Brutus-Cassius relationship, which moves in the opposite direction: from cynical exploitation to true friendship. Wisely, Burge shows Octavius as cocommander with Antony at Philippi, whereas Mankiewicz made the mistake of ascribing the victory to Antony alone, thereby diminishing the parallel pairs. Burge includes the key moment of confrontation between the two sets of generals before the battle, each man revealing his true self and value system—which Mankiewicz unwisely cut. Burge at least attempts to convey Shakespeare's ironic treatment of the four key characters. He makes us like Brutus and Cassius moments before they die, even as we like Antony and Octavius less than we originally did when they conquer.

The key moment in any *Julius Caesar* is Antony's funeral address. His oration stands not only at the center of the play's narrative but at the heart of its dramatic greatness. Nowhere else does Shakespeare so completely convey his understanding of practical politics or his deep-seated fear of the easily swayed masses. In mere minutes, the populace, who was ready to crown Brutus, is begging for his blood. Mankiewicz played the speeches by Brutus and Antony in an identical manner, each speaking directly to the crowd. Burge took a cue from Heston, effectively employing it to reveal the contrast between the speakers and their speeches.

Here Brutus stands on the forum steps, at a distance from the public. He speaks, as a political innocent would, logically, sharing reasons for doing what he did. For the moment, this approach works; people are taken by the sincerity of his liberal idealism. By addressing the crowd en masse, he is visually established as a leftist who perceives the community as an entirety. Then it is Antony's turn, and Heston's as well. This Antony is a conservative and a realist who believes in the concept that would eventually be defined as "rugged individualism." So Antony descends *into* the crowd, speaking successive lines to specific people, carefully isolating them, one-on-one. Cynically understanding that emotion will win out over logic, Antony plays on their basest emotion—greed—and makes them aware of the riches Caesar intended for them, turning the listeners into a mob.

The sequence works due to Heston's underscoring of subtexts in a way Brando did not. Every time this Antony repeats the phrase "honorable men" in changing contexts, the line rings with a different intonation and an altered meaning. Brando paced his speech nicely; Heston gives us pacing *and* variety. Brando's Antony appeared totally sincere; Heston's conveys Shakespeare's concept via a double image. This man is at once sincerely moved by the death of his friend while delighting in his ability to manipulate the masses.

Burge attempted, at every turn, to make the film a visual experience, though limited resources (and, in truth, limited talent) reigned him in. Near the beginning, he briefly shows Antony running in the games rather than merely have Casca report the event. Burge vividly portrays Calpurnia's dream of the bleeding statue, though this makes her later recitation redundant. When the conspirators bend to wash their hands in Caesar's blood, Burge cuts to a down angle, visually communicating Shakespeare's moral vision of them. He shows Antony reclining, on the eve of battle, downing grapes and wine, conveying the man's essential hedonism. Second-unit director Joe Canutt (son of legendary stunt man Yakima Canutt) staged the battle so that we see distinct strategies, whereas Mankiewicz presented an ambush from a studio western.

Finally, when Pindarus climbs up a hill to watch his companion Titinius ride, we see the chase over Pindarus's shoulder, making it purely cinematic. None of this is to suggest that the film is, overall, better than Mankiewicz's. However, this *Julius Caesar* is considerably more interesting, worthwhile, and venturesome than anyone has previously noted.

## One Final Note

*Time* once commented: "*Julius Caesar* is a play that lends itself fairly easily to filming. Melodramatic, rather than introspective, it is a gangster picture with an ancient setting." The truth of that statement makes the fact that this play hasn't been filmed more often incomprehensible; there's a *Hamlet,* as well as an *Othello* and a *Romeo and Juliet* for each successive generation. Why filmmakers have not retold *Julius Caesar* in nearly thirty years remains a mystery.

# 8

# I KNOW NOT SEEMS
## *Hamlet*

*To be or not to be; that is the question.*
—Hamlet

By 1599, Shakespeare had reached the height of his powers. It was the perfect moment from which to stretch the boundaries of tragedy beyond anything existing in the Western world. Would it be possible to write a tragedy in which fate played little, if any, part? Could the hero's ultimate demise be determined entirely by forces within the man himself, without regard to what *Romeo and Juliet's* Friar Laurence described as "a power greater than we can contradict"? It could, and the result would be *Hamlet*, the first true tragedy of character and, many insist, the most complex, confounding play ever written.

"Along with the King James Bible," *Life* once noted, "*Hamlet* has passed into the language so completely that millions of people who have neither seen nor read the play unknowingly repeat fragments of its stirring lines in everyday conversations to describe their own situations and emotions." *Hamlet* isn't an important artifact from our collective past, rather, it is central to our ongoing culture.

First and foremost, Hamlet is as universal as Oedipus of old. Hamlet's specific story touches something in every theatergoer, whether living in 1600 or the year 2000. Hamlet is one man; simultaneously, he is Everyman. As such, he is the ultimate literary creation, the apotheosis of any dramatist's goal: Convey the general truth of the human condition through the story of an individual character. No wonder *Hamlet* is often performed in modern dress, a bare stage suggesting that Elsinore exists altogether out of time—a state of mind rather than some concrete castle in Denmark.

Paradoxically, though, *Hamlet* is the most *modern* of Shakespeare's tragedies, sharing as much with Arthur Miller's *Death of a Salesman* as *Oedipus the King,* by Sophocles. He is, in a word, *existential.* From the rightfully famous "To be or not to be . . ." speech to the wise-guy, stand-up-comic attitude this protagonist assumes to the central issue raised by the play (is life, in Hemingway's words, nothing more than a dirty biological trick?), Shakespeare raised questions that, four centuries later, would be debated by artist-philosphers, including Camus and Sartre. Is, as Nietzsche insisted, God really dead? Are we all, in Kurt Weill's words, lost in the stars? Or is it possible to continue believing there is "providence in the fall of a sparrow," God's hand evident in the smallest act?

We live in an age of doubt, but Hamlet was created when the idea of the great chain of being still offered reassurance that the world was a perfectly ordered, smooth-running machine. Hamlet stepped from out of the shadows as a precursor to the twentieth-century existentialist as antihero. A Scandinavian intellectual, Hamlet would seem more likely to have been created by Ingmar Bergman (who did indeed mount a stage *Hamlet*) than Shakespeare. Bergman is the modern dramatist who most profoundly analyzes the search for meaning in what appears a God-abandoned universe, while Shakespeare was an Elizabethan of provincial origin and conservative leanings. At a time when literary figures were still defined by some humour (a single, overriding personality trait), due to one of four bodily fluids. Hamlet presaged the psychologically complex characters of post-Freudian drama.

Ironically, Shakespeare conveyed such revolutionary ideas through what was, on the surface, a humble genre piece. *Hamlet* belonged to a popular type of lurid tale considered no more likely to result in profundity than the typical western or gangster film of today. The "revenge tragedy," which had flourished in the late 1580s, was staging a comeback. The public devoured plays—good, bad, or indifferent—dealing with some central character who sets out for vengeance. Crude, bloodthirsty, playing to a lowest-common-denominator audience and contemptuously dismissed by serious-minded theatergoers, the Elizabethan era's revenge tragedies (including a roughhewn *Hamlet,* probably written by Thomas Kyd) peaked, then waned in popularity.

In 1597, a rival company revived Thomas Kyd's *Spanish Tragedy*, and the public loved all the blood and violence in this tale of revenge. Burbage suggested that Shakespeare find material for a similar production. Whether Will recalled seeing Thomas Kyd's unmemorable *Hamlet* or discovered the tale during his own reading is debatable. Hamlet was by this time well known, already in the process of passing from folk fable into myth. The story can be traced back to the ninth-century oral tradition. When Saxo Grammaticus wrote *Historia Danica* (approximate date, 1189), he included a character named Amlethus of Elsinore. The ending was epic, as Prince Amelthus dispensed with his uncle and ascended to the throne. Some four hundred years later, French scribe Belleforest translated this story, opting for a sad finale due to the organizing principle of his anthology, which was called *Histoires Tragiques*.

Kyd most likely drew on Belleforest's volume, adding the play within a play, the battle with Laertes, and the arrival of Fortinbras, prince of nearby Norway, who restores order. Such elements contributed to the theatricality, allowing this crude version to succeed with a rowdy Elizabethan audience, but Kyd's poetry was uninspired, and his characterizations were simplistic. What Shakespeare achieved with such seemingly unrewarding material was thus all the more remarkable.

Indeed, the Bard did such a beautiful job that a "problem" led to heated debate during the following centuries. Hamlet has the opportunity to kill King Claudius early in the play, but he refrains from avenging his murdered father. This lack of action seemed implausible to audiences and critics in a character supposedly bent on revenge. Shakespeare himself offered an explanation that was consistent with his worldview: Like all his heroes (other than the notable exception, Macbeth), Hamlet wants to do the right thing even when it's difficult to discern what that may be. So Hamlet may mean precisely what he says: He doesn't kill the king when he believes Claudius is praying, since the hated enemy's soul would go to heaven. As Shakespeare's creation came to seem like more of a real man than a literary figure, critics (particularly during the early nineteenth century) attempted to determine the *real* reason Hamlet delays. In so doing, they re-created Hamlet in their own image.

To be fair, there is a justification for their notion of a problem. Shortly after Hamlet confronts the spiritual incarnation of his father, he assures best friend Horatio: "It is a true ghost." If he's certain, why, then, would Hamlet decide to test the ghost? Hamlet sets out to make sure it isn't the devil in disguise planning to trick Hamlet into killing an honest man, thereby dooming Hamlet to hell for eternity. This can be explained by viewing Hamlet as an intellectual who, once his initial emotional reaction has passed, logically thinks things through and is willing to delay a while for absolute certainty. Then again, Hamlet may have some secret reason, one he hides even from his conscious self.

Romantics perceived Hamlet as being weak of will and essentially effeminate; for such a poetic soul to be ordered to kill was, according to Goethe, like "a great action laid upon a soul unfit for it." Subsequently, there were two stage traditions: actors like David Garrick and John Philip Kemble offered a dignified, if bombastic, Elizabethan prince, whereas Edmund Keane and Edwin Booth opted for an eccentric, inwardly troubled coward. In time, the latter interpretation won out; little matter that it contradicted Shakespeare's intended action hero, if one more cerebral than most. The softer, gentler Hamlet became the rule, unchallenged for so long that—for better or worse—the public came to accept Hamlet as an indecisive, effeminate man.

## Silents, Please

No wonder, then, that one of the more notable Hamlets of the early twentieth century was enacted *by* a woman. Sarah Bernhardt won acclaim in the part, though audiences had difficulty accepting her as Macbeth or Othello. In addition to popular stage performances, the legendary star performed in an early (1900) film version, a brief rendering of the climactic Hamlet-Laertes duel. Surprisingly, this antique, completed more than a quarter century before *The Jazz Singer*, was a crude sound movie; music and voices, recorded on phonograph records, were played simultaneously with the brief (less than five minute) film. Following Bernhardt's minispectacle, there were numerous other *Hamlets*, all silent, the most memorable directed by George Melies (France, 1907), Luca Comerio (Italy, 1908), William George Barker (England, 1910), August Blom (Denmark, 1910), Cecil Hepworth (England, 1913), and Eleuterio Rodolfi (Italy, 1917).

Each starred a man in the lead role; however, one silent film, discussed next, took Hamlet's "effeminacy" to its illogical conclusion.

## Goodnight, Sweet Prince
## *Hamlet: The Drama of Vengeance*
Art-Film Germany, 1920; Svend Gade

In 1920 Asta Nielsen starred in a Berlin-based version directed by Danish filmmaker Svend Gade, with the screenplay by Erwin Gepard. This *Hamlet* was, by the collaborators' own admission, only peripherally related to the play, derived from an 1881 American tome by Edward Vining, *The Mystery of Hamlet*. The book's central conceit explains why Nielsen offered something altogether different from Bernhardt—a woman playing a man whom many believed to be effeminate. Nielsen incarnated the idea that Hamlet was actually a woman who spent her life disguised as a man. Thus, Nielsen is a woman playing a woman pretending to be a man who is perceived as feminine—a unique, if debatable, solution to Hamlet's "problem."

Rather than Shakespeare's tragedy of enclosure, Gade crafted his film in the epic-history-as-human-melodrama approach Griffith initiated five years earlier with *The Birth of a Nation*. Gade opened with rapid crosscutting between old Hamlet, off fighting a battle with old Fortinbras (whom he kills), and the birth of young Hamlet at Elsinore. Gertrude gives birth to a girl; she is fearful her husband may die and worried whether the population will accept a woman as head of state, so she swears her nurse to secrecy, then announces that a prince has been born. Years later, Gertrude (resembling wicked Lady Macbeth more than Denmark's morally ambiguous queen) and Claudius conspire to kill old Hamlet. Hamlet delays his/her vengeance owing to a crisis of sexual identity rather than any failure of nerve. Attracted to friend Horatio, (s)he must repress such yearnings so that the secret will not be revealed. This Hamlet woos Polonius's daughter only because Ophelia and Horatio are falling in love; Hamlet can best keep Horatio free for him(her)self by seducing the competition.

The gender-bending approach is so similar to the heroines disguised as boys in Shakespearean comedies that one wishes Gade had gone all the way, giving his film a happy ending. Nonetheless, Gade employs the cinematic vocabulary created by Griffith to drive home points in visual terms, most notably animal symbolism. Hamlet, returning from Wittenberg, discovers Gertrude and Claudius (in long shot) feasting; the camera tilts down to a closer shot of two snarling dogs at the royals' feet, gnawing on bones, establishing a connection between two sets of beasts. Even as Hamlet confronts his enemies, Gade crosscuts to young Fortinbras and his troops, hurrying to enact a last-minute rescue not unlike the one that concludes Griffith's monumental 1915 movie. Hamlet's often erratic behavior, perversely feminine for a supposed macho man, makes sense in this different context.

The impact of this widely seen film was to further the image of Hamlet as an essentially feminine figure, whether woman or man. So the romantic stage convention of (in one critic's words) "delicate dreamers" deepened in the public consciousness despite the fact that no significant filmed *Hamlet* appeared for three decades.

## The Undiscovered Country

### *Hamlet*

Rank of England, 1948; Laurence Olivier

In 1948, Laurence Olivier, basking in praise for his resounding wartime success *Henry V*, announced that he and Arthur Rank would join forces again. Their *Hamlet* would be shot in black and white on Denham Studio's soundstages, forgoing the detailed on-location work basic to their previous collaboration. "I see *Hamlet* as an engraving," Olivier said, "rather than a painting." Olivier's approach derived from his sense of this play as an intimate character study. Moreover, he was strongly influenced by current vogues in filmmaking, which had drastically altered since the war's end. In Hollywood, a style emerged that expressed the difficult tenor of the times: film noir. French critics dubbed it—"films of the night," grim stories of confused characters disillusioned to find everything changed for the worse.

Simultaneously, movies were becoming more psychological. The general population ceased to conceive of analysis as something for a few mad undesirables, but rather as a necessary medical treatment for the walking wounded who composed a "lonely crowd." Hollywood reflected this by providing Freudian variations of traditional genre pictures: The gangster (Raoul Walsh's *White Heat*), the cowboy (Howard Hawks's *Red River*), and the thriller (Alfred Hitchcock's *Spellbound*) film now featured inwardly troubled heroes suffering neurotic impulses owing to some deeply felt, if consciously repressed, childhood trauma. Today that era's strict Freudianism (on film as in life) seems naive due to its insistence that a single problem rests at the root of all mental illness. At the time, though, Olivier was as immersed in reading psychological tracts as he was busily watching recent film noirs. Not surprisingly, his *Hamlet* emerged as a representative work for the postwar years.

Before embarking on the $2 million film's six-month gestation period, Olivier consulted noted analyst-author Ernest Jones, who had written extensively about Hamlet as suffering from an oedipal complex; not coincidentally, Olivier played Oedipus onstage to great acclaim earlier that same year. As Olivier and Alan Dent cut *Hamlet* by one-third, Sir Laurence arrived at his own conclusion: "This," he announces at the film's beginning, "is the tragedy of a man who could not make up his mind." The movie proceeded from that conception (or, if you will, misconception); general audiences wrongly assumed the opening words were by the Bard. The mainstream press responded positively, enjoying the castle's horror-movie appearance as well as the accessibility achieved by streamlining. Academics, particularly in the literary field, complained that Olivier pandered to public taste and misrepresented Shakespeare's meaning by providing a reductive interpretation which removed the ambiguity that makes *Hamlet* great.

No question that his film was, as Robert Hatch of the *New Republic* wrote, "overwhelmingly visual—it pours out images and impressions with a prodigal richness you would suppose exceeded your capacity to assimilate." Olivier had been highly impressed by the use of deep focus in the work of Orson Welles, particularly *Citizen Kane*. By presenting several visual planes with the same sharp clarity, he thereby brought a new realism to the screen. In fact, *Kane* had, in 1941, served as something of a precursor to film noir, as had Alfred Hitchcock's *Rebecca* of the previous year, in which Olivier starred. Those directors shared a fascination with long, winding staircases, which separate the hero's house into upper and lower levels, suggesting the character's own higher consciousness and lower Freudian id.

Likewise, Olivier transformed Hamlet's Elsinore into a symbolic estate on the order of Kane's Xanadu or Max de Winter's Manderley. Olivier opens with a dissolve montage through a mist, toward the hero's foreboding home; shots of surf crashing nearby could be outtakes from Hitchcock's *Rebecca*. Olivier's hero, a cinematic second cousin to Kane or Max, emerges as more confused than complex, while the royal bed becomes a visual key that unlocks the movie's meaning, much as the Rosebud sleigh does at the end of *Citizen Kane.*

As in 1930s horror classics by James Whale (*Bride of Frankenstein*) and Todd Browning (*Dracula*), Olivier slowly tracks down the castle's gloomy corridors. This technique enabled him to create a sense of narrative continuum (basic to the cinematic experience) rather than the short, separate scenes of a play. The traveling shots take up so much time (some lasting three minutes) that the text of *Hamlet* had to be cut more drastically than *Henry V.* Fortinbras, essential to Shakespeare's view of civil order restored, had been dropped from many stage productions, as had the second gravedigger. Olivier also eliminated Rosencrantz and Guildenstern, Hamlet's betraying schoolmates. Some famous speeches (the self-loathing "O what a rogue and peasant slave am I"; the paranoid "How all occasions do inform against me") were excised; other difficult lines, modernized. ("Recks not his own rede" here becomes "Minds not his own creed.")

Conversely, Olivier depicted sequences only reported in the play, including the drowning death of Ophelia, here inspired by Millais's rightfully famous painting. This provides a successful fusion of sight and sound, where the speech is pruned so that image and words compliment rather than repeat one another. Conversely, the weakest is (as Professor Robert A. Duffy noted) Ophelia's report to her father of Hamlet's private visit; the image merely illustrates rather than adds to what she says. Professor Duffy also delineated Olivier's use of *mise en scène* and lighting for Ophelia. Whenever Hamlet approaches her, an open window allows a view of the greater world outside, behind the girl who was played as highly intelligent by Jean Simmons, then nineteen years old. Olivier makes visually clear that *his* Ophelia is *not* part of the conspiracy; if Hamlet only realized this, she might offer him escape from the suffocating enclosure the castle has become for him. Other people appear guileless but are guilty; Ophelia seems part of the plot but isn't. The inability of Olivier's character to grasp this seals Hamlet's tragedy. He falls victim to the discrepancy between appearance and reality.

Olivier transposed the order of scenes, in some cases improving on the original. Hamlet's legendary "To be or not to be . . ." occurs after, rather than before, his harsh confrontation with Ophelia. During their meeting, he comes to believe that she is in on the plot and berates her badly. It stands to reason that Hamlet would consider suicide only *after* being convinced (if wrongly) that the woman he loves is among the nest of vipers. In keeping with the psychological interpretation, Olivier presents most of that speech (and other soliloquies) as a voice-over, which is set against images of crashing surf, thematically suggesting inner turmoil. Working closely with set designer Roger Furse, Olivier achieved a balance between unique and universal elements. The castle is at once actual and surreal, specific enough to satisfy the cinema's demand for a grounding in reality and symbolically shaded to suggest that what happens in this microcosm mirrors the universe itself.

As to the character, Professor Peter Donaldson saw the interpretation as "narcissistic," and Hamlet's "deep and persistent doubts about the value of the self" were traceable to Olivier's life (as revealed in his biography, *Confessions of an Actor*). If we all discover something of ourselves in Hamlet, it makes sense that Olivier would, too, but as an auteur rather than interpreter, presenting his Hamlet. Shakespeare had done much the same thing when he had Hamlet write a play, then request a naturalistic acting approach ("Speak the speech, I pray you, trippingly on the tongue"); thus, Hamlet *is* Shakespeare.

Philip T. Hartung noted in *Commonweal* a striking contradiction in interpretation: "Hamlet is well established in the film as a man who could not make up his mind, (but) is portrayed by Olivier as a man with a delightful sense of humor and a confidence in himself that belie the gloomy Dane." Throughout most of the movie, Olivier's passive Hamlet threatens to dissolve into the castle walls; at other moments, including the sea battle, he becomes a Douglas Fairbanks–like swashbuckler, leaping about in dazzling displays of derring-do. Perhaps, though, this is not such a contradiction. During Olivier's school days at All Saints, he was forced to play Katharina in *The Taming of the Shrew* (doing so, by all reports, brilliantly), though he'd rather have acted Petruchio. The character, perceived as feminine, desperate to prove his masculinity, is essential to Olivier's autobiographical approach. But the character's dichotomy stretches beyond the personal. Olivier, though relying on the romantic view of Hamlet, also wanted to include hints of the Elizabethan man of action. This can be taken as an attempt to fuse the two traditions, much as his filmmaking approach fused cinema with literature.

As to that, in the *Saturday Review*, John Mason Brown expressed fascination with what he perceived as Olivier's basic stylistic problem: "to find an outward form for an inward tragedy. Not such a form, mind you, as a stage designer would have evolved. No, a form three-dimensional, spacious, filmworthy." Brown argued that with its great spatial expanses the play *Henry V* had all but begged to be filmed, whereas *Hamlet*, essentially a one-set story, defied effective filmization. Brown's misconception is that since the camera can go anywhere, it *ought* to; the truth is, the camera, properly understood, is employed by the director to reveal his locale(s) as he desires us to perceive it (them).

Films which leap about from place to place (westerns, spectacles, and picaresques) are not necessarily more inherently "cinematic"; they only qualify as such if the director employs those spaces creatively, as is the case with John Ford or D. W. Griffith. Thus, a one-set film can be entirely successful as long as the director approaches that single place with a creative camera. Alfred Hitchcock's *Rear Window* exemplifies how truly cinematic (and nontheatrical) a single-set movie can be.

Whatever one's complaints about this *Hamlet*, its enduring importance stems from the fact that Olivier often succeeded in his attempt to search for ways in which technical devices of cinema could heighten the impact of a stage play, rendering the notion of "canned theater" ever more remote. Though his Hamlet is, in many respects, aesthetic and soft, there's enough adventurous bouncing about to suggest that the time had come to put the romantic cliché to rest, reviving the earlier, virile Hamlet who dominated what was essentially an Elizabethan *Death Wish*.

## Hamlet, Sturm und Drang
### *Hamlet: Prinz Von Danemark*
Bavaria Attelier, 1960; Franz Peter Wirth

Swiss-born Maximilian Schell, hailed by many critics as the Continent's equivalent to Olivier, mounted his own *Hamlet* onstage in Munich during the August festival of 1960. Schell modernized the language ("To live or not to live," he called out; "Get thee to a nunnery" became "get thee to a whorehouse," in keeping with Shakespeare's intention); Schell directed the production himself. William Glenesk, who visited the city's music hall, reported in *After Dark* that old-guard audiences found Schell too antitraditional, whereas young people swarmed the place. They discovered themselves in his melancholy prince, perfectly suited to the sixties. Hamlet was an idealistic activist standing up to Denmark's corrupt Establishment. This Hamlet barely stood still long enough to appear to be thinking, much less lost in thought; "The stage is not the place to think," Schell explained. "Theater is action, present tense. I do my thinking *before* the play. You, as audience, see it in the action."

So soliloquies were spoken in the active rather than the passive voice. Schell's Hamlet, Glenesk continued, is all "Sturm und Drang, strident, cool, yet heavy with the weight of his own aggressive approach—a Prometheus, a titan." The production was filmed specifically for broadcast on Eurovision by director Franz Peter Wirth, who sensed that the correct approach would be to play *Hamlet* as an intimate chamber drama. He ignored any and all possibilities for epic proportion—those very elements theatrical filmmakers emphasize, which explains why there are no exterior shots.

The result came pretty close to being the ideal televised *Hamlet*; in America, *Variety* praised "Wirth's imaginative staging within the confines of the small screen." Problems began, though, when director Edward Dmytryk (who had given Schell his first important Hollywood role several years earlier in *The Young Lions*) became convinced that this *Hamlet* ought to have a theatrical release. Those same close-to-medium-range shots, so right for television, came off as disturbingly claustrophobic when shown in American movie theaters.

Dmytryk convinced Schell, against the actor's better judgment, to dub the film into English rather than use subtitles. Schell opened his mouth and articulated words in German, though what we heard was British verse. The lines in their original, abbreviated German ran considerably shorter than the added Shakespearean counterparts, creating the awkward situation of Schell closing his mouth before a soliloquy was concluded. Only the multilingual Schell dubbed his own lines; other members of the German cast were dubbed by Brits, causing *Variety* to complain that "frequently the voices sound detached from the bodies."

There were moments of inspiration, however, most notably having Schell deliver the "To be or not to be . . ." speech with the camera trained exclusively on his eyes. The result was a striking alternative both to the earlier Olivier approach (voice-over) and the later Zeffirelli decision to have Mel Gibson speak the words aloud, theatrical fashion. Having Hamlet speak—but not allowing us to see his lips moving—does seem the most satisfying cinematic solution to a stage soliloquy contained in a film.

There were fascinating dramatic decisions as well, such as Gertrude purposefully seizing the goblet (which she knows to be poisoned) and drinking rather than allowing Hamlet to do so. Less successful was having Hans Canineberg play Claudius as a stock villain, without Shakespeare's subtle emotional shading. Prof. Lillian Wilds, of the California State Polytechnic University at Pomona, hailed Schell as "the least quirky" of the filmed Hamlets. Utterly without neuroses, particularly in regard to his mother, he is "at once a suffering human being and the humanistic Prince . . . the much written about private and public persons into which traditionally the Renaissance ruler was divided," particularly in the plays of Shakespeare.

It made sense, then, that for their unifying symbol Wirth and Schell chose not Olivier's luxurious oedipal bed but the twin thrones, always empty. Central to the opening shot, the camera returns to them throughout; at the end, Claudius, dying, struggles to crawl back onto his throne. Hamlet chooses to sit on that throne and expire there, dying a king. Such visual symbolism makes it clear that this *Hamlet* is actuated not by modern Freudianism but by Shakespeare's own insistence on the need for a proper ruler if a city-state hopes to avoid falling into chaos and ruin.

## Neither Fish nor Fowl
### *Hamlet*
Warner Bros., 1964; John Gielgud-Bill Colleran

To commemorate the 400th anniversary of Shakespeare's death, Sir John Gielgud (himself a legendary Hamlet in the soft, romantic tradition) directed Richard Burton in what would emerge as the twentieth century's most macho stage incarnation. Due to Burton's ongoing affair with Liz Taylor and rumors that America's Queen Elizabeth would be in the audience for most performances, the show sold out. On nights when Taylor did not make an appearance, a sizable portion of the audience walked out. Yet ticket sales are ticket sales. The production, which premiered on April 9, 1964, at the Lunt-Fontanne Theatre, ran for 138 performances.

The Gielgud-Burton *Hamlet* represented an intriguing, if doomed, attempt to develop a new means of sharing top Manhattan productions with the entire country. On June 30 and July 1, seven electronic Theatrofilm cameras were assembled in the orchestra and the stage's wings, recording three separate performances (one matinee, two evenings) from beginning to end, with the audience present. One camera remained close on Burton, another in medium on Burton and costars, a third for long shots, etc. This recording, akin to a TV image, was fed to a truck outside the theater, where a new process called Electronovision allowed for immediate transference to 35-millimeter film. The three recordings were quickly edited into a single print. A thousand prints were struck by Warner Bros., and in late September, *Hamlet* was shown four times (two matinees, two evenings) at theaters nationwide for one-fourth of what people had paid to see the show on Broadway.

The intended effect, as Robert Koehler later reflected in the *Los Angeles Times*, was "to create the illusion of putting moviegoers in a seat at the Lunt-Fontanne." The experiment did not work. As critic Bob Thomas noted, "With normal stage lighting, the sets were murky much of the time, the actors [voices] often indistinct." Leonard Harris added: "Apparently unsure whether he wanted to try movie techniques or merely record the stage play, Bill Colleran, the film director, tried a bit of each and ended up with an unhappy medium" that even provincial audiences sensed was neither fish nor fowl. Rather than a happy blend of the two, this proved a sorry bastard form.

The film did rate as a commercial success. With the $1.1 million cost returning grosses of $6.5 million, Hollywood briefly hoped the technique might provide a new source of revenue while at the same time raising the nation's level of theater sophistication. In fact, most ticket buyers had been attracted by the novelty (much like the brief-lived 3-D phenomenon of the mid-fifties) and by Burton's box-office appeal. One year later, an attempt to similarly share Olivier's *Othello* (see chapter 9 for details) did less business; a third, of the Anthony Newley–Lesley Bricusse musical *Stop The World—I Want to Get Off!*, bombed. The concept would not take hold until, a quarter century later, pay-per-view allowed the public to see such broadcasts in the privacy of their homes (and often live, which added to the impact). The smaller TV screen proved more conducive to such a concept, since a huge theatrical image blew already larger than life stage performances out of proportion.

Whatever its aesthetic failings, the production had a major impact on the public's perception of *Hamlet*. Millions of people saw a performance of the Prince that, as Howard Taubman put it in the *New York Times*, was marked by "sweeping virility"; that did much to restore Shakespeare's intended notion of Hamlet as a thinking man's action hero rather than an ineffectual dreamer. Richard L. Coe of the *Washington Post* added that Burton's "superb" Hamlet was "imaginative, stirring, and wholly sane . . . far from a weak man, far from a mad one. [Burton] has had the perception to see what our age so self-consciously neglects, sensitivity in virility." We need not necessarily choose between the Elizabethan Hamlet and the Romantic one; the two conceptions could (perhaps should) coexist in one frame.

Gielgud had staged the production in "rehearsal clothes," actors wearing sneakers and sports coats or suits and ties while carrying swords. So the Bard's concept of anachronistic dress as well as the universal notion of a play altogther out of time were conveyed via film. Perhaps most important, due to the new freedom of the swinging sixties, the Oedipus complex could at last come out of the cinematic closet. Considering the tight censorship in 1948, Olivier had at best been able to suggest such a situation via visual focus on the "royal bed," which, in Prof. Peter Donaldson's words, was "immense, rumpled, and suggestively canopied . . . female anatomical symbol."

Olivier (forty years old at the time) had played opposite the attractively youthful Eileen Hurlie. She, a mere twenty-seven years old then, appeared more likely to be cast as leading lady than mother. As the *New Yorker* nervously noted in 1948: "In some of their affectionate scenes together, there is a hint of incest." When Burton kissed his Queen (again played by Eileen Hurlie, now more matronly) square on the lips, lingeringly and lasciviously, audiences gasped in amazement at what was more than a mere hint. Finally, they understood the perverse nature of this rugged Hamlet's true problem.

**Not to Be**

## Gamlet

Lenfilm, 1964; Grigori Kozintsev

*Gamlet* (1964) was likewise created specifically as a contribution to the worldwide Shakespeare quadricentennial. Russians have always admired the Bard's plays, and at any one time, a dozen stage productions are likely to be on display in Moscow and St. Petersburg. Though best known for his epic novel *Dr. Zhivago*, Nobel Prize winner Boris Pasternak spent far more of his life translating Shakespeare into Russian than creating original prose and poetry. Likewise admired for realpolitik filmmaking, such as *New Babylon* (1928), director Grigory Kozintsev also penned a respected tome, *Our Contemporary William Shakespeare*, focusing on elements that make the Bard accessible to modern audiences.

Not surprisingly, the two joined forces on what they hoped would be the definitive Russian *Hamlet*. Considering the project's growing prestige, acclaimed composer Dmitri Shostakovich signed on to create a symphonic score, while the Soviet Union's most highly regarded actor, Innokenti Smoktunovsky, agreed to play the lead. Filming began early in January 1963 at Leningrad's Len-film Studio, where authentic weapons and sets of armor, dating back to the sixteenth century, were borrowed from the nearby Hermitage as well as Moscow's Historical Museum. In fact, though, less than one-half of *Gamlet* was shot on soundstages.

Scenes originally written as interiors were reconceived for exterior shots; such sequences were filmed in black-and-white wide screen for a somber epic along Estonia's Baltic coast, fifteen miles west of Talinn. There a Danish-style castle had been constructed over a ten-month period. The movie was shot during autumn months, taking advantage of seasonal winds and menacing clouds, thereby visualizing the gloomy aura so essential to this reading.

The result was the most "external" *Hamlet* ever, which struck critics as a fascinating new approach to, or total misreading of, Shakespeare's most "internal" play. Even Hamlet's death was played outside, with hundreds of peasants crying (suggesting Shakespeare's notion of Hamlet as "loved by the general"); Horatio's famous farewell ("Good night, sweet prince") was eliminated. Such cuts were questionable; still, *Gamlet*, appearing simultaneous with the Gielgud-Burton version, did much to reinstate the character as a man of action. *Esquire* duly noted: "This is a Hamlet who rides and duels a lot more than he reflects; Smoktunovsky looks a little like Burton and plays the part in the Burton style, as a vigorous type much more at home with horses and women than with ideas." In addition to any sense of weakness being removed, also gone, sadly, was Hamlet's ironic wit.

The Russian Hamlet barely paused for reflection. Most soliloquies (including the essential "To be or not to be . . .") were cut, as was what many consider Hamlet's moment of truth: his decision *not* to kill Claudius at prayer, moments after the Ghost has been proven honest. Absent also was any hint of an oedipal complex. As to Hamlet's problem, the *Saturday Review* noted that this Hamlet "lacks not will, but opportunity"; he's here ready to kill the king from that moment when the ghost first appears, though someone or something always interferes. Shakespeare's "Oh how all occasions do inform against me" is *not* included, though that line encapsulates the film's conception of Hamlet's problem. No question, though, that this is a work of cinema. Courtiers dash about in cloaks and capes, while women wear furs and finery; the rich detail of clothing compensates for a stark gray sky overhead, ever-present symbol of an encroaching darkness that threatens to extinguish those bright little lights deluded humans burn to convince themselves they are the be-all and end-all in the universe.

Stylistically, *Gamlet* seems less a new cinematic treatment than Kozintsev's own application of previous approaches not only to *Hamlet* but filmmaking in general. He was obviously influenced by Olivier's version, particularly the image of a pounding surf just outside Elsinore castle; whereas Olivier employed such visions on occasion, Kozintsev made them the film's central motif. He returns again and again to the sight and sound until the surf all but overpowers the film, conveying the theme of inevitable natural power in the universe. From Olivier, Kozintsev also borrowed the technique of Hamlet's soliloquies heard on the soundtrack, suggesting they take place in his mind. The overall sensation was akin to watching Richard Burton's virile Hamlet step into Olivier's imagined world.

The images of Fortinbras's army were shot with the same sense of hard-edged period realism that Sergei Eisenstein employed for works like *Alexander Nevsky*—particularly the famed battle-on-the-ice sequence. Bosley Crowther concluded that this "Hamlet flows from strong expressions and vibrant actions more than from words. This, I would say, is performing Shakespeare cinematically"—that is, reimagining Shakespeare for the medium of cinema.

## Loneliness of the Long Distance Avenger
### *Hamlet*
Woodfall Productions, 1969; Tony Richardson

Burton and Gielgud had taken pains to let the audience in on the fact that theirs was an experimental form. "This is *not* a motion picture," Sir John's voice could be heard announcing before their filmed stage play began. Not so Tony Richardson's *Hamlet*, adapted from the controversial London production starring Nicol Williamson. A character actor turned leading man, he offered larger-than-life (and occasionally over the top) portraits of flawed, angry working-class men. This was advertised as a true film, whatever its origins; even those who had championed the stage production admitted that, as such, the result was disastrous.

Richardson failed to create any tangible mood for Elsinore; the problem is not that we disagree with his interpretation-through-image but that there is no visual scheme. This is obvious from the first scene, in which palace guards confront the ghost. Two inconsequential men stand against a dull brick wall; Richardson apparently took his cue from the prologue of *Henry V*, asking us to fill in, like an Elizabethan audience, missing details. We are not an Elizabethan audience but modern moviegoers and expect Shakespeare to be adjusted for that reality.

Columbia Pictures and Filmways compounded this problem by attempting to sell Richardson's *Hamlet* to the very teen audience that two years earlier had responded to Zeffirelli. The advertising read: "From the author of *Romeo and Juliet*: the love story of Hamlet and Ophelia." Although Marianne Faithful, a rock star, played Ophelia, any hope for young romance dissipated when she performed opposite balding, paunchy Williamson, who looked more like her father than her lover.

At 114 minutes, this *Hamlet* is abridged to the point of embarrassment. Claudius falls to his knees, attempting to pray. The scene allows the villain a guilty conscience and degree of integrity (he can't force a prayer he doesn't feel), making him three-dimensional. The moment also reveals so much about Hamlet, who has at last tested the ghost, finding him honest beyond doubt; yet he still delays. Unaccountably, Richardson included Claudius's pathetic half prayers but left out Hamlet entirely. Shakespeare's intent is so distorted that the scene would have been better dropped.

The *mise en scène* (a kindness to call it that, so minimalist is the imagery) was constructed entirely in close-up. This approach worked well enough for Maximilian Schell, the play reimagined specifically for television, but this is a theatrical film. Even the pacing of players was noncinematic, losing the key element of *Hamlet* as a pre-Hitchcock exercise in suspense. Claudius's cry of "Lights!" ought to shock us with an explosion of long-repressed emotion gone suddenly out of control, ringing like the scream of a wounded animal. Instead, Claudius appears as if drugged; Richardson directed Anthony Hopkins to hesitate before screaming. Perhaps intended as a pregnant pause, this deflated any sense of mounting intensity.

*Hamlet* is Shakespeare's funniest tragedy, its hero a forerunner of today's stand-up comics. Most unforgivable is Richardson's cutting every bit of humor, resulting in a leaden, dull version. Polonius is no fun to watch, while gags are missing from the Gravedigger's scene. To compensate, Richardson added graphic sensuality. Rather than play the Hamlet-Ophelia or Hamlet-Gertrude confrontations for sexual intensity, however, Richardson suggested an incestuous relationship between Laertes and Ophelia. Gertrude-Claudius court dialogues were shifted to their bedchamber, which might have served to heighten a sense of their "luxurious" relationship. Instead, Richardson has them call for a servant to bring food, attempting a redux of his famous sex-while-eating scene from *Tom Jones*; sadly, he was unable to match the earlier film's impact.

Richardson appears eager to destroy Shakespeare's richness of texture, reducing beautifully realized supporting characters to cardboard caricatures. He did away with Shakespeare's appearance-reality theme, which stands at the heart of the play—indeed, at the center of the Bard's ongoing vision. In the text, Claudius and Gertrude go to great lengths to appear honorable rulers, keeping up appearances to hide their corruptness. Richardson's King and Queen proudly parade their vulgarity. Judy Parfitt as Gertrude looks and acts like some sort of madam and was directed to play a cackling villainess on the order of the Wicked Queen in Walt Disney's *Snow White and the Seven Dwarfs*. Other films depict Ophelia as a simple innocent used by her father or a confused girl trying to hang on to Hamlet. Although we might have expected a 1969 film to offer Ophelia as a wide-eyed hippie done in by the corrupt Establishment, Marianne Faithful's Ophelia is a predecessor of punk, since she is corrupt, snarling, and backbiting.

Williamson's interpretation is a reaction against Olivier's exalted elocution. He delivers famous lines so matter-of-factly, the audience could not later recall whether they had heard them or not. This destroyed the most basic element of Hamlet's personality: the notion that, whether effeminate or macho, he is a *gifted* individual, a true prince among men. While Burton restored strength, Williamson rendered Hamlet crude. Shakespeare's vision was of a sensitive talented man tragically cast by life in the role of avenging prince rather than artist. Hamlet thus combined his desired role with his destined one by directing the play within the play. Neither as ill fitted for prince as Richard II nor as perfect for that position as Henry V, Hamlet rates as truly tragic, a man inwardly torn assunder. Such a sense of burning genius is precisely the quality ultranaturalistic Williamson couldn't convey. His performance was less Hamlet for Everyman than Everyman as Hamlet. Crying in his mother's arms, he appears pathetic. Ironically, one moment rings truer than ever before in Hamlet's advice to the players. Williamson doesn't merely speak it; he lives it.

## The Prince as Byronic Hero

### *Hamlet*

Hallmark Entertainment, 1970; Peter Wood

Like the Richardson-Williamson version, Hallmark's version (originally broadcast on NBC, November 17, 1970) was adapted from a British stage production. The film, starring Richard Chamberlain, was similarly intended as a rethinking of *Hamlet* for its era. Within the tight limits of a 115-minute running time, it was a happy update and an effective reconsideration of a stage production for the camera. Director Peter Wood had not mounted (or, for that matter, even seen) the stage version; therefore, he was free to think in original and cinematic terms. The preponderance of close-ups rendered it ineffectual for theatrical screens; yet it was perfect for TV.

Due to a long-standing prejudice against American performers, none had dared essay the prince on British boards since John Barrymore in the 1920s. This was particularly gutsy for Chamberlain, typecast as a bland TV star in the *Dr. Kildare* series (1961–66). He initially turned down an offer by Peter Dews to headline a production with the Birmingham Repertory Theatre. Then, taking the risk, Chamberlain dedicated two years to the part; his time and effort were not wasted. Critics in England, then America, were surprised at his efficient, respectable, impressive performance. Harriet Van Horne of the *New York Post* cited the "quiet dignity and authority" Chamberlain brought to "the most taxing and difficult role in all English drama," noting that the actor delivered "a pretty, peevish prince."

Chamberlain himself insisted, shortly before the broadcast: "*Hamlet* has always seemed a contemporary play." As such, it not only *can* be adapted to reflect on any temporarily modern period but literally *demands* such an approach. "It is surprising," Chamberlain continued, "that someone hasn't pressed the play into service as part of the student protest, with Hamlet as victim of the generation gap." The actor doth protest too much: That's precisely what he and Wood opted for.

Their choice of a nineteenth-century setting (England's picturesque Raby Castle served for exteriors) was not a case of imaginative interpreters arbitrarily picking a fascinating period, then plopping some Shakespearean play into it. The decision was dictated by, in Chamberlain's words, this era's being closest "to our own in fashions and attitudes, so the play's contemporary qualities are emphasized" despite a period presentation. The star's costumes, including fluffy shirts, looked like Carnaby Street fashions; even Chamberlain's sideburns were as in vogue for the peace-and-love era as they had been for Regency England. More important was the emotional similarity. In England and America, the youth movement rejected everything recent in society, including intellectual psychiatric analysis, while openly embracing the values of Shelley or Keats. Chamberlain admitted: "Our version is avowedly and unashamedly *romantic*," turning away from the postwar period's neurotic Hamlet, reviving an "earlier rendition that includes Irving, Barrymore, Gielgud and Redgrave—the prince as Byronic hero."

A Hamlet reimagined for the hippie era had to be, Chamberlain insisted, "a man caught in a power struggle, with aspirations beyond such mundane matters, finally forced into intrigues and destroyed by them," For contrast, Claudius (Richard Johnson) was portrayed as an unpleasant, Nixon-like corporate executive, suffering from five o'clock shadow, often found at a desk completing paperwork. Gertrude (Margaret Leighton) is highly sensual and remains married to a powerful man in a suit while claiming to enjoy the Beatles. Mary Lois Vann of *Women's Wear Daily* tagged her a socially nervous aristocrat, "uneasy with the onset of age and particularly vulnerable to confrontation with youth." Her internal conflict is less incestuously sexual, between deceased husband's brother and her son, than generational; Gertrude can't decide whether to stick with Claudius's Establishment or join Hamlet on a commune.

Intriguing, too, was the decision to make this the most supine Hamlet ever. The great speeches are delivered with the prince on his back, staring up into space, including critical words to Gertrude in her bedchamber. Most often Hamlet was glimpsed lying outside the castle, "grazing in the grass," as a pop tune of the time put it. This choice transformed the character's body language into a visual metaphor for a generation that chose to tune in, turn on, and drop out. Chamberlain's Hamlet does not appear all that different from Peter Fonda, ruminating while on LSD, in Roger Corman's *Trip* (1967). Likewise, director Wood's choices for individual scenes reflected the antipsychological, proromantic point of view; whereas Olivier led his audience down dark tunnels, Wood favored brightly sunlit courtyards leading into green gardens—truly, a flower-power *Hamlet*.

Claran Madden, the pretty, talented unknown cast as Ophelia, clicked nicely with Chamberlain; they provided the youth-cult chemistry that had worked so well in Zeffirelli's *Romeo and Juliet*. Two legendary stage Hamlets appeared in supporting roles. Michael Redgrave avoided the cliché of a bumbling, doddering Polonius, making him a vital servant of the system. John Gielgud's ghost, decked out in, as one critic noted, "a Bonaparte bonnet worn at a rakish angle," struck some viewers as eccentric; actually, this is the perfect "father" to Chamberlain's Hamlet—a romantic-era ghost.

What emerges is an entirely original interpretation, a notable alternative to previous offerings. As Jay Halio noted in "Three Filmed *Hamlets*" (*Literary/Film Quarterly*, 1973), Wood cinematically emphasized Christian elements inherent (but never before emphasized) in the story. Here the ghost leads Hamlet away from the castle into a churchyard, where their confrontation takes place beneath a dominating cross. Hamlet's "To be or not to be . . ." speech is intercut with images of Ophelia, on her knees before an altar. When Hamlet heads toward his mother's "closet," the camera films him from behind a statue of Madonna and Child. The same week this *Hamlet* was broadcast, George Harrison's recording of "My Sweet Lord" topped the record charts. In the early 1970s, the youth culture was turning conservative, Students for a Democratic Society giving way to the Jesus movement. This *Hamlet* caught that moment of transition in a work of popular culture.

In Chamberlain's mind, the play was "primarily concerned with the meaning of action. Most people act on firmly held convictions that, if examined, have little logical basis but proceed rather from emotional processes to which they themselves may be blind." Laertes, one of Hamlet's many foils, is such a man; he never thinks things through, always acting on impulse. Laertes symbolizes the simple attitude that he who hesitates is lost. Then again, one can also be lost (as Laertes almost is when he wrongly turns his wrath on Hamlet) by failing to think things through. Hamlet's is the opposite approach: Look before you leap. Its downside is that intellectual consideration may lead, in Chamberlain's words, to total stasis. "If, like Hamlet, you begin to doubt your reasons for action—you may be lost."

The following spring, the show received five highly deserved Emmy Awards; that it is not readily available on home video today is inexplicable.

## The Name of Action
### *Hamlet*
Warner Bros., 1990; Franco Zeffirelli

By the time Zeffirelli mounted the most ambitious *Hamlet* since Olivier's, the screen enjoyed relative freedom of image and idea. The director made the most of it, expanding Olivier's oedipal suggestions by graphically dramatizing them. On the other hand, Zeffirelli abandoned Olivier's most questionable and limiting element, the conception of Hamlet as a man who could not make up his mind. In the person of Mel Gibson, Zeffirelli's Hamlet is anything but indecisive. Yet even an ultramasculine hero may be plagued by other intense inner problems.

So Zeffirelli emphasized the similarity Freud himself noted between *Oedipus the King* and *Hamlet*. For Freud, the two plays and characters stood the test of time, serving as lasting touchstones for mankind due to something deep and dark in the human condition these seemingly different narratives addressed, which was the universality of the Oedipus complex. For the Greeks, Oedipus may have seemed a strange story about a man who inadvertently kills his own father, then sleeps with his mother; in Freud's view, the tale represents an emotional period through which each male must pass. Every boy, at some point, resents the father who intrudes, at workday's end, into a home that mother and son have up to that point shared.

Freud saw Hamlet much as Shakespeare did, as a strong man of action, and cites the scene in which Hamlet, while at sea, defeats a shipload of pirates. Freud says, "Hamlet is able to do *anything—except* take vengeance on the man who did away with his father and took his [old Hamlet's? or Hamlet's?] place with his mother, the man who shows Hamlet the repressed wishes of his (own) childhood realized." No wonder Hamlet is split down the middle on this, and only this, issue, to the point of his feigned madness becoming all too real. As a decent man of moral convictions, how can he bring himself to kill a man who performed a wrongful act that is precisely what Hamlet, in his own most awful fantasies, wanted to do but never would? To kill Claudius would, in essence, be to kill himself—or at least the dark side of himself. As Freud himself had put it: "The loathing that should drive (Hamlet) on to revenge is replaced by self-reproaches, scruples of conscience that remind him he is literally no better than the sinner whom he is to punish." This is the Zeffirelli-Gibson Hamlet in a nutshell.

Zeffirelli took precisely the same approach he had earlier assumed for *The Taming of the Shrew* and *Romeo and Juliet:* Make the Bard easily accessible to modern audiences by stripping away all semblance of theatricality, replacing archaic conventions with the more immediate sensation of a mainstream "movie-movie." The result was as naturalistic a production as possible, with authentic settings rather than symbolic sets, dialogue mercilessly pruned, and actors encouraged to deliver lines as if they were prose rather than poetry. Even the casting of Mel Gibson, star of the *Lethal Weapon* trilogy, made clear that this would not be an artsy, elitist *Hamlet* but a visceral rendering.

Though Hamlet was something of a stretch for an actor associated with hard-edged action, Gibson was (thankfully) *not* encouraged to try for reverse typecasting. Likewise, Zeffirelli's visual approach is full of action. The camera is constantly on the move, darting, slipping, and finally rushing madly through the film's Elsinore. Camera and character are at one. Both are robust and athletic, if deeply troubled or even schizophrenic. Surprisingly, serious actress Glenn Close (who, as Gertrude, everyone assumed would overpower Gibson) offers the film's weakest performance, appearing more like calculating Lady Macbeth than a willfully oblivious queen even the Ghost cannot bring himself to condemn. Perhaps wishing to avoid appearing as a retrowoman, Close attempted to make her Gertrude an equal in evil to Claudius.

If she is his equal, then she deserves equal punishment. Twitchy, neurotic, and mannered, Close's sexual predator rings shrill, a far cry from the fleshy, foolish woman Gertrude must be if the Ghost's decree is to make sense. This couldn't help but have an impact on and ultimately alter Zeffirelli's perception of the Hamlet-Gertrude relationship as well as his approach to staging their scenes together. Zeffirelli extends the oedipal impulse to an almost obscene limit. Hamlet speaks his famous lines to his mother not only while beside her on the bed but literally mounting her. If he weren't sidetracked by the realization that someone else is in the room, this Hamlet would surely rape Gertrude.

He is, in fact, ready to do so when his orgasmic shrieks elicit a scream of horror from hidden Polonius, whom Hamlet leaps up and kills. Hamlet was, at a moment of crisis, about to come out of the closet in terms of his true feelings for his mother. Instead, Hamlet seizes his actual sword and, assuming that the interloper is Claudius, redirects his insane anger, using it to kill as a means to avoid employing his sexual sword. Gertrude's room is precisely where Hamlet would love to do in his competitor and secret sharer. Killing that man would serve as a substitute for killing the perversity inside himself; in Shakespeare (or at least Zeffirelli's vision of Shakespeare), as in Hitchcock, the victim turns out to be the wrong man.

When Hamlet leaves for England, he says his goodbyes to Gertrude not as a dutiful son taking leave of a caring mother but as a lover—in thought if not deed—parting with his mate. Other films leave doubt as to why Hamlet rejects Ophelia; not here. She was the easily available, socially acceptable woman he diverted sexual energy toward in denial of coveting his mother. At his most bitter, Hamlet hurls accusations at the stunned girl, misdirecting his anger for Gertrude. Then he literally forgets Ophelia the moment that he and Gertrude acknowledge their forbidden feelings.

Other interpretations are ambiguous as to Ophelia's motivation for degenerating into madness; here the reason is obvious. She has seen the man she loves reject her for his own mother; this is more horrific than her simple, sweet mind can bear. As in Olivier's film, Hamlet here recites his famed "To be or not to be . . ." speech *following* his important confrontation with Ophelia, improving on Shakespeare's placement of the scene. Important, too, is that Helena Bonham Carter's none-too-bright girl-child is completely innocent, unaware her father is spying when she insists Polonius went home, then sincerely shocked when Hamlet (having spotted Polonius hiding) abuses her.

Though it was necessary to cut the play, Zeffirelli went way too far. At 135 minutes, his film is 3 minutes shorter than his *Romeo and Juliet*, based on a briefer tragedy. The controversial cuts begin at the beginning; there is no initial confrontation between Horatio and the guards, a scene that establishes the Ghost's existence outside of Hamlet's imagination; even the unforgettable "Something is rotten in the state of Denmark" is gone. The bitter-cold mood of physical and psychological chill is absent; in its place, a springtime setting, which does justify the play's description of drowning Ophelia grabbing on to green plants and madly playing with flowers.

Unable to find a single castle that came close to resembling Denmark's Elsinore, Zeffirelli visited various structures in England and Scotland. He noted which sections of them best suited his purposes for specific scenes, then employing them for appropriate moments. A parapet from one place serves as a backdrop for an open-air scene atop the tower, while a suitably encroaching arch, employed for a key moment when Hamlet catches Polonius (Ian Holm) spying, makes the imagery appear as claustrophic as Hamlet then feels.

Besides allowing for a color epic, this approach visualizes Zeffirelli's point of view: Hamlet, isolated in his melancholy, considers Denmark a prison without bars. We, however, see an appealing place, as others do. Zeffirelli's *mise en scène* is objective, emphasizing the contrast between Hamlet's inner vision of Elsinore and everyone else's; Olivier's monster-movie terrain insisted we view the setting subjectively, through Hamlet's embittered eyes.

Hamlet's lengthy advice to the players is gone, though Zeffirelli might have included those all-important opening words: "Speak the speech, I pray you, trippingly on the tongue"—expressing the Bard's own belief in naturalistic acting. The great irony is that Olivier included the speech, though his play within a play is presented as dumb show, without the speeches Hamlet referred to; Zeffirelli includes dialogue (the play is done in true Elizabethan style, with a male taking on the Queen's role) but dispenses with Hamlet's acting instructions. In Zeffirelli's version, only the king is overcome with guilt at what he sees; other members of the court are oblivious to the immediate subtext. In Olivier's version, the entire court gradually goes berserk, sharing Claudius's sense of guilt. The situation is less a case of one director being right, the other wrong, than our having two intriguing interpretations to consider.

The one that cannot be forgiven is the deletion of a single line by Claudius when, following the Ghost's testing, Hamlet spies him on his knees at prayer. True to his character, Hamlet again delays. He wishes to kill Claudius while in sin, consigning his uncle to eternal damnation rather than sending him, caught in confession, directly to God. Zeffirelli unaccountably leaves out Claudius's capper after Hamlet's exit: "My words fly high, but my thoughts remain below; words without thoughts never to heaven go." Shakespeare is an ironist; he wants us to see and hear more than Hamlet does, knowing Hamlet could at this point have achieved his goal. It would have been better to cut the entire sequence.

Fortinbras, the Norwegian prince who finally restores order, is gone. Yet the omission undercuts Shakespeare's intent. The appearance of Fortinbras is necessary for the author's vision of chaos replaced by a return to order; without Fortinbras and the stability he symbolizes, the carnage we have witnessed is, in the words of Shakespeare's Brutus, "savage spectacle"—violence without purpose. We are left hanging, uncertain whether the bloodshed has led to positive closure. Furthering this dark vision, the final shot peers down at dead Hamlet, Horatio weeping for him, implying a pessimism that is Zeffirelli's, not Shakespeare's. Though Olivier eliminated Fortinbras, he did approximate the notion of catharsis achieved through terrible sacrifice; the camera moves up, up, up, following Hamlet's body, which is carried to the very top of the tower.

New material is added, replacing wordy exposition with short, sharp visuals. At the outset, Zeffirelli brings his characters (and viewers) deep down into the castle's crypt as the deceased king is sealed in his coffin. The sequence begins with a medium shot with all in attendance seen as a group for the first and last time. Then Zeffirelli cuts to a close shot of Gertrude as she cries; it's impossible to tell whether her tears are real, feigned, or a combination of the two. The camera cuts to Claudius, attempting to maintain his innocent façade while secretively watching Gertrude, still jealous of any feelings she harbors for the murdered man. Finally, Hamlet himself, a hooded figure who considers first his mother, then Claudius, observant eyes making clear that this young man realizes that some subterfuge has taken place. Effective editing prepares us for his later reaction to the Ghost's revelation: "O my prophetic soul!"

Zeffirelli made difficult decisions regarding Shakespeare's anachronisms. In the play, the final duel between Hamlet Laertes is fought with the lightweight rapier so popular in Renaissance England. However, since the story is drawn from a tale that hearkens back to medieval times and Zeffirelli early on decided the film's atmosphere ought to evoke the Dark Ages, it was consistent with his approach that rapiers be abandoned for heavy-duty broadswords. This diminished the sensation, so strong in Olivier's version, that the duel begins as a courtly performance, then gradually degenerates into an out-of-control bloodbath; in Zeffirelli's film there's an unromanticized banging about that's as unique a reversal of the cliché as was his interpretation of the Mercutio-Tybalt fight in *Romeo and Juliet*.

With a Zeffirelli adaptation, we are never watching canned theater, but a work that is truly cinematic from beginning to end. We see Shakespeare's play entirely reimagined for the camera. Yet Olivier's film, for all its considerable cuts and questionable interpretation, came closer to communicating the full scope of the original. As David Denby noted in *New York* magazine: "The physical action has been expanded, but the play's amazing reach is gone—its sense of man as godlike but corruptible, a paragon who decays—the range that makes it the universal drama of Western literature." The paradox is that while carefully constructing a movie that beautifully plays to a modern audience, Zeffirelli allowed something of Shakespeare's eternal wisdom to slip away.

## A Winter's Tale
### *Hamlet*
U.S/British, 1996; Kenneth Branagh

Branagh's announced intention to film the entire play (the popular first folio, plus a scene and several lines from the less authoritative second folio) for the first time caused even Bard buffs to wonder if, like one of Shakespeare's tragic heroes, Branagh suffered from overwhelming ambition. However, his film belied such concern. "All other movie versions," Richard Corliss marveled in *Time*, "seem like samplings." Despite the 242-minute running time (the second-longest English-language film ever, about a minute less than *Cleopatra*), *Hamlet* was squarely aimed at the mass audience, with clarity, not complexity, the goal. It was shot on 65-millimeter film stock for projection in 70 millimeter and was intended for malls, not the art houses.

Which makes sense, since Branagh, who grew up watching matinee movies (American films at that), came to Shakespeare late in life. When he did, the budding actor-director sensed that Shakespeare's plays were intended for Everyman, not the Old Vic's elite. Quietly, he glowered at a classy men-in-tights approach, secretly fantasizing: Today the Bard begs to be done as a movie-movie. Branagh held steadfast to that concept. His *Hamlet* is intentionally big, influenced by Cecil B. DeMille and *The Ten Commandments*. (That film's legendary star, Charlton Heston, makes an appearance.) DeMille, of course, was the greatest showman since . . . well, since Shakespeare.

There are more cameo performances here (Robin Williams as a *Birdcage*-inspired Osric; Billy Crystal, the First Gravedigger as a Borscht-belt wise guy, and Charlton Heston as the Player King) than in any film since *Around the World in Eighty Days*. Branagh wanted movie stars, persuading Julie Christie (not a Shakespeare fan) to come out of semiretirement for Gertrude. Still, he did not overlook live theater, picking Derek Jacobi for Claudius. Significantly, Jacobi was the first live Hamlet Branagh ever saw, and he later directed Branagh in the role onstage. The coupling of Christie with Jacobi as a married couple can be taken as a key to the film's attitude, where the best of movie-movies and serious art are married in a single work.

There are arty influences besides Jacobi. The Russian look for Fortinbras's troops is reminiscent of the Soviet *Gamlet*, while the Norwegian army's final siege of Elsinore brings to mind St. Petersburg during the Russian Revolution, as incarnated in Sergei Eisenstein's *Ten Days That Shook the World*. Branagh is as much in love with cinema as with Shakespeare. In filming each successive work, he pays homage to cinema as the logical descendant of such plays and therefore our proper means of expressing them.

Basic to his interpretation is a rejection of the oedipal complex, returning us to a tragedy of revenge. This is implied in Branagh's choice of time and place. He sets the film in a European palace during the late 1800s, just before the world discovered Freud. Thus, we see the play as it might have been presented one minute before the birth of modernism, an age that transformed *Hamlet* into a mirror for our neuroses. Gone is the gloomy medieval fortress; in its place, exterior shots of the duke of Marlborough's swank Blenheim Palace at Christmastime. For interiors, great gobs of gilt, red carpeting, checkered tiles, multiplane mirrors, and falling confetti fill the screen. The experience is more like watching some Ruritanian romance, perhaps *The Prisoner of Zenda*, than the dark *Hamlet* of our century.

Branagh's *mise en scène* includes the dead of winter, the tale set against a backdrop of eternally falling snow. There are moments when this strains credulity; what is one to make of Gertrude's lines about Ophelia's grasping for blossoms while floating downstream? Still, Shakespeare didn't present time realistically; why should Branagh? The perennially icy palace is a symbolic place; this is an Elsinore of the mind, not some spot in Denmark.

From Hamlet's first confrontation with his mother, it is clear that any attraction is as banished as Romeo from fair Verona. As Stanley Kauffmann pointed out in the *New Republic*: "In Gertrude's key moment, the closet scene, Christie bursts with the frightened despair of a guilty woman who thinks her [salacious] behavior [with Claudius] may have driven her son mad." Also, Branagh's prince is rightfully angry about being denied his throne—possibly Shakespeare's most essential point, however obscured by a century of post-Freudian pontificating. Claudius wears the crown that should be Hamlet's. David Denby wrote in *New York* magazine: "This Hamlet *very much* wants to be king." And well he should; the crown belongs to Hamlet, and him alone; that is the central issue of the history-chronicle plays, here carried over to the realm of tragedy. *Commentary*'s Donald Lyons questioned Branagh's "effort to turn the play into a political epic," though this might better be described as Branagh's effort to return the play to what Shakespeare created, which is nothing if not a political statement.

Branagh insists that Hamlet and Ophelia (Kate Winslet) were sexually involved, a point left ambiguous in previous films. Branagh thus motivates Hamlet's eventual bitterness as well as his intense reaction to her death. Ophelia's protestations to brother and father (the terrified girl insists she has resisted Hamlet's advances) are included, though Branagh directed Winslet to speak the words awkwardly. During her self-defense, Branagh cuts to shots of Hamlet and Ophelia "'twixt the sheets," undercutting the distressed girl's lies. Although the look in Polonius's eyes makes it clear that he wants to believe his daughter, he is perceptive enough to see through her charade. When he continues to insist that Hamlet's mental problems result from sexual rejection, which denies Hamlet a physical outlet, Polonius seems less the sex-obsessed fool of other films than a wise man.

Branagh insists, in direct opposition to earlier films, that Ophelia is part of her father's conspiracy. Hamlet's sudden anger at her lie (father is "at home") is no error on his part. Ophelia lies to Hamlet for her father's sake, even as she lied to her father for Hamlet's sake. She is not wicked, only weak, false with people she sincerely loves (father, brother, lover) in a pathetic attempt to survive. Hamlet's line—"Frailty, thy name is woman"—takes on special meaning, implying for the first time on film what Shakespeare intended four hundred years ago. Other versions have Hamlet speak unpleasantly to Ophelia from the scene's opening, which makes no sense; Branagh's Hamlet initially approaches Ophelia smiling with anticipation, trusting her as fully as he does Horatio. Then he catches her lying and, understandably, grows furious. There are only two women in the self-contained "world" of the play; both—100 percent of the available female population—prove false. No wonder Hamlet sighs in despair; there could be no other reaction to his situation.

Also effective is Ophelia's oncoming madness and eventual suicide, ordinarily the most difficult element for a viewer to accept. Branagh suggests a hint of potential neuroses in Ophelia from her first scene rather than having it descend on her in mid-play. Winslet speaks tenuously; she grows flustered whenever things do not go as planned. This increases with every scene; following the vicious rejection by her lover and subsequent cold-blooded murder of her father, Ophelia naturally loses control. Branagh dares show her struggling in a straitjacket, cutting away to flashbacks of Ophelia and Hamlet in bed, letting us grasp how all these events and lies could cumulatively crack an already shaky soul.

By including the complete text, Branagh emphasizes an important element that, sadly, often gets lost: the sincerity of Claudius's love for Gertrude. Jacobi's talent, coupled with the character's additional screen time, makes us aware of Shakespeare's full achievement in presenting a multidimensional human. Branagh (notably generous to his costar) seems willing to suggest that Claudius may be the tragic hero. Hamlet, after all, is presented as good throughout; Claudius better fits the classic definition of a good man who does bad things. Unlike any earlier tragic heroes (misguided but not evil), he does so consciously. Branagh's film makes clear that Claudius was Shakespeare's dry run for Macbeth. He appears to have murdered his brother less out of ambition than owing to honest emotions for the woman, thus becoming strangely sympathetic.

If we consider Hamlet the hero, however, then Branagh's interpretation is of a man who wants, more than anything else, to do the right thing. Branagh's Hamlet is a moral absolutist. This (and this alone) explains his bitterness toward Gertrude, Ophelia, and ultimately even himself. As a moralist, he knows he must do what the Ghost commands; as an absolutist, he must have proof positive. So he hesitates not out of cowardice but out of idealism. After the player's performance catches the conscience of the king, he knows for certain and is ready to act; however, circumstances make this impossible.

Happily, Branagh includes the oft-missing "Oh how all occasions do inform against me" speech. On his way to England, Hamlet spots the army of Fortinbras marching off to battle. This is the play's turning point as well as the pivot for Hamlet's transformation: A man who lost "the name of action," appearing less guilty (the modern notion) than *embarrassed* about not avenging earlier, particularly in contrast to these noble fellows. They, like the earlier tears in the eyes of the Player King during his Hecuba speech, cause Hamlet to reconsider his own now-questionable decision that anything less than *total* certainty "must give us pause." Branagh begins the "all occasions" speech with the camera close on his face; behind him, we barely perceive Fortinbras's army. As the speech continues, our hero takes himself to task; the camera slowly pulls back, revealing the immense scope of men ready to do what a man must do without any proof positive they're in the right. Simultaneously, Hamlet is swallowed up by the epic frame. Employing cinematic technique to convey Shakespeare's concept, Branagh allows us to see how this situation makes Hamlet feel about himself. No wonder he vows to do the act at first opportunity.

As an actor, Branagh combines elements of both Olivier and Gibson. His appearance is marked by a bleach-blond hairstyle, recalling Olivier's; yet the cut is austere and military, more on the order of Gibson. Like Olivier, this Hamlet is sensitive yet masculine, like Gibson. Branagh gives us, for the first time, the best of both worlds. John Simon, in the *National Review*, mentioned this Hamlet's "brawn with guidance from the brain," acknowledging the difficult balancing act. Branagh also makes the issue of Hamlet's madness comprehensible. Previous versions remained ambiguous, insisting we decipher whether at some point Hamlet's "playing mad" descends, without his knowing, into true madness. Branagh's Hamlet begins as sane man, assumes the "antic disposition," gradually cracking under extreme stress; then the sight of Fortinbras's army provides a stiff shock to the system, and he regains his senses.

As to Fortinbras, this is the only major English-language film in which he appears; as in the Russian *Gamlet* (and perhaps inspired by that movie), Branagh includes shots of Norway's army on the move, as well as the face of Fortinbras, until his visage becomes a recurring motif. As a result of crosscutting, which suggests predetermination, Branagh makes clear that his Fortinbras is fated to arrive at Elsinore when most needed rather than showing up by happy accident. Here, though, Branagh departs from Shakespeare, not the text but the intent. Fortinbras was the Bard's device to portray order restored via a proper prince. Branagh's Fortinbras, however, appears so menacing throughout that we feel queasy about his assuming control. In contrast to Shakespeare's vision of a friendly visit, Fortinbras's men attack Elsinore. Fortinbras's first command, as newly crowned king, is to pull down statues of old Hamlet. To visually convey Shakespeare's vision, they should rather raise up old Hamlet's statue, which Claudius had knocked down.

The film is not without weaknesses. Jack Lemmon, as the guard Marcellus, sounds so out of place that he threatens to ruin the film before it begins; thankfully, he soon disappears, and the rest of the American casting works well enough. (Heston, as the Player King, is nothing short of inspired.) Twice director Branagh makes the mistake that all but ruined his film *Mary Shelley's Frankenstein*, in which his camera continuously circled characters to no noticeable effect. The camera should move only when it *must* and not perfunctorily to merely prove it *can*. The constant use of such a distracting technique made it clear that Branagh was directorially insecure while filming *Mary Shelley's Frankenstein*. In *Hamlet* he's more secure, allowing the strong material to speak for itself, except for two scenes where he uses the distracting circular approach: early on, when Claudius, Polonius, Gertrude, and Ophelia discuss what must be done with Hamlet; and again, when Claudius plots with Laertes to kill Hamlet. On both occasions, Claudius initiates a conspiracy; perhaps Branagh adopted a circular movement to convey the roundabout approach by which Claudius plots.

Unfortunately, the technique calls attention to itself, which is disastrous in a movie that otherwise makes us all but forget the camera's existence. As Hamlet might have put it, "More matter, with less art." At other moments, Branagh does not visualize what he should. The confrontation between Hamlet and the sea pirates, the death of Ophelia, and the eventual fate of Rosencrantz and Guildenstern are reported but not shown. Although Branagh decided to keep Shakespeare's language intact, he might have cut away to the action, since it's wise to make a movie visual whenever possible.

On the other hand, if there is a single sequence that proves Branagh's directorial gifts, it's his handling of the "To be or not to be . . ." speech, the play's most glorious soliloquy and yet the most troublesome for filmmakers. What is one to do with all these words? Olivier offered one approach: speaking the speech while cutting away to images of the ocean crashing on rocks. Zeffirelli went the other route, having Gibson speak the speech into a static camera, suggesting there are indeed moments when the cinema need not add anything. Branagh's approach is more satisfying than either, so right that we wonder why no one thought of it before.

Hamlet begins speaking into a mirror, unaware it's a one-way window. Claudius and his coconspirators stand on the other side, observing. Branagh cuts back and forth between Hamlet's confrontation with himself through his image, and the antagonists voyeuristically learning about a side of the prince he would never knowingly reveal. Then Polonius makes a noise; as Hamlet continues, he does so with the realization that the walls literally have ears. Without adding extraneous material, Branagh refuses to sit still for a set piece; integrating the words, he makes the soliloquy play cinematically as never before.

After everyone is killed at the end, Olivier had us look up at Hamlet's dead body, suggesting positivism, while Zeffirelli insisted we gaze down, implying negativism. Branagh, again refusing to simplify, combines the best of both. First, as Hamlet's body is carried away, Branagh shoots the scene with the camera angled depressingly downward, perhaps overdoing the symbolism by allowing himself, as actor, to spread out his arms, Christ-like. This is followed by an up angle, as Hamlet ascends, suggesting that from the negativity of this great man's death, something positive has been achieved. By refusing to make a *Hamlet* that ends with the old, positive Elizabethan vision (Olivier) or the more modern negative one (Zeffirelli), Branagh suggests that Shakespeare's script contains elements of each, incorporating both into what rates as not only a sturdy film of *Hamlet* but a virtual apotheosis of all twentieth-century *Hamlet*s.

What we here encounter is both the Shakespeare of our collective imagination and "the real Will," too often obscured by existential, oedipal, and academic approaches. Janet Maslin of the *New York*

*Times* commented that "Branagh remains a great popularizer of Shakespeare," and her point is apt. Branagh brings Shakespeare to the contemporary equivalent of those who first discovered him, the public itself. That, of course, is our modern moviegoing audience. Branagh has fashioned not only a *Hamlet* for the common man but a commonsense *Hamlet* stripped of the interpretive layers successive generations imposed. This is a *Hamlet* that has returned to its essential meaning, as discovered in Shakespeare's words, which prove less ambiguous than scholars and directors have suggested.

"There can never be a definitive production of a play," *Time* once noted, "about which no two people in the world agree." That may be true; still, Branagh's *Hamlet* comes close to delivering the definitive film.

## Variations on a Theme

The universality of *Hamlet* allows not only for abstract "rehearsal clothing" productions but also transference of the play to specific settings and diverse periods. Literally dozens of films can be traced, in some respect, to this greatest play in all of Western culture; what follows is a sampling of the most important and original works.

One approach is to update the basic story line without including the poetry or depth of purpose that accompanies the Bard's words. Without this element, the story reverts to what it had been before Shakespeare: an intriguing tale of personal vengeance. In 1945, cult director Edgar G. Ulmer (*The Black Cat*) directed a B-budget film noir for Poverty Row's PRC studio. While *Strange Illusion* hardly rates as a forgotten masterpiece, it was the first postwar attempt to bring the then-radical concept of psychology to the screen. James Lydon, previously known as the happily oblivious Henry Aldrich, was here cast as a troubled youth, a precursor to James Dean. He's a sensitive, confused, alienated teenager who cannot understand why his recently widowed mother (Sally Eilers) would have married the local lounge lizard (Warren William). Bizarre nightmares cause the boy to look further into this matter while assuming a modern variation of Hamlet's "antic disposition," where he becomes a juvenile delinquent but a rebel *with* a cause.

The sense of general displacement following World War II lent itself to another notable update, the German film *The Rest Is Silence* (1960) by producer-director-writer Helmut Kautner. The main character, played by Hardy Kruger, is an American-raised intellectual teaching existential philosophy at Harvard; he returns to Germany following the mysterious death of his industrialist father and his mother's subsequent marriage to a scheming uncle (Peter Van Eyck). An anonymous phone call serves as a realistic replacement for the Ghost's telling the lad that something is rotten in the state of Düsseldorf.

Eventually, this Hamlet catches the conscience of his stepfather by suggesting changes in the program that a touring ballet company performs. Laertes was portrayed as an ex-Nazi living in denial of his past, while guilt over the Holocaust causes the film's Ophelia substitute to grow ever more schizophrenic. *The Rest Is Silence* rates as a fascinating idea that almost pulls off its attempts at narrative parallels.

There have been more exotic versions. In 1955, writer-director-producer-star Koshore Sahu filmed an Indian *Hamlet* in Bombay, though it has never been made available for viewing in America. Ten years later, the story was shifted to northern Ghana by Joe deGraft, head of the University of Ghana's Drama School, with students (mostly Ga tribesmen) taking all parts. *Hamile*, based on a university stage production, was directed by British documentarian Terry Bishop. The film concerned a prince of the fra-fra people in the Tongo tribe. Bishop insisted "the only script changes were those needed to have it make sense in [an African] setting." He substituted local references for classical mythology, and Hamile's adversary, Laitu (Laertes), departs for neighboring Togo rather than Paris; upon returning, he wrestles instead of sword fights with, Hamile. "*Hamlet* makes sense set in northern Ghana because, like Denmark, it was once an area of feudal kingdoms," Bishop said of his two-hour black-and-white film, completed in thirty days on a set (depicting an ancient Ghana king's compound) built on the plain near Accra.

A number of filmdom's heavyweights have tried their hand at adaptation. Claude Chabrol, a member in good standing of the French New Wave, wrote and directed *Ophelia* in 1962. *Ophelia*'s plot encapsulates the most basic themes of *nouvelle* vogue: Each and every one of us are products of what we see and read, unconsciously perceiving the real world through pop culture; moviemakers are unique in that they attempt to understand their own lives and what old movies mean by making new movies supposedly about reality but patterned after influential films.

Yvan (Andre Jocelyn), living in a provincial Gallic town, deeply dislikes the uncle (Claude Cerval) who marries Yvan's recently widowed mother (Alida Valli). While strolling the streets, Yvan hears snickering remarks about the possibility that these two actually got away with murder. Yvan decides to escape from his waking nightmare by slipping into a theater, where he can daydream in darkness; but the film happens to be Olivier's *Hamlet*, its powerful presentation convincing Yvan that his own life parallels the legend too completely for coincidence. To catch the uncle's conscience, Yvan sets out to make his own movie, a substitute for the play within the play. To accomplish this, he must talk the family retainer's daughter (Juliette Meyniel) into playing the part of Ophelia; while shooting the film, Yvan verbally abuses her offscreen as well as in front of the camera as reel and real become inseparable.

The film ultimately serves as a cautionary fable about the folly of living one's life as if it were a movie. At the end, having driven the uncle to suicide, Yvan realizes too late that the dying man is not only innocent of any crime but may be his own biological father. The film's best moments include a modernization of Hamlet's advice to the players where Yvan argues with the performers about billing in the credits and Hamlet's sarcastic thrift speech in which he suggests that leftovers from the funeral furnish a cold repast for the marriage, wordlessly conveyed through such rapid crosscutting between funeral and wedding ceremonies that the viewer cannot tell precisely where one ends and the other begins.

Japan's greatest director, Akira Kurosawa, felt the story would also make sense in the land of the samurai. Whereas Kurosawa would retell *Macbeth* and *King Lear* as costume dramas, he chose to do *Hamlet* as a modern critique of Japan's 1963 business world, which is depicted as a false cover for criminal activities of the type associated with that land's gangsters, the Yakuza. In *The Bad Sleep Well* Toshiro Mifune plays a young executive offered the hand in marriage of a corporate bigwig; however, he cannot forget the unsolved murder of his own father, whom he suspects was done in by the company's president (Masayuki Mori). As he uncompromisingly seeks personal revenge, the hero goes out of control, perhaps even mad. Kurosawa maintained only the barest element of Shakespeare's vision, though he did turn out a turgid example of journalistic-exposé cinema in which he pulled no punches in decrying the scandalous situation within the contemporary Japanese business community.

A considerably less ambitious version appeared in 1972, at the height of an international craze for spaghetti westerns. *Johnny Hamlet* shifted the story to America's old west, though the film was shot entirely in Italy. Chip Corman (a.k.a. Andrea Giordana) played the title character who returns home following the Civil War to discover his father dead and his uncle now married to Johnny's mother and running the ranch. With the help of a Horatio-like foreman (Gilbert Roland), Johnny sets out to learn the truth and afterward exact revenge. The idea sounds better than it plays due to an obvious script (Shakespeare's words were *not* used) by Sergio Corbucci and Enzo G. Castellari as well as uninspired direction by Castellari. Although the movie was produced by Leone Film, it lacks the storytelling brilliance Sergio Leone brought to such classics as *The Good, the Bad, and the Ugly.*

Certainly, though, it is more watchable than producer Walter Hill's *Blue City* (1986), an embarrassing adaptation of Ross Macdonald's crime novel. Judd Nelson plays a teenage tough guy who returns to his Florida hometown after the murder of his father and brings down the criminal Establishment. Ally Sheedy, who costarred with Nelson in *The Breakfast Club* and *St. Elmo's Fire*, is his non-suicidal Ophelia; at the end, they are victorious in this botched attempt to do a film noir for the Brat Pack generation. Far better, in its own modest way, was *Strange Brew* (1983), the comic reworking of *Hamlet.* This film proved to be the only screen vehicle for the MacKenzie Brothers of Canada's *SCTV*, appealingly played by Rick Moranis and Dave Thomas, who also cowrote and directed. Their propensity for beer brings them to Elsinore Castle, where clever situations provide nice in-jokes for Shakespeare buffs.

Last if not least, Tom Stoppard's *Rosencrantz and Guildenstern Are Dead* (1990) deserves at least passing mention. Stoppard himself directed the film version of his own highly regarded theater-of-the-absurd play, with Gary Oldman and Tim Roth as the fated duo. Perhaps the least important characters in the original, they are here the point of focus, licking their lips with anticipation as to the reward awaiting them in England, little suspecting that seemingly oblivious Prince Hamlet (Iain Glen) has cleverly sealed their fates. Their conversations are always clever, often dripping with existential meaning, but there is so much talk here and so little action that it's easy to understand why the vehicle failed as a film. It had succeeded, however, on the off-Broadway boards, where intimate character studies are the order of the day.

# 9

# THE GREEN-EYED MONSTER
## *Othello, the Moor of Venice*

*It is thought abroad that 'twixt my sheets*
*He has done my office.*

—Iago, on Othello

With *Hamlet*, Shakespeare proved it possible to diminish the force of fate while heightening the importance of character, still achieving full tragic impact. The next experiment led him further in that direction. Hamlet's final decision—to kill or not to kill—was up to him; still, a ghostly figure had served as catalyst. Would it be possible to invent a new, more realistic kind of play in which the hero's impetus had *nothing* to do with metaphysical forces, growing entirely out of what Freud would have called his psyche? Will found his source in *Hecatommithi* (1565), an Italian novella by Giraldi Cinthio. The sketchy story had some basis in truth; a "Disdamona" did marry an officer in the Venetian military, only to be killed by him when a rejected suitor, seeking vengeance, made the husband incorrectly believe his lady had been unfaithful.

This fable was based on a 1508 incident involving Christopher Moro, who was not black. During the imprecise process of translation, Moro somehow transformed into Moor, historically incorrect but fraught with dramatic potential. Shakespeare provided the name Othello while heightening narrative power, creating complex characters, and interpolating his own ideas about life and love. Appearance versus reality, the duties of a prince, madness, romance, and rebellion were among the themes he further explored here; the play also deals with such modern issues as racial hostility, spousal abuse, and the playing of mind games. Literary critic T. M. Parrott pointed out that *Othello* can be considered the earliest example of a domestic tragedy, shifting high drama from the throne room to the middle-class household.

In 1604, Shakespeare's immediate challenge was to surpass *Hamlet* by offering an original, even alternative, hero. The melancholy Dane had been destroyed by his own ultralogical mind; Othello, on the other hand, is a slave to his illogical emotions. Taken as a set of compliments, the plays warn against extremism of any kind. To avoid a tragic fate, the wise man treads a balanced pathway between head and heart.

## The Stage Tradition

In Shakespeare's time, Richard Burbage played Othello with the expected bombast, all but exploding onstage; generations later, Edmund Kean did the part, as might be expected, by quietly imploding before his audience. At the Globe in 1604, Joseph Taylor enacted Iago as a literal demon; Edwin Forrest, opposite Kean, scaled the role down to human dimensions. The cinematic Othellos and Iagos of our century necessarily chose between the two possible extremes.

## Early Efforts

The first-known *Othello*, with a running time of five minutes, was shot in Italy late in 1906 by director Mario Caserini. It remains (at this writing) among the lost Shakespearean films. Likewise lost is the first sound *Othello*, shot in Germany the following year. Adapted from Verdi's opera *Otello* (itself derived from the play), this featured actor Henny Porten delivering "The Death of Othello" (actually lip-synching to a phonograph record played simultaneously while the movie was projected).

The oldest *Othello* in existence was produced in Austria in 1908 by Pathe Freres. An ambitious experiment that ran a then-impressive half hour, this was an early talkie. A plus was the striking exteriors shot on location in Venice, although the acting was in the overly histrionic approach popular at the time. The first American version was produced in 1908 by J. Stuart Blackton at Vitagraph, with popular actor William Ranous starring and directing. During the 1910s, *Othello*s (each progressively more ambitious in technique and length) were produced in Italy (one by Gerolamo LoSavio in 1911;

another by Arturo Ambrosio in 1914) and Germany (Max Mack, in 1918).

## Cinthio's Othello
### *Othello*
Worner Film, 1922; Dimitri Buchowetzki

In 1919, the German golden age began with *The Cabinet of Dr. Caligari*. Werner Krauss, who played the title role, was picked by director Dimitri Buchowetzki for Iago in his Teutonic variation; this made sense, since Caligari, like Iago, is a master manipulator. The era's other great star, Emil Jannings (*The Last Laugh; The Blue Angel*) always allowed full tragic dimension to anguished souls; he seemed the perfect choice for the anguished Othello. What seemed a likely classic instead emerged as a disaster. It was a commercial failure in its day and notably inferior in hindsight to the era's enduring milestones.

During a scene in which frantic Iago attempts to eat the incriminating evidence of the handkerchief, Krauss is guilty of embarrassing overacting. Jannings, an expert at playing physically unattactive characters, proved a poor choice for the charismatic Moor. Film historian Robert Hamilton Ball complained: "What emerges is more like Cinthio's narrative than Shakespeare's play, a bald and not very well told story of primitive passions without nobility, romance, or poetry, a complicated and unbelievable melodrama of unsympathetic characters." Though there are marvelous moments, including some strikingly surreal shots, they play as artificial rather than functional, art for art's sake that in no way reveals character or theme.

## Citizen Othello
### *The Tragedy of Othello, the Moor of Venice*
Mogador/Mercury Productions, 1952; Orson Welles

Orson Welles's Hollywood career was over by 1948. In seven short years, he had degenerated from boy genius to unemployable has-been. At age thirty-six, Welles became an artistic gypsy, traveling through Europe's diverse movie communities during that period when film became internationalized. He had long hoped to do a movie of *Othello* and scraped together money from individual investors, embarking on a four-year quest. Welles began filming in Rome, with popular Italian actress Lea Padovani as his Desdemona and Micheal MacLiammoir (a trusted friend from Ireland's Abbey Theatre) as Iago. They ran out of cash, and the production was put on hold. Meanwhile, Welles dashed off to appear in another film, earning enough to forge ahead with the dream project. When he returned six months later, Padovani had moved on to other work, so it was necessary to start over. Welles attempted to lure *Citizen Kane* costar Agnes Moorehead to Europe, but she was otherwise engaged; in the end, he chose Suzanne Cloutier, a blond beauty virtually without stage or screen experience.

The company moved to Morocco where Welles could shoot cheaply. After several weeks money ran out again. Welles once more put *Othello* on hold to take another acting job, afterward moving his patient company and crew to Venice for exteriors. Following yet another break in filming, they continued on to Tuscany, and in 1952 the film was finally finished. Welles had worked in an opposing approach to his studio-bound *Macbeth* (see chapter 10), vividly filming the entire *Othello* (even interiors) on location. This was the right approach for the "open" Othello, as opposed to the claustrophobia of a castle-cave, which appeared proper for Welles's "trapped" Macbeth.

Somehow during the elongated process Welles managed to keep his unique vision firmly in place. Often situations that promised disaster actually provided inspiration. While readying for the conflict between Roderigo and Cassio, Welles was informed that only Iago's costume had arrived. Rather than surrender to despair, Welles hurriedly rewrote the scene, setting it in a Turkish bathhouse with everyone wrapped in towels. All the derring-do takes place amid clouds of steam, and this sequence is the film's finest. Necessity truly was the mother of invention.

Welles was fully aware that Shakespeare had been a pre-Freudian psychologist, adding a key concept not found in Cinthio when Brabantio, father of Desdemona, bitterly spits out: "Look to her, Moor; she has deceived her father, and may thee." Though Othello shrugs this off with "My life upon her faith," the seed of doubt has been planted. Moreover, Iago, having overheard it, becomes a gardener, verbally watering that semantic seed via hints that bloom into suspicion in Othello's mind. In the view of Welles (particularly in the early 1950s, when psychological cinema was at its height), the original play justified his Freudian interpretation.

As MacLiammoir noted in his published diary of the filmmaking process, *Put Money in Thy Purse*, Welles saw the essence of the story thus: Iago is impotent and a closet homosexual. He married Emilia as his cover, needing to appear normal. Iago has developed a crush or hero fixation on Othello. He's stunned and as jealous as a spurned lover when Othello bypasses him for promotion. Insult is added to injury when Othello reportedly beds Iago's frustrated wife. When he observes Othello and Cassio, second in command, bound together as brothers, it is too much for Iago. Welles insisted that MacLiammoir appear (via makeup and performance) castrated.

Though the running time is a mere ninety-two minutes, Welles's film plays as economical rather than abbreviated because potent images so effectively take the place of words. Welles includes only the dialogue that is absolutely necessary for our understanding of the plot. Nor surprisingly, such a film received mixed notices, depending on one's preexisting point of view. Speaking for *Shakespeare Quarterly*, a publication that holds the literary text as primary, Margaret F. Thorp chastised the director "for the liberties he has taken . . . wrenching Shakespeare's proportions all awry." As the primary voice of France's *Cahiers du Cinema*, the first magazine to propose an auteur theory, André Bazin marveled that Welles remained "profoundly faithful" to the play, cinematically communicating the essence of Shakespeare, if not necessarily adhering to the surface. In retrospect, film historians Kenneth S. Rothwell and Annabelle Henkin Melzer pointed out that Welles's *Othello* had been attacked by "those who quantify the value of a Shakespearean film into a textual balance sheet," reducing the complex issue of "quality" to a simple addition problem: How many lines were cut and how many left intact? The more words included for such purposes, the merrier.

Welles constructed his *mise en scène* so that iron bars on the windows suggest entrapment of Othello; Shakespeare, working in an entirely different medium, had his characters articulate the very same thing. "Othello is a tragedy about agony," Rothwell and Melzer insisted, "and the Wellesian technique of skewed angles, funhouse mirror effects, [and] surrealistic visions captures those kinds of emotional destabilizations."

However faithful to or divergent from Shakespeare, Welles was primarily, as always, making an Orson Welles film. His movie begins with an extreme close-up on the face of Othello (Welles), precisely how his first film, 1941's *Citizen Kane*, began. Welles offers up two simultaneous, if seemingly unrelated, actions: the funeral procession for Othello and Desdemona, crosscut with the raising of frightened Iago onto the wall of Cypress in a makeshift cage. The citizenry cheer this villain's torture even as they weep for the deceased heroes. Likewise, *Kane* began with the protagonist's death, traveling back in time to trace events that inexorably led to such an outcome. At the end of both films (and most others by Welles), we conclude where we began, now with a full sense of what happened and a partial sense of why.

Due to this sense of predetermination, Welles's *Othello*, unlike Shakespeare's, is a tragedy of fate. What follows is an attempt to let us understand an aloof man's dark, distracted mind—whether he is Welles, Kane, or Othello. Like Kane, Othello is unable to understand the woman in his life; like Kane, he achieved great power despite humble origins; like Kane, he alienates friends by failing to treat them properly; like Kane, he's a public person who finds himself all alone. The Othello we meet here is a strangely satisfying combination of Shakespeare's creation and Welles's own continuing protagonist, always an alter ego of himself.

Gerald D. McDonald, of the New York Public Library, tagged the film as "a series of cinematic studies on the Othello theme," instead of an attempt at faithful adaptation; Welles himself would have heartily agreed, particularly considering McDonald's afterthought: "It is the motion picture treated as a distinct medium." McDonald appreciated Welles's control of cinema's plastic elements despite the director's tendency to show off more than absolutely necessary: "The photography is mannered, arresting, often quite wonderful, with its composition so studied that it verges on abstract design." Not everyone concurred; Shakespearean scholar Roger Manvel found that the film's "strictly formal beauty" detracted from the essential power of the piece by distancing an audience via impressive pictorialism that engages the eyes more than the heart or mind, "transform[ing] the scenes into a photographic exhibition."

Yet to deny Welles the right to do this is to deny Welles the right to be Welles. His aesthetic purpose, beginning with *Citizen Kane*, was clearly to forge a new cinematic language as well as an alternative to conventional Hollywood cinema that immediately involves an audience with emotions and ideas. Such traditional filmmaking reached its zenith in the work of John Ford, but the essence of

Welles's art would change the nature of moviegoing, forcing a viewer to see in an entirely new way—that being, of course, Welles's way. It's a way that subsequently influenced the later films of Stanley Kubrick, who in movies as diverse as *2001: A Space Odyssey, Barry Lyndon*, and *The Shining* insisted on playing down conventional drama in favor of photogenic elements. Though Welles's *Macbeth* was shot in a studio and *Othello* on actual locations, they ultimately express the same attitude: that of a man who creates his own world out of the raw materials at hand, whether artificial or real. He is the director as God, and each individual film serves as one of his planets, with the auteur's entire *oeuvre* constituting an alternative universe.

There is a strong dose of Sergei Eisenstein in Welles's visualization of the past. In particular, he appears taken with the operatic quality and a stark sense of the past as existing halfway between history and legend, as expressed in that director's *Ivan the Terrible*. Even the editing is Eisensteinian: For example, as Welles the actor becomes consumed with jealousy, repressesing it so no one will notice, Welles the director cuts to the fortress's cannons, firing one after the other, expressing his hero's hidden feelings. Onstage it would have been necessary for the performer to convey feelings through controlled use of vocal tones and body language; in the cinema, editing *is* acting. Likewise, when Welles the director cuts from an image of Welles the actor snuffing out the candle to Desdemona, we know by the symbolism in the montage that her fate is sealed.

"I have no objection to Mr. Welles having himself photographed as he dashes through a liberal selection of Italy's architectural gems and curiosities," Robert Hatch ventured in the *Nation*.

> He is a splendid figure of a man and the chase is invigorating. But I wish he wouldn't try to tell a story at the same time—particularly, a story so terrible, one touching so closely the general madness of humanity. His voice is an impressive instrument, but I could not hear half he said, he panted so; and I cannot attend closely to Othello's tragedy when he sticks his head right out of the screen and drips sweat in my lap. *I* haven't got the damned handkerchief!

Clever as Hatch's gag may be, Welles attempted to create a cinematic equivalent of the intimacy of live performance, with soliloquies and asides conveyed by direct address to the moviegoer. The very words Hatch employs to suggest Welles's failure may convince some that Welles achieved the difficult effect he opted for by making an audience feel actively involved rather than as passive observers, which is the case in most movies, even most Shakespearean movies, though never with Shakespeare onstage.

"Take the music," the *New Yorker* complained. "It really isn't music—it's sound." The point is on target, although it may not be a failing, as the critic believed. Welles knew that music, at its most cinematically sophisticated, shouldn't merely serve as a backdrop or to prop up weak scenes. Music *must* reach a point at which it is no longer distinguishable as music, melding into the movie's whole being and becoming an integral part of the cinematic composition. Hitchcock realized this better than anyone other than Welles; *The Birds* represents his ultimate experiment with pure sound as a component of pure cinema. Welles achieves much the same thing in *Othello*, where his discordant notes convey his very theme.

One serious problem is the performance of MacLiammoir, who lisps his way through the role. MacLiammoir managed, over the film's four-year gestation period, to maintain his concept of walking cadaver, dead in spirit, if still moving about. The versatile actor provided his director with what he asked for; Welles, not MacLiammoir, must be blamed for the fact that an audience cannot grasp why Othello would listen to such an obviously venomous person. We believe an intelligent Othello could be taken in by a man who appears honest, but only a fool would believe anything this reptilian Iago says.

Virtually alone among popular publications of the time, *Newsweek* championed the film, noting those very qualities film historians would point out years later in defense of Welles:

> It is a disturbing experience, as it should be, whereas it might have been simply a translation, from stage to screen, to be admired without being felt—or, worse, one of those free translations in which the words of Shakespeare are lost in an uproar of physical activity. As Welles has produced it, not only is the action suited to the word; the artful suitability of all the picture's elements to one another makes it a dramatic success.

Such praise was rare in America.

Still, the film won the Grand Prix at the Cannes Film Festival in 1952. Despite that honor, *Othello* would not be released theatrically in America until 1955, and then shown in only three theaters, where it soon disappeared from sight. Long considered lost, a print of it was discovered in the 1980s. *Othello* (now hailed as a masterpiece) was fully restored and reissued in 1992.

### Black Narcissus
### *Othello*
Mosfilm, 1955; Sergei Yutkevich

The Russians initiated their Shakespearean films with Sergei Yutkevich's 1955 adptation, working from a script by poet, novelist, and Shakespearean translator Boris Pasternak. Yutkevich himself was an expert on the Bard, having published a volume, *Shekspir i Kino*, exalting Shakespeare for presaging socialist art. Indeed, Shakespeare had created a populist theater, simultaneously entertaining and informing an illiterate public, much like postrevolutionary Soviet film. Like such contemporaries as Eisenstein, Yutkevich had early on hoped to rescue drama from the elitist domain of aristocrats, emphasizing theater's relationship to such popular forms as the circus and music hall. The hope was to create an unpretentious, accessible "group theater," thereby catching the attention of the working man, much like the plays Shakespeare had devised for the Globe.

Yutkevich, fifty-one at the time, worked on a grand scale; crowd scenes were ironically reminiscent of those staged by the most decadent of American capitalist filmmakers, Cecil B. DeMille. Running 108 minutes, *Othello* featured Sergei Bondarchuk (later to direct the monumental Soviet *War and Peace*) as Othello. The movie was shot in lush Sovcolor with Russian actors speaking in their native tongue, though the print eventually released in America was dubbed by British performers. Reviewing for the *New York Times*, A. H. Weiler hailed the film as "a most beautiful, colorful, and motion-filled version that dwarfs any *Othello* constricted by confines of stage and proscenium arch." Most critics took note of the pictorial beauty; Yutkevich had been a painter in his youth and launched his filmmaking career as a set designer. When he eventually turned to directing, he emphasized the relationship of film to graphic rather than theatrical arts. Not surprisingly, the acting seems overdone and is less impressive than the magnificent tableaus Yutkevich so painstakingly mounted, mostly on exterior locations.

Yutkevich himself insisted that his version was not an alternative to Welles's but its polar opposite. The Russian director bridled at Welles's decision to start the film with its conclusion; Yutkevich began by tracing Othello's earlier adventures, expanding the tragedy to epic proportions. "I start from life," Yutkevich insisted, "Welles from death." In this respect, Yutkevich comes closer to Shakespeare, emphasizing the free will of characters who determine their own fates rather than any sense of predestination.

Yutkevich Sovietized the film, playing the final death scene by an open window, allowing a view of the Crimean seaside during purple dusk, with pounding ocean waves drowning out Desdemona's frantic plea for mercy. In fact, he transformed this into the tragedy of Desdemona, beginning the film with a shot of the lady spinning a globe to discover the places Othello told her of. The movie assumes her point of view on mood-shifting Othello rather than perceiving her through his eyes. Critics found the film "warm," "romantic," and "lyrical," a true celebration of this woman's love for a man who as clearly hails from Mars as she does from Venus. One fascinating costuming touch was having Desdemona arrive on Cypress wearing a tight, dark man's suit. In a self-consciously arty shot, we notice Iago viewing her arrival as reflected in his sword's hilt. The notion of possible homosexuality, though never emphasized here, takes on new meaning as he perceives his archrival in masculine garb, not unlike a heroine in a Shakespearean cross-dressing comedy.

Yutkevich's production is hardly a filmed play. This *Othello* is dominated by traveling and tracking shots, which convey a sense that the audience moves alongside the characters. To further decrease theatricality, Yutkevich staged Othello-Iago scenes on a ship at sea and while riding on horseback. Yutkevich was too talented to falsely believe merely transferring moments from interiors to exteriors automatically qualifies them as cinematic. Pure cinema occurs only if the director creatively organizes his *mise en scène*, so that the manner in which we see a confrontation is as important as what is said. As Iago initially attempts to convince Othello of Desdemona's faithlessness, Othello resists; they walk on a beach near huge hanging fishnets. Yutkevich alters his camera angle until the nets—initially a realistic element—take on symbolic significance, seeming to swallow up Othello. The camera angles make the nets appear ready to descend on him, ironically countermanding his vocalized insistence that Desdemona is true.

Whereas most moderns insist on a complex, imperfect Othello and at least somewhat sympathetic Iago, Yutkevich saw the story baldly: pure good and absolute evil. He goes so far as to underplay Shakespeare's key motives (career and spousal), harkening back to Cinthio's simplistic original, suggesting Iago may be motivated by lust for Desdemona. The Russian *Othello* received the "best direction" award at the Cannes Film Festival in 1956, the committee clearly defining direction in a visual rather than a dramatic sense.

## "I Hate the Moor!"
## *Othello, the Moor of Venice*
Eagle Films Ltd.; Stuart Burge, 1965

By 1965, Olivier was acutely aware of the growing black population in England. He was fascinated by those immigrants from the West Indies working in restaurants, as conductors on Red Rovers, or selling newspapers. Their way of speaking, manner of moving, and choice of clothes were all highly intriguing. Olivier was a true actor, working even during his off-hours by creating a mental catalog of mannerisms and filing away details in the computer of his thespian's mind. Then along came an offer from John Dexter of the National Theater to star in a new production of *Othello*. Olivier jumped at the chance, for he already knew the approach he would take.

His decision to contemporize the character by portraying Othello as a modern Caribbean created a frenzy of public interest as well as a storm of controversy. Such debate caused the production to become a huge commercial success. Since the filmed transcription of the Burton-Gielgud *Hamlet* had been a box-office winner, Warner Bros. was contracted to immortalize this performance in much the same manner. Director Stuart Burge ever so slightly reconceived the work via three camera setups to allow for minimal editing. The major difference was that *Hamlet* had been taped before a live audience and then transferred to film; *Othello* would be remounted on a soundstage at Shepperton Studios and filmed in Technicolor and wide screen. The settings by William Kenner were modeled closely on those created for the stage by Jocelyn Herbert. The finished work would, like *Hamlet*, be shown for four performances over a two-day period.

"The whole object was to capture the absolute magic of the theater," producer Anthony Havelock-Allan stated, so "we have put the best cinema resources *at the service* of great drama." As to the validity of this approach, there was a variety of opinions. Hollis Alpert of the *Saturday Review* lauded the device: "Very little has been done to make this *Othello* cinematic, [so] as a result, we have the play itself, living proof that theater and film can serve each other and serve us all." Such an approach proceeds from the aesthetic (considered naive today) that film is essentially a recording device rather than, as Rudolf Arnheim put it, an original art form. Conversely, *Time* insisted that filming a stage play violates rather than immortalizes a theatrical experience: "The camera's merciless eye often annihilates the indispensable illusion of theater, leaping the distance that might lend more credibility to Olivier's performance. His makeup looks false, and through the blackface gleams a supreme actor's intelligence, timing every phrase, calculating effects, revealing the mechanics of his trade in monstrous close-ups."

Such reasoning proceeds from the assumption that turning *Othello* into a movie should be as extreme a conversion as Verdi transforming Shakespeare's story into opera. Striking a middle ground between the extremes, the *New Yorker*'s Brendan Gill wrote that if approached as a recording, this unquestionably was "a valuable addition to our theatrical archives, but as cinema [it's] like a literal translation of a poem, playing us false by remaining all too grimly true to the original."

Which is not to imply that the production is without merit. While preparing for the role, Olivier studied the interpretation of F. R. Leavis, the critic who rejected the widespread notion that *Othello* is a realistically retold good-Faust-seduced-by-evil-Mephistopheles fable, insisting Othello is more responsible for what happens than Iago. Whereas the villain of Cinthio's piece had been miffed after rejection by Disdamona, Shakespeare's Iago is furious that Cassio, lacking battlefield experience, received the promotion due to his military-school degree. The supposedly wise Othello is overly impressed by the white Establishment's paper chase, although he, as a black man, should know better.

Indeed, it was experience and not a university pedigree that won Othello his position. Worse, Iago believes his commander casually bedded Iago's wife. Far from the "motiveless malignancy" Samuel Taylor Coleridge once dubbed him, Iago is a man with justifiable complaints. His deep hurt, if not his subsequent action, makes sense. Who wouldn't say, "I hate the Moor!" under such circumstances? There is a terrible perfection and a poetic justice to his plan. Villain and hero suffer from the same flaw: jealousy. Olivier was indebted to his mentor Hitchcock and couldn't miss the similarities between Shakespeare's situation and the "original sin" or "transference of guilt" theme running through works by the master of suspense.

Hitchcock's villains serve as doppelgängers to his heroes, secret sharers of the protagonists' deep, dark failings. There is a bond between hero and villain in *Shadow of a Doubt, Strangers on a Train, Frenzy,* and dozens of other movies. Hitchcock's heroes are never the pure Protestant ideal; rather, they are troubled, flawed (implicitly Catholic) individuals, valiantly struggling toward the light; the villain, who is the flip side of the same coin, embraces the darkness wholeheartedly. Each serves as the other's good or evil twin. Though Shakespeare's *Othello* preceded Hitchcock's *oeuvre* by some four hundred years, their effect is essentially the same. No one is completely innocent in the shadow worlds of Shakespeare, Hitchcock, or Olivier.

Olivier had always admired Hitchcock's *Suspicion,* about a wife who suspects her husband is planning her murder, though he is not; with *Othello,* Olivier could mount his own companion piece, an inverse situation in which a wife does not suspect her husband is planning to murder her, though he is. Also serving as a foreshadowing of Hitchcock is Shakespeare's infamous handkerchief, which is emphasized in this version. It's what Hitchcock (who likewise explored the theme of madness) would, four centuries later, refer to as a "MacGuffin": some simple object, blown way out of proportion by the characters, which then becomes the center of all human activity.

In a striking image halfway between the theatrical and the cinematic, Othello made his grand entrance dressed entirely in white, carrying a blood-red rose, with his black skin glistening under hot lights. Whether the symbolism derives from Dexter, Burge, or Olivier, it effectively announces that this hero is doomed not by his love (the traditional approach) but by an insecurity complex that makes him vulnerable to the Establishment he has seemingly joined. Despite his conscious appearance of self-assurance, this Othello is not what he seems. Certainly he wouldn't so easily be won over by Iago's plot were he not already in fear of eventually losing his wife. He creates his own inner hell based on anxiety, then projects that subjective vision onto the world around him. Hamlet told us "nothing's either good nor bad; thinking makes it so." Othello has a position of power and a beautiful, faithful wife; yet what should make him happy only makes him sad, then mad, owing to the manner in which he thinks about it.

That happens because he remains consciously aware of being a black man in a white world. So Olivier's Othello has crinkled hair, rolls his eyes, smacks his pink lips, and is blacker than black. This qualified the film as the first screen version to insist on a civil-rights approach; ironically, it also exposed Olivier to charges of racism. For he was likewise the last white actor to don blackface for a major film. *Time* noted:

> Pantherlike, vain, and arrogant, his skin is dark as charcoal, his bass-toned speech richly thickened in a kind of classic calypso rhythm. Rolling his r's and his hips, he swaggers. . . . The approach is valid, but Olivier overworks it, for his portrayal appears geared primarily to the task of impersonating a Negro. In his accomplished mimicry, there is often too much mammy singer . . . [Othello] emerg[ing] as a modern stereotype.

Not everyone agreed that Olivier reduced Othello to Al Jolson as Uncle Tom. *Newsweek* insisted that what transpired on-screen was a dramatic emancipation proclamation:

> Olivier has set Othello free from acting conventions that sentimentalized him into the gentlest of warriors. . . . This new Othello is pontifical, fatuous, self-satisfied and removed from reality almost to the point of psychosis. He is a model of gorgeous decadence. . . . Olivier has found an artistically valid notion of how the role should be interpreted [for our time] and found the courage to set it forth. He makes the play more engrossing—and more convincing—than it has ever been for a modern audience.

It could be argued, then, that Olivier, like Shakespeare before him, was a civil-rights activist. He takes a complex black man as his central character and shows him as worthy (if imperfect) as Brutus, Hamlet, or Lear. Conversely, one could complain that Olivier, like Shakespeare, incarnated the offensive notion of the black man as a noble savage, ultimately done in by a residue of primitive passions within him, which is (odious by politically correct standards) part of his racial identity. Thus interpreted, the tragic ending suggests that however fit (indeed, superior) he may seem, the black man is ultimately incapable of accepting a dignified position. His overly emotional origins cause destruction for himself and those who believe in him.

Hugh O'Kenner of the *National Review* noted the social relevance and topical immediacy of this approach: "Olivier's black man is shut off from [other] men by something James Baldwin's contemporaries understand . . . a self-hypnotizing assurance that the white establishment is too trivial to worry about. He comes onstage a Black Narcissus. . . . Nothing will shake him and the security of his black otherness modulates rapidly to hysteria." Perhaps, though, O'Kenner is wrong when he speaks of "security"; more likely than not, this is bravado, to cover the deep sense of worthlessness Othello—at least Olivier's Othello—suffers from. Although his status may be earned (he is indeed the greatest warrior), his confidence is feigned. He must constantly strut, convincing whites that he believes himself superior. A show, however, is just a show; when Iago sees through his act, he can prey on Othello's hidden anxieties.

Whereas Welles had reduced the lines to almost an afterthought, Olivier insisted on an old-school approach of perfect diction, striking delivery and self-conscious stage presence. This was, after all, not a realistic movie but a classical play performed nearly in its entirety. Owing to the virtual completeness of text, Olivier conveys, to a greater degree than Welles, the essence of Shakespeare's attraction to this story. How often Will must have fantasized about killing Anne Hathaway, the wife he believed unfaithful. If he did, he would go directly to the hangman. Art, however, provides a safer means for a cathartic experience; by having Othello, his alter ego, perform such an act, Shakespeare could experience relief, since, on a literary level, he had done the deed in such a way that he earned accolades. Freud would insist that the artist and the insane man are similar; the artist merely escapes detection as psychotic by channeling neurotic urges into a publicly lauded craft.

Olivier emphasizes Othello's epilepsy, which Welles all but omitted. Of Maggie Smith's Desdemona, one critic put it perfectly, insisting she accomplished the near impossible task of making "virtue as exciting as vice." Actor Frank Finlay suggested the possible homosexuality of Iago, more so even than in the Welles version (if only because he has more screen time), without overly insisting on that approach. Due to a sustained lower-working-class accent, Finlay insists on the notion that Iago hails from contemporary East London's worst slum. Iago emerges as a lower-class white, seeing in the black man a natural ally as a former underdog. When Othello hands over the promotion that Iago feels is his due to an upper-class snob, Iago rightly feels betrayed. This black man has lost touch with his own humble origins and now aligns himself with the ruling class.

Burge was highly experienced both in theater and television. His *Othello* looks like live theater reimagined for the small screen due to a preponderance of close-ups. Only once does Burge go for a truly cinematic effect; as Othello falls into his most severe fit, Burge cuts to a striking crane shot, visually conveying the hero's disorientation. As the only such moment in the film, however, it draws attention to itself. Burge would have done better to shoot the entire picture imaginatively or excise his one instance of improvisation so it would not serve as a foil and remind viewers of how noncinematic the rest of his film happens to be.

## A Fascinating Footnote

## *Othello*

Howard University, 1980; Liz White

Though virtually unknown, there was a motion picture (not of Hollywood origin) starring a black actor as Othello before Oliver Parker's 1995 version with Laurence Fishburne, although Parker's film is universally (though incorrectly) considered the first to feature such casting. Indeed, not only Othello but *all* roles were played by blacks, mostly Howard University students. Also fascinating is that the 1980 *Othello* was directed by a woman, Liz White. She assumed a feminist attitude, envisioning this as a classic case study of spousal abuse among African Americans. White shot the film at Martha's Vineyard, Massachusetts as well as at Cobbleclose Farm, New Jersey. Ethnic jazz, composed by Gwangwa Jones, was featured on the soundtrack. Character actor Yaphet Kotto portrayed Othello, with Audrey Dixon as Desdemona and Richard Dixon as Iago; director White cast herself, intriguingly, as the whore Bianca. Though not commercially available, the 115-minute film remains in limited availability, through Howard University's cultural committee.

## The Tragedy of Iago
### *Othello*

Columbia, Castle Rock, Dakota, Imminent, 1995; Oliver Parker

At a time when other adapters were placing *Richard III* in a World War II battlefield and setting *Romeo and Juliet* to a hip-hop beat, Oliver Parker created a surprisingly traditional *Othello*. Trimming away more than a third of the words, he broke lengthy sequences into short scenes, playing them in varied interiors and exteriors to make crystal clear that his was a movie rather than a filmed play. Despite the richly appointed period costumes and settings, the actors were encouraged to take a naturalistic approach, making this an easily accessible *Othello*. Numerous critics complained that Parker's film aped the surface appeal while missing the artistic essence of Branagh's and Zeffirelli's direction. Their films are open to modern audiences, thanks to bright colors, fast pace, extreme condensation, attractive young stars, brief nudity, and realistic characters. Yet each precedes from a strong point of view about the particular play. Not so, most reviewers complained, with this *Othello*. Parker, more experienced as actor than director, had been content to provide a journeyman's servicing of material, guiding a strong cast through a series of well-played acting exercises.

No wonder, then, that Parker's *Othello* failed to receive the extreme raves or pans more outrageous films elicit. Critical reaction ranged from mildly positive ("standard . . . a solid reading"—Richard Corliss, *Time*) to genially dismissive ("conventional—realistic, unimaginative, even depressingly literal-minded"—David Denby, *New York*). In Stanley Kauffmann's view, the degree to which Parker successfully transformed this play into a film spelled its downfall as Shakespeare. "I know of no drama in the whole history of art, including the Greeks, that surpasses *Othello* in the sense of a force launched at the start that drives unremittingly to the end, gathering speed and power as it goes," he wrote in the *New Republic*. The film's problem derives less from the pruning away of dialogue than the reconstruction of narrative line. The very necessity of translating theater into film, even when effectively done, doomed (at least, in Kauffmann's mind) the possibility of successfully representing what was essential to the play's greatness. Kauffmann continues: "Parker shuns complete scenes, complete at least in shape even if condensed. So what we get is an assemblage instead of unbroken onrush."

Most critics have written this film off as a handsome, respectable, but ultimately negligible *Othello*. Its chief value is, for high schools and such, as an acceptable means of introducing the uninitiated to the Bard. In fact, Parker's film is far more worthy than anyone has yet acknowledged. It is truly cinematic, while offering a unique take on the play.

Any production of *Hamlet* rises or falls on the performance of the actor in the lead; *Othello* presents a more complex problem, since Othello and Iago are equally important. That seems especially relevant, as this was regarded as the first film in which a black man played Othello. "Fishburne's soft-voiced, tentative, and mysteriously uncharismatic performance is the result of his own discomfort with the material," the *New Yorker* noted. "Fishburne looks lost . . . he has never played Shakespeare before." Fishburne appeared so intimidated by working with the Bard that he ceased doing what he does best, which is naturalistic Method acting. Instead, he enunciated every word, and the final result was elocution, not acting. Fishburne simmered and projected surliness (his stock in trade) but never created any sense of a character who arcs during the course of the story. As critic David Denby noted, "Fishburne is awfully tight. The point [of the play], however, is that Othello loses his command of himself, and Fishburne won't let himself out."

On the other hand, Branagh was rightly praised for, as *Commonweal* noted, "an Iago so radically perverted that he seems to think he is doing the right thing when he works havoc." The *New Yorker* concurred: "Iago is a hearty, bluff, soldierly type whose artless manner enables him to win the trust of those he means to destroy. It's a welcome twist on the customary interpretation—in many productions, Iago is so glib and oily that we can't imagine anyone's believing a word he says."

On subsequent viewings, the dominance of Branagh over Fishburne seems less an unfortunate accident than a quietly expressed attitude. Parker has transformed *Othello* into the tragedy of Iago, making it work as that. Certainly this is a radical but satisfying approach. It's not for nothing that in this version Iago has more screen time than Othello; in his intense identification with the audience through direct address, Branagh's Iago resembles Richard III, with Othello reduced to one of Gloucester's puppets.

This Othello becomes a foil for Iago instead of the other way around. Were this not the case, Fishburne's superficial portrait would, in comparison to Branagh's three-dimensional Iago, prove more problematic than it does. Never, in a film version, has the contrast between Iago's nasty reality (when confiding his bitterness to us) and his show of false affection (when speaking with anyone else) been so effectively communicated. In large part, this plays because Parker and Branagh worked out a series of visual transitions between those two Iagos where his gestures, as he slips back and forth from public persona to cruel confidant, allow us to see his essential dishonesty during wordless moments. The experience is akin to watching Dr. Jekyll turn into Mr. Hyde and back again.

One striking example occurs after Iago pretends friendship with Roderigo, who hurries off to put money in his purse. Iago turns to us, ready to offer cynical pronouncements, only to be interrupted as Roderigo unexpectedly returns. Iago has to slip back into his public persona but barely manages this as he turns to Roderigo and feigns affection. Once more rid of the nuisance, Iago eyeballs the audience and shrugs off his deception impishly. Branagh is so effective an actor and so charming a personality that it's impossible for a viewer *not* to chuckle. The moment we do, *we* are, like Othello, lost and complicit in his scheme. We, like Othello, are seduced by the attractiveness of evil without knowing it.

This approach allows Parker to communicate the essence of a key Shakespearean theme: *Othello* is ultimately *about* acting. Shakespeare used the theatrical form to comment on what he perceived as a nearly universal phoniness in the world. In his view, life is a form of theater, most everybody pretending to be something they are not. Even the sincere Hamlet ("I know not seems") necessarily feigned madness (thereby acting) to survive. Fortunately, he appreciated the truthfulness of one human being: namely, Horatio. No wonder Othello believes the worst about Desdemona; in a corrupt world someone who seems pure *must* be pretending.

The notion that Iago is impotent, perhaps homosexual, is neatly expressed through visual arrangements, despite the fact that Branagh is an extremely virile specimen. What he and Parker achieve, then, is all the more impressive, suggesting that beneath their Iago's surface of conventional manliness, a closet queen struggles to break out. The sequence in which Emilia innocently carries Desdemona's handkerchief to her husband, due to Iago's repeated requests, is notable. Finding Iago sleeping, she seductively slithers over him, but Iago pushes her away. He insists she's a "common thing," and like Othello, he assumes his wife's guilt without, Hamlet-like, testing the issue. Realizing she has brought the object of his desire, Iago leaps up. Now he's ecstatic, even sexually excited by the prospect of what mischief he can achieve. Emilia, misunderstanding his arrousal, readies herself for sex; Iago, lost in delirious expectations, unconsciously joins her. In seconds, he is spent; unwilling to acknowledge his instantaneous self-loathing, Iago blames her, turning away as if his failure were her fault. Then he smiles wickedly, taking alternate pleasure in the coming power play.

This is the only filmed *Othello* to suggest a dynamic relationship between Iago and Othello. Iago is initially seen at the periphery of the action, while Othello is accompanied by Cassio. Branagh's manner of considering the two suggests not only resentment at being passed over but repressed jealousy that Cassio (a handsome, long-haired, High Renaissance gentleman) is so close to the man Iago covets, in ways that are perhaps ambiguous even to himself. As Iago spins his web, Cassio is gradually physically distanced as Iago slips ever closer. The tone of their conversations change; Othello at first keeps a polite distance, then loosens up with Iago, and finally falls under his spell.

Parker creates a stunning image for that moment when Othello surrenders entirely. We see the two embrace, a physical encounter which means something very different to Othello than Iago. "I am yours," Iago whispers to Othello. Iago is on the verge of tears—sincere tears at that! This is the one moment when it's impossible to tell whether Branagh's Iago is speaking to Othello, to us, or both; even he may not know for certain. Iago holds Othello tightly but tenderly; he casts a glance in our direction, then averts his eyes, embarrassed that we see him so emotionally naked.

We realize that the nasty sophistication of his asides may have been as much show as his seeming honesty. Possibly there's a vulnerable, threatened, frightened human being here, striking out for satisfaction in the only way he knows. Though secretly in love with his commandant, Iago would happily repress the sexual element. Iago could suffer the sight of Othello retiring with Desdemona if only he were allowed alternative satisfactions: career advancement and respect. Having been denied these, he self-destructs, taking everyone down with him. But not before winning his prize, which, in this rendering, is not widespread bloodshed but a transcendental moment: the brief but all important embrace when he and Othello admit they belong only to each other.

This is what Iago always wanted; if he could have achieved it without causing pain, that would have been fine. Since he couldn't, he secured what he wanted and needed via the only avenue open to him. Brian D. Johnson in *MacLean's* complained that "Iago is a bad boy with an idle mind and a mischievious wit, but he does not seem especially evil." Intended as criticism, Johnson's words make clear his recognition that director and actor achieved precisely the interpretation of Iago they were after.

The major flaw in the film resulted from Parker's decision to cut Desdemona's final lines. After she has been killed in the play, help belatedly arrives, and to everyone's surprise, she literally comes back from the dead. Filmmakers, especially directors opting for a realistic approach, are stymied by such patent theatricality. Writing about the Olivier *Othello* (which *does* include Desdemona's final lines) in 1966, Warren Coffey of *Commentary* observed that the scene failed because "there is something very questionably operatic, at least if [seen in the context of] a realistic, wide-screen, color movie . . . in having Desdemona smothered with a pillow then throttled, only to revive. The pathos of the scene might well carry the bad physiology of this in a more stylized production, but not here." That scene, mind you, was in a film shot on a theatrical set. Who could blame Parker, whose movie is considerably realistic, for dropping it?

Cutting it, however, creates another problem. Her final words are so significant to the play's impact that to drop them amounts to telling a two-hour joke, then failing to deliver the punch line. When she opens her mouth, Othello shudders, fearing incrimination. Instead, when asked to name her killer, she insists, "Nobody; I myself. Commend me to my fair lord," then expires. Othello realizes three things: Desdemona is innocent; she still loves him so much that she exonerates him; and having lived a pure life, she dies with a lie on her lips, condemning herself to hell for eternity. She has knowingly given up salvation of her immortal soul to save the man who brutally murdered her; greater love than this no man knows. The power of Shakespeare's conception is inherent in this conceit, however difficult it is to pull off.

On the other hand, Parker effectively handles another problem. Contemporary viewers are stunned when the strong and liberated Desdemona passively allows Othello to go through with his announced intention; in the Welles and Olivier-Burge versions, such an approach (true to Shakespeare) confuses the modern viewer, unable to understand why she doesn't struggle. In fact, Desdemona is the perfect Elizabethan wife; so perfect that if her husband decides to murder her, she submits, as she does to all else. Parker's Desdemona fights for her life while saying Shakespeare's lines. The moment is made palatable for today's viewers without detracting from the original meaning. It is one more ingenious directorial decision in a film that is far more committed to an original, if noncontroversial, interpretation than director Parker has been given credit for.

## Variations on a Theme

The first cinematic attempt to modernize Shakespeare's story occurred in Denmark in 1911. Directed by August Blom, *Desdemona* ran a then-hefty eighteen minutes. Generally regarded as the first European film to break away from straight adaptations of classics (termed *film d'art*), this Nordisk production was promoted as "not unadulterated Shakespeare, but a good modern play," as Desdemona's purity gave way to "the terrible vengeance a husband exacts from his *erring* wife"! Ejnar and Maria, a husband-wife acting team, perform *Othello* at the Rococo Theatre. A fellow thespian, Preben, is intoxicated with Maria, though she rejects him for another suitor. Bitterly, he plots vengeance, making her husband suspicious as all three rehearse. Ejnar loses himself in the role so completely that he soon believes himself to be Othello. On opening night, when Othello kills Desdemona, the audience is dumbfounded by the onstage realism.

A similar approach was offered in *Carnival*, the 1921 British-Italian coproduction. Set in Venice, the story concerns a modern woman who appears anything but faithful, causing her actor-husband to strangle her onstage. The outcome is less gruesome this time, as a standard happy ending involving unlikely reversals is provided. Simonetta (Hilda Bayley) somehow survives the attack and explains (via flashback) that she resisted the advances of Andreone (Ivor Novello), though everything we've seen implies involvement. England's Harley Knoles directed *Carnival* from a screenplay by H. C. M. Hardinge and Matheson Lang, based on their London stage play. Lang also played Silvio/Othello.

A 1931 remake of *Carnival* called *Venetian Nights* likewise starred Matheson Lang, with Dorothy Bouchier and the esteemed Joseph Schildkraut. The improbabilities of the original conception remained problematic and were rendered even less tenable by the static theatrical quality of early sound production. Far superior was *Men Are Not Gods* (1936), the title derived from Desdemona's speech about the nature of masculine behavior. Produced by Alexander Korda, famed for his classy productions of *The Thief of Baghdad* and *The Jungle Book*, this film was directed by Walter Reisch.

Edmund Davey (Sebastian Shaw) bombs badly in a new production of *Othello*, and he is so devastated by negative reviews that he vows to lose himself in the part to redeem himself with the critics. His secretary (Miriam Hopkins) realizes the now-obsessed Davey is likely to strangle his leading lady (Gertrude Lawrence) during performance, but everything turns out for the best.

The fifth and final film (so far) of this type is by far the greatest. *A Double Life* (1947) was directed by George Cukor from a screenplay by Ruth Gordon and Garson Kanin. It won two Academy Awards, one for Ronald Colman as Best Actor and another for Miklos Rozsa's memorable score. Anthony John (Colman) is a once-respected actor who has abandoned serious plays to make money performing potboilers. His agent suggests he regain his lost status by appearing as the Moor. John hopes to lure back his estranged wife and onetime partner (Signe Hasso), a perfect Desdemona. Meanwhile, he becomes involved with a pretty waitress (Shelley Winters). While in rehearsal for the role, John inadvertently strangles the girl during one of their romantic trysts. The film is convincing in a way earlier variations were not. Critic Leonard Maltin hailed it as "brilliant."

Like *Hamlet*, the *Othello* story has been stripped of its poetry and relocated in various time periods and far-flung places. *Jubal*, a rugged 1956 westernized version by Delmer Daves, was based on a novel by Paul I. Wellman that focused on Cassio. Easygoing ranch hand Jubal Troop (Glenn Ford) is promoted to foreman by ranch owner Shep (Ernest Borgnine) over longtime hand Pinky (Rod Steiger). Embittered and desperately attracted to the boss's wife, Maie (Valerie French), Pinky manipulates innocent Shep into believing that Maie and Jubal are involved. In fact, Maie is hardly a Desdemona; she would welcome such an affair, though Jubal repulses her. Intriguingly, most modernizations eliminate the woman's purity, perhaps an unintentional commentary on our times. More surprising is that the racial issue was eliminated despite the fact that this was the era of civil-rights cinema.

*All Night Long* (1961), yet another British variation, set the story in the world of jazz. Paul Harris plays Aurelius Rex, whose girlfriend, Delia (Marti Sevens), is coveted by Johnny Cousin (Patrick McGoohan). Hoping to install her in his band as vocalist, he gets her friend Cass (Keith Michell) high on pot, causing him to insult an influential music-world mover and shaker. Johnny slips a cigarette lighter (the film's handkerchief) into Cass's pocket so that Rex will believe she gave away his recent present. There's a nick-of-time happy ending, but not before jazz greats, including Dave Brubeck, jam. The plot parallels to *Othello* seem forced. Still, McGoohan's villain makes one wish there were a legitimate *Othello* film in which he could play Iago.

Clearly taken by *Othello*, McGoohan directed *Catch My Soul*, a 1974 rock-opera version, appearing simultaneously with the better-known *Jesus Christ Superstar*. At a desert commune, Othello (Richie Havens) is a rock performer and charismatic cult leader, and Desdemona (Season Hubley) is a hippieish devotee. Iago is played by Lance LeGault as a Charles Manson clone. Instead of getting drunk, Cassio (Tony Joe White) experiences a bad drug trip; musicians Bonnie and Delaney Bramlett include as much Shakespearean poetry as possible in their songs. When the film flopped on the art-house circuit, it was retitled *Santa Fe Satan* and rereleased as a drive-in exploitation flick. Though not particularly distinguished, it remains a real curio. The same cannot be said for *Black Commando*, a 1973 Spanish-lensed action flick about a mercenary who, while on assignment in Africa, is attracted to the daughter (Joanna Pettet) of a visiting U.S. senator, also coveted by Iago (Tony Curtis). Shakespeare's name was spelled incorrectly in the credits. Star Max H. Boulois adapted and directed.

# 10

# FATAL VISION
## *Macbeth*

*It is a tale told by an idiot
full of sound and fury, signifying nothing.*

—Macbeth

The queen is dead. Long live the king!

Following Elizabeth's demise in 1603, her nephew King James of Scotland arrived forthwith to accept the crown. To Shakespeare's probable surprise and relief, civil war did not immediately break out. Nevertheless, an extremist conspiracy to assassinate the king culminated in the Gunpowder Plot of 1605 and resulted in the much-publicized arrest and execution of Guy Fawkes. Shakespeare sensed that the time was ripe to revive his great recurring theme—the killing of a king—while maintaining the domestic issues he had recently explored in *Othello*. As always, the Bard made his point by adapting a story from the past to comment on the present.

Because of King James's origins Scotland was enjoying a great vogue, so Shakespeare searched for suitable material to exploit that. Then James (as great a fan of the Bard's plays as Elizabeth) probably wrote Will (according to a tradition recorded by Oldys), calling the author's attention to the Macbeth story. James was descended from Fleance, son of Banquo, so the tale thus justifies James's divine right by lineage. Moreover, the presence of witches in the plot delighted James, who had authored *Daemonologie* (1599), a well-regarded book on the subject. Holinshed's *Chronicles* provided the Bard with diverse information on Macbeth. He also happened on an entirely different story that equally intrigued him: that of King Duff, who was killed in the castle of Forres by Donwald, against Donwald's own better judgment following incessant urging by his ambitious wife.

For a fuller, richer play, he could graft that tale of a difficult marriage onto Macbeth, which did not feature a strong female lead. Elsewhere, Will discovered the story of a different murderer, Malcolm, who killed Scotland's king Kenneth, then was unable to sleep at night; guilty dreams had long since become a staple of Shakespeare's plays. Yet another story told of Siward's invasion of Scotland from England to rid that land of an evil king. Lastly, he had long been fascinated by two tales from prehistoric (and not necessarily Scottish) folklore: the moving forest and the man of no woman born. By mixing and matching these elements, he created a composite to equal *Hamlet* and *Othello*.

Indeed, many literary critics insist that *Macbeth* surpasses them. For here, and only here, Shakespeare is at his "most Greek," working in the tradition of Sophocles. If he did not know that author firsthand, then this is a case of great minds separately moving in the same direction. The early *Romeo and Juliet* had presented a simple, straightforward tragedy of fate; in the more mature tragedies (*Julius Caesar, Hamlet, Othello*), he had discarded predestination and created a modern tragedy of character. Only in *Macbeth* does Will balance the two, much as Sophocles had nearly two millenia earlier, in *Oedipus the King*, in which a fated character, attempting to exercise free will, brings about his own dark destiny.

Witches greet Macbeth and Banquo, predicting kingship for the former and a lineage of kings for the latter. Had the witches not met them, Macbeth would never have considered killing Duncan; in a sense, he *is* fated by their prediction. Yet Banquo hears similar predictions and never consciously attempts to alter the future. Something in Macbeth's character, in precarious relation to the edict, causes his downfall. Fate and free will are finely fused in this most structurally impressive of all Shakespeare's plays.

Macbeth struggles with a horrible truth he discovers: the potential for evil within himself. Here was the great challenge for Shakespeare, who wanted to avoid repetition at all costs. Hamlet, however psychologically disturbed, is motivated by the desire to do the right thing. Othello and Brutus, despite their terrible mistakes, are guilty of naïveté, not evil. Would it be possible, Will mused, to transform a man who, like the villainous Richard III, deliberately performs evil acts into a sympathetic tragic hero? This, never achieved previously, was a challenge the Bard couldn't resist. Macbeth, though marvelously specific, is his portrait of universal mankind, torn apart by the opposing forces of good and evil within each of us.

The great challenge for actors, then, is to convey the full measure of this man by making the audience love *and* hate him. Viewers feel moved, even if they can't understand why they emotionally experience extreme feeling for a killer. Both live and film productions succeed or fail based on how effectively they elicit this complexity of emotion.

## Early Efforts

The earliest *Macbeth* movies were too brief to convey anything but simple villainy: Attempts in America (*Death Scene from 'Macbeth'* in 1905 from American Mutoscope and Biograph Company), Italy (*Macbeth* in 1909 by Mario Caserini for Cines of Rome), and France (*Macbeth* in 1910, Calmettes of the Comédie-Française) were brief, ranging between two and fifteen minutes. Their primary interest is historical rather than aesthetic, featuring primitively staged action scenes and histrionic acting. A more ambitious *Macbeth* was produced in Germany in 1913, directed by Ludwig Landmann and running a full forty-seven minutes. This was a key precursor to feature films as we know them. Unfortunately, the film remains lost.

Also missing is the version produced by D. W. Griffith in America in 1916, immediately following the release of his landmark *Birth of a Nation*. As Griffith was absorbed with the creation of his immense *Intolerance*, the impressario allowed John Emerson to direct Sir Herbert Tree as Macbeth. This marks a notable early appearance by an acclaimed actor in the still-déclassé medium of motion pictures. Griffith's own cinematic pleas against social disorder as well as his love of threatened characters in an epic scope made him a prime candidate to bring Shakespeare to the screen. The two artists were both complimentary in conservativism of philosophy and originality of approach.

Films of *Macbeth*, most lost, continued to be produced in Europe throughout the 1920s and 1930s. Hollywood, in the wake of the commercial failure of both *A Midsummer Night's Dream* (1935) and *Romeo and Juliet* (1936), avoided Shakespeare for more than a decade.

## Dagger of the Mind
# *Macbeth*

Willow Productions, 1947; David Bradley

Fortunately, there were filmmakers who operated outside the studio system's confines. One was the independent David Bradley, who in 1947 shot a very low budget *Macbeth* in and around Chicago for less than five thousand dollars. Bradley was a graduate of the Todd School in Woodstock, Illinois, where he had arrived to begin studies shortly after Orson Welles graduated. During World War II he served in the motion-picture section of the army signal corps, turning out filmed projects. Bradley received a free graduate-level education, courtesy of Uncle Sam, at a signal-corps school in Hollywood, followed by another session at Long Island's Astoria Studios. A longtime Shakespeare buff and aspiring moviemaker before the war, Bradley seized on the notion of someday applying this new knowledge to a project of his own choosing. He worked up a *Macbeth* scenario during free hours while stationed in London so as to be ready when the war was over. Bradley's earlier films, including an *Oliver Twist*, had been silent; now he understood how to shoot in 16-millimeter sound.

While still in high school, he had been painfully aware that his chums, who did not share David's high regard for Shakespeare, would rather catch a movie. The way to effectively bring the Bard to them, then, was simple: Film the plays. Bradley was not interested in art for art's sake, but saw a viable money-making possibility. Since Hollywood steered clear of the classics, someone might make a nice profit by turning out films that could then be sold directly to the nation's schools for educational purposes.

While overseas, Bradley shared this dream with his fellow signal-corps students. They were eager to become involved and agreed to meet him on the North Shore following the armistice. Throughout the war, Bradley kept in touch with each by mail. Thomas A. Blair, who would direct and play Banquo, prepared his ideas for a low-key lighting approach while serving with the marines in the South Pacific; Rodney Maynard, chief cameraman and electrician, devised his technical plans while serving with the air force in southern Europe. Young hopeful Charlton Heston of Wilmette, Illinois, who had played the lead in Bradley's *Peer Gynt* and would later enact Mark Antony in *Julius Caesar*, designed the eighty-three costumes for this seventy-three-minute production while still serving in the army in Alaska.

Bradley's coworkers had been discharged before him. Upon his homecoming on April 23, 1946 (the anniversary of Shakespeare's birth and death, which Bradley took as a good omen) the twenty-six-year-old filmmaker was happily surprised to find everyone waiting for him. They set to work in late June, employing two motion-picture and three still cameras. First, though, it was necessary to find material for costumes at rummage sales. Bradley's mother, Mrs. A. Ballard Bradley, brought them to life from Heston's designs. Props were purchased at junk stores, helmets fashioned from papier-mâché, swords cut from wood, and scabbards composed of paper towels and newspapers. Bradley himself chose to play the lead, with Jain Wilimovsky, daughter of an art-institute professor, as his Lady Macbeth.

For the banquet and castle scenes, Bradley brought the cast and crew to Rockford, Illinois, where he recalled seeing suitably ancient buildings. Then they moved on to a quarry in Racine, Wisconsin, for heath and cavern sequences involving the witches. The Deering Library of Northwestern University in Chicago was picked for Lady Macbeth's sleepwalking scene, while portions of Christ Church in his hometown of Winnetka, Illinois, could be photographed so as to suggest a fortress backdrop. The group traveled caravan style, appearing to people in a hundred-mile radius of Chicago like some pack of artistic gypsies, applying makeup en route while sharing sandwiches Bradley's mother had packed.

He then edited and adapted the film to its sound track at home, having transformed his basement into a makeshift studio. All sound was dubbed in afterward, including the dialogue that had to be lip-synched. On-location sound had proved impossible due to low-flying planes and suburban noise just out of camera range. After hometown premieres in Winnetka and Chicago, the film was shown at the New York Public Library, where it was enthusiastically received. Although there would be several other features from this fascinating and forgotten figure, Bradley's dreams never panned out. His planned *Cyrano de Bergerac* and *Romeo and Juliet* failed to reach fruition because distribution to schools proved more difficult than Bradley had imagined. His eventual move to Hollywood led to obscurity rather than, as in the case of collaborator Heston, fame and fortune. Still, Bradley deserves a footnote in the history of Shakespearean cinema, truly rating as the Orson Welles of independents.

## "Oot, Damne Spat!"
## *Macbeth*

Republic Pictures/Mercury Films, 1948; Orson Welles

Welles, already established as a controversial stage interpreter of the Bard, made his first stab at cinematic Shakespeare with *Macbeth*. His earlier Mercury Theatre mounting of the play, at the Utah Centennial Festival in Salt Lake City, dazzled casual theatergoers, but purists complained that all the billowing smoke, excessive sounds, and razzle-dazzle lighting effects drowned out Shakespeare. With 1941's *Citizen Kane* a mere memory and a seven-year string of flops behind him, Welles considered himself lucky to get *Macbeth* into production at Republic Pictures, which was known for shoestring-budget westerns starring Roy Rogers. For the company, it was an opportunity to upgrade their image; for Welles, it was a chance to make the movie he wanted to make, if not necessarily under the circumstances he would have preferred.

A tight twenty-one-day shooting schedule, all on the Poverty Row company's back lot, and minuscule financing drastically restricted his every move. What he accomplished under such circumstances remains remarkable. His *Macbeth* is a stylish movie in which Welles realizes a vividly detailed, fully believable world: What we see combines equal measures of Sergei Eisenstein's ancient Russia from *Alexander Nevsky* and the cave of the Clay People in the Saturday morning serial *Flash Gordon's Trip to Mars*. Whether *that* world is the one Shakespeare envisioned remains highly debatable.

In keeping with the film-noir approach so popular in the postwar years (which Welles himself initiated in the early forties), the director opted for a stark, barren ambience. A sense of gloom hovers over this fabricated Scotland; fog drifts in endlessly, while dirty animals dash across the courtyard and belie any audience expectation of a romantic past. Rock formations are threateningly jagged; trees appear twisted and misshapen, like Snow White's forest in the Disney cartoon; and constant drizzle descends from foreboding darkness. Macbeth's bizarre helmet is a take-your-breath-away thing to consider; on close consideration, it would be more appropriate for a Mongolian monarch or Viking warrior than Scottish lord.

Our first image of Macbeth's castle suggests the home of Count Dracula. Apparently, Welles cared little about Duncan's words as he unwisely enters Inverness: "This castle hath a pleasant seat." Shakespeare opted for his appearance-versus-reality theme, the good old king arriving at a place that seems safe but is not. This Duncan enters a man-made cavern worthy of Paris's Grand Guignol. A problem arises when a filmmaker who is himself a genius approaches the plays of a literary master. Someone like Welles cannot limit himself to servicing the existing work like a semitalented journeyman, acting as an interpreter or go-between, bridging an old classic and a contemporary audience. As an auteur, Welles can't refrain from imposing his point of view on a script by Herman Mankiewicz, a novel by Booth Tarkington, or even a play by the Bard. Even as Will rethought the Macbeth of the *Chronicles*, reinventing him to serve the playwright's purpose, so did Welles do the same thing to Shakespeare.

The Macbeth we meet here has more in common with Kane and Amberson than with Shakespeare's Macbeth. We encounter a hollow man intimidated by his whining little wife. He lives in a huge house that, in its emptiness, symbolizes this powerful person's inner vacuum. From his first film, Welles departed from earlier masters of American moviemaking, such as John Ford, Howard Hawks, and Frank Capra, by giving the audience a dislikable protagonist. He here takes pains to do the same with Macbeth. Certainly he succeeded in transforming the character into a true Wellesian antihero, but in so doing, Welles created a film that fails to elicit the emotions Shakespeare achieved. The Bard had a knack of evoking surprising sympathy for a man who does the wrong thing, knows it, yet continues down the wayward path, consequences be damned.

Like Olivier, who had decided (rightly or wrongly) that *Hamlet* had been about "a man who could not make up his mind," Welles took a particular slant to *Macbeth*. His film portrays Scotland as a recently civilized country, always in danger of slipping back to a more primitive natural state. His witches represent the Old Religion, agents of anarchy on earth and Satan below, hoping to overthrow the still-new Christian domain of Duncan. To achieve this, they manipulate Macbeth. No wonder, then, that the three weird sisters not only open the story (as in Shakespeare) but close it. (They do not in the original.)

As a foil for their pagan religion, Welles invented an entirely original character: a Holy Man (Alan Napier) who first cheers the victorious troops of Macbeth and Banquo (Edgar Barrier), delivering key lines about mankind's need to beware of "agents of darkness." Banquo will remember those words; Macbeth, to his eternal regret, will not. Macbeth lives in a castle worthy of Frank Lloyd Wright, not merely *on* a hill but *of* the hill, a natural extension of the horrific landscape. The house mirrors the man; Macbeth's tragedy is that there is too much of nature in him and not enough civilization. He gradually loses all constraint and reductively degenerates into a natural man. His crown, like his helmet, is horned; at one point, he stops sipping out of silver goblets to gulp wine from animal horns. In every detail, from costuming to props, Welles communicates his notion of Macbeth as more bestial than ambitious.

When the rebellious Thane of Cawdor is executed, the Holy Man leads everyone in prayer. Macbeth stands on the sidelines, failing to join in, and plots with his wife (Jeannette Nolan). The audience here revisits the witches before Macbeth does via an additional scene penned by Welles. They serve as a corrupt chorus, observing and commenting on all that transpires. In the opening, the witches create a likeness of Macbeth, which they use to manipulate events in the world. When Macbeth is executed, Welles the director cuts from an image of Welles the actor to a close-up of the doll as its head is severed; by implication, we sense what has happened to the character without seeing it. If Welles's set design hearkens back to German golden-age Expressionism, his editing is pure Russian. Rather than show an act, a truly cinematic artist implies it through symbolic cutting.

The Holy Man, not Ross, tries to warn Lady Macduff of impending danger. It is he who joins Malcolm (Roddy McDowall) and Macduff (Dan O'Herlihy) in England, where they meet beneath an immense cross; Siward (Lionel Braham), the English warrior joining them, dons a Crusader's white armor, in comparison to Macbeth's dark visage. England has been Christian longer than Scotland, so the New Religion has taken root there. When the allies invade, they do so not only to kill a tyrant but to crush a revival of barbarism. In this context, Macbeth's killing of the innocents is akin to human sacrifice; men of the cross must wipe out paganism and return Scotland to the light.

When Siward's army approaches Macbeth's castle, his soldiers' headpieces sport crosses on top, while Macbeth's men prefer horned helmets. More of Malcolm's soldiers carry crosses than pikes or lances. The symbolism may be obvious, but it effectively communicates Welles's theme. Even the trees of Birnham Wood, descending through monster-movie mists toward Macbeth's castle, look fresh and healthy, contrasted with the grotesquely misshapen forest surrounding the fortress. When Macbeth calls for his servant Seton, a thick brogue makes the word sound like "Satan."

Today the film is considered a classic; in its time, however, most reviews were negative. After admiring the unique look, *Time* complained that *Macbeth* was ultimately unsuccessful due to Welles's take on the character. This was "not quite the great tragedy of a noble man gone wrong . . . his Macbeth is no once-honorable soldier whose muddled aspirations trap him into a crime . . . Orson has robbed the play of tragic impact by substituting a conniving heel who kills as he climbs." *Newsweek* agreed, insisting: "His Macbeth is a static, two-dimensional creature as capable of evil in the first scene as in the final hours of his bloody reign." Missing amid all the notable sound and fury was the notion of a great soul gone bad. He is a once-great hero who makes a conscious decision to surrender to his dark side, though not without soul-searching and deep doubt, eventually descending into self-loathing.

One complaint about *Macbeth* was that Welles, and the other performers, were too bombastic. They always go for the big effect, whereas Olivier and his *Hamlet* company had recently offered a quieter, gentler version of that play to the delight of reviewers and audiences. "Mr. Welles has had the idea," *Life* sniffed, "that 11th Century Scotsmen appearing in a 17th Century play should express themselves in the [extreme] accents of Sir Harry Lauder on the vaudeville stage of the 20th." Other critics likewise complained about Welles's insistence on an arch and inconsistently delivered Scots burr for his entire cast. This approach made the already difficult poetic language almost impossible for the average person to understand. "Oooot, damne spat," Lady Macbeth cursed, causing confusion for the general public while eliciting chuckles from sophisticates. One British wag suggested the film would be fine, though only if accompanied by English subtitles. Such an argument, however, considers the piece as though it were a stage play. It was, in fact, a movie, and any attitude about the character is communicated less through acting than what Eisenstein and other early theorists referred to as the plastic elements, those building blocks of the medium.

Lighting tells us what we need to know about the moral state of Macbeth at any one moment. Early, we see his face fully; as he and his wife enter into the plot to kill, shadows begin to appear on one side. Following the deed, half his face slips into shadow; finally, after the massacre of Macduff's innocent household, his visage all but disappears into darkness. Welles claimed that his later *Othello*, "whether successful or not, is about as close to Shakespeare's play as Verdi's opera. I think Verdi [was] perfectly entitled to change Shakespeare in adapting him to another art form; and, assuming that film is an art form, I took the line that you can adapt a classic freely and vigorously for the cinema." That line of reasoning holds true for *Macbeth* as well.

Assuming agreement with his approach, the film's most serious flaw derives from the economic necessity that caused Welles to violate his own basic principle. "I believe the cinema should be dynamic," he once wrote. "For me, cinema is life in movement, projected on a screen. I don't believe in [a movie] unless there is movement" to catch a viewer; indeed, the term *cinema* is derived from the Greek word for movement. Too often, though, his *Macbeth* is static—not only the character but the camera itself. Lengthy sequences feature Macbeth and Lady Macbeth conversing without moving, with an obviously artificial backdrop behind them. At such moments, it's impossible to shake the sensation that we're watching canned Shakespeare.

The great moments occur early, before Welles, like Hamlet, loses "the name of action." Macbeth and Banquo riding through a storm rates as one of the great moments in cinema. Another element Welles effectively communicated was the notion of Macbeth and Lady Macbeth as predecessors of today's middle-aged, middle-level, white-collar executives; no longer young, they have settled into an unsatisfying secondary situation, only to sense a possibility of achieving their long-repressed secret ambitions. Middle-age precipitates their sudden rampage. This is, in their minds, the last chance to achieve what they have always wanted while still young enough to enjoy it. Although this hardly justifies their actions, it does allow us to understand their motivations, however misguided, and understanding is the first step toward sympathy. This is necessary if the tragic effect is to occur. Critics and *cinéastes* will forever debate whether such tragic impact occurs in Welles.

Ultimately, the film's great achievement is its economy—not only the financial economy with which Welles created his near-great work but the economy of storytelling. Although this *Macbeth* lasts less than eighty-nine minutes, it conveys more of the play's essence than other productions running three hours. Welles excises anything he perceives to be extraneous; Donalbain, second son of Duncan, is gone, along with the mysterious third murderer of Banquo. They are not missed much, and all of the greatest lines of poetry are present. So we're free to revel in Welles's basic belief that a picture truly is worth a thousand words; while incorporating Shakespeare's masterful phrases, Welles eliminates all the rest, replacing lengthy speeches with some single sharp image to convey all the information we need. He is as in control of his medium, the movies, as Shakespeare was of his, the stage play.

## Culture for the Masses
### *Macbeth*

Grand Prize Films, 1960; George Schaefer

There could be no greater contrast to the Welles *Macbeth* than the one directed by George Schaefer in 1961. It was originally broadcast on television (NBC; Sunday, November 20, 1960) and then received limited theatrical release. Schaefer's *Macbeth* rates as one of the earliest made-for-TV movies since the networks, which were still providing live and taped plays, wouldn't begin airing features in prime time until the following fall, and original films didn't take their bow until two years later. Indeed, *Macbeth* was a redux of a live production Schaefer had directed with Maurice Evans and Judith Anderson in 1954.

This was an era, long gone, when the networks still believed that it was their solemn duty to bring culture to the masses. In addition to nightly servings of situation comedy, detective drama, horse operas, and quiz shows, they would occasionally offer something more ambitious, and a surprising number of dutiful, social-climbing surburban parents responded by sitting their children down in front of the sets. However noble such intentions, these tasteful, literal productions missed the vitality and vulgarity that characterized Elizabethan theater and its natural descendant, the silent cinema.

Will's work had, during the past half century, become the domain of high-minded types who wished to better themselves by exposure to the finer things in life. The name Shakespeare gradually became synonymous with dullness in the impressionable minds of youngsters whose first exposure to the Bard was through such noncontroversial middlebrow entertainment. *Hallmark* TV productions were not unlike *Classics Illustrated* comic books, stripping old stories of their darker edges, simplifying complex works so that an upwardly aspiring audience could comprehend tales on their most elemental level. Lost, ironically, were the more difficult elements that caused these plays to be considered classics.

For the bigger-budget 1960 film, Schaefer brought his cast and crew to Scotland. The actors were decked out in colorful, realistically designed period tartans. This was far from Will's own anachronistic approach to costuming, which had found its logical cinematic equivalent in Orson Welles. "By comparison," film professors Rothwell and Melzer noted in *Shakespeare on Screen*, "the Welles *Macbeth*, though teetering on the absurd, nevertheless fearlessly plunges into the depths of the human soul for [visual] codes to represent the inner agony of the Scottish king. . . . The anxiety to make a faithful copy of the Shakespearean text [here] works against the need to re-create the play in the exciting new medium of film." The entire movie was shot in bright light, apparently to make the most obvious use of color film, though this play's mood grows ever darker as evil acts accumulate; any carefully thought out cinematic version would reduce the amount of sunshine as the drama wears on. Critic Roger Manvell noted: "The film has the respectful earnestness of a routine production in some conventional theater."

If Schaefer's restrained, matter-of-fact direction was the opposite of Welles's auteurist approach, then Evans's performance in the title role was likewise the polar opposite of Welles's debatable but mesmerizing interpretation. Writing about the 1954 stage version, critic Alice Griffin noted that Evans "recited rather than acted" the role; that was even more true in the 1960 redux, where celluloid film rendered such a refined type of performance still less acceptable. Never do we sense that this Macbeth is a physically strong man with a surprisingly weak psyche. Evans stands stock-still, a papier-mâché manqué, reciting each and every word like some self-conscious student in a sophomore elocution class.

The film also inadvertently proves that stage acting, even at its best, has little to do with screen performance. Judith Anderson's reputation certainly survives; her role as the demented, repressed housekeeper in Alfred Hitchcock's *Rebecca* assures her a place in the scene stealer's hall of fame. However, her Lady Macbeth, a role she all but patented onstage, appears even more awkward than Evans's work. Anderson was unable to readjust her stage interpretation for a radically different medium. To make matters worse, director Schaefer emphasized close-ups (for the TV broadcast) while also attempting to utilize epic film technique (for theatrical release), so Anderson's performance is, like the piece itself, neither fish nor fowl. She appears to be auditioning for the Wicked Witch in *The Wizard of Oz*; it's impossible to distinguish her from the weird sisters. We get no sense of a sensuous, ambitious, confused woman—only a screeching shrew.

The biggest problem derived from the actors' age. Neither Evans (59) nor Anderson (62) was a spring chicken, so they wrongly convinced viewers that Shakespeare's Macbeths were old. That misses the point, as this is a tragedy of middle age. These people are hysterically attempting to break free of a mid-career rut and give in to their worst impulses out of desperation. Having addressed the problems of youth in *Romeo and Juliet*, Shakespeare would deal with old age in *King Lear. Macbeth* ought to be appreciated for what it is: a bridge between those plays, completing the Bard's vision.

## An Epitaph on Aquarius
### Roman Polanski's Film of Macbeth
Columbia Pictures, 1971; Roman Polanski

When Roman Polanski's version appeared in 1971, the theme of middle-aged angst was again absent, though for the opposite reason. Polanski's interpretation gradually took shape during the period following Zeffirelli's *Romeo and Juliet*, a film that proved the commercial possibilities for Shakespeare when produced with the youth audience in mind. Partly for such commercial dictates and partially due to Polanski's take on the piece, Macbeth and Lady Macbeth (Jon Finch, twenty-eight, and Francesca Annis, twenty-five) emerged as a strikingly handsome young couple. They resembled Zeffirelli's Romeo and Juliet, but were a little older and transformed from peace-and-love Yippies to selfish, ambitious Yuppies. Shortly, these Macbeths would go the way of Arthur Penn's *Bonnie and Clyde*, who were a rural Romeo and Juliet turned violent.

There is a historical rationale for Polanski's decision. Since the expected lifespan in ancient Scotland was fifty, people approaching thirty would have been considered middle-aged. Though Polanski's Macbeths might appear youthful for modern audiences with expectations of characters caught in midlife crisis, thirty-somethings would indeed have been perceived as middle-aged during the Middle Ages. There was also an interpretive reason: Critic turned adapter Kenneth Tynan and Polanski (then thirty-seven) hoped to suggest the sensuality of Lady Macbeth; in their view, her ability to manipulate, even corrupt, her husband derived from his intense sexual obsession. "This way it's a more fascinating personal story of an ambitious couple, very much in love, in some ways rather vulnerable and pathetic, who believe in an existing prophecy and make the mistake of taking shortcuts to achieve it," Tynan insisted.

Intriguingly, there were those who agreed with this approach but felt that Polanski failed to milk the Macbeths' sexuality for all it was worth; Stanley Kauffmann of the *New Republic* complained: "Why doesn't he make *more* use of the sex motivation by which Lady M. rekindles M. after he has faltered in his intent to kill? To play this scene, Polanski even moves them out of privacy on a balcony, into a room full of other people. For the most private and—potentially—most sex-charged dialogue in the drama!" In fact, Polanski, who is often charged with directorial excess and rarely with subtlety, attempted (and to a degree succeeded) in conveying such sexuality through hints of body language and eye contact between the two.

In comparison to Welles's twenty-one-day studio shoot, Polanski's lavish budget allowed for six months of filming on locations in northern England and Wales. While most filmmakers schedule a shoot to carefully avoid inclement weather, Polanski relished shooting during the winter season. For this allowed him to capture the contrast of clammy poison-gray skies as set against tranquil picture-book settings. To keep his cast from falling too ill to work, Polanski insisted they take daily doses of vitamin C; the actors did, even as hailstones fell around them.

Polanski's approach to poetic dialogue was groundbreaking; every line is played realistically, including the words of the witches, who are not spirits from the metaphysical but accurately drawn period portraits of Wiccans. Such an approach did cause one major problem: the "dagger of the mind" that leads Macbeth to Duncan's death chamber. Polanski, fearing the audience would be confused or disappointed if he left that dagger to the character's imagination, showed it. Although the special effects are acceptable, the dagger's appearance insists, however unintentionally, on its existence. In a film that otherwise plays as a realistic costume epic rather than a fairy tale, the decision violates the director's overall attitude.

Hugh Hefner, publisher of *Playboy* magazine, was at the time anxious to expand his popular men's magazine into an entertainment empire. Hefner had already produced several films, including a movie version of Desmond Morris's sociological tract *The Naked Ape*. When Polanski had been unable to find financing elsewhere, he approached "Hef" during a party at the Playboy mansion; Hefner responded positively to the idea of his company being associated with a world-class director, not to mention the world's greatest author. There was one condition, though: Lady Macbeth must be played by a beautiful blonde, and her sleepwalking scene must be staged in the nude.

When the press got hold of this, word quickly spread that the world would be treated to the first nudie Shakespeare film; Tynan had, after all, recently mounted a breakthrough Broadway nude hit, *Oh, Calcutta*! Considering Polanski's own recent brush with violence (his wife Sharon Tate was killed by a crazed cult), there was a widespread rumor that he would ladle on huge helpings of gore. Shakespeare purists mounted a letter-writing protest campaign. "Both groups," Polanski said, chuckling, "will be disappointed." He insisted that sex and violence would be presented as logical extensions of the drama, now honestly depicted in the postcensorship age. As for Ms. Annis's brief nudity, Tynan defended it by explaining: "In the Middle Ages, they hadn't heard about nightdresses."

The violence, however, is intense and incessant. "Perhaps it is the force of history or the workings of Polanski's own bizarre psychology," Paul D. Zimmerman noted in his *Newsweek* review, "but parallels between the Manson murders and the mad, bloody acts of these beautiful, lost Macbeths keep pressing themselves on the viewer—as though Shakespeare's play provided Polanski with some strange opportunity to act out his own complicated feelings about Satanism, mystic ties, blood, evil and revenge." Polanski had been intrigued with the relationship of sexuality to violence for some time, as the earlier movies *Knife in the Water*, *Repulsion*, and *Rosemary's Baby* clearly indicate. Recently, horror had leaped out of the sacrosanct world of movies and exploded in his own everyday life.

The process of making the film, then, served as a cathartic experience for the director, who transformed haunting emotions into art. Which is all well and good, considering that one element of art is self-consideration; Shakespeare himself had employed the old tale for personal expression. On the other hand, art must also communicate, speaking not only *for* the artist but *to* the audience. Shakespeare achieved that in his greatest plays, including *Macbeth*; whether Polanski did in his filmed *Macbeth* is another matter.

Whereas Shakespeare kept the murders offstage, Polanski made the graphic (and ritualistic) killing of Duncan his film's centerpiece. In his *Macbeth*, knives are driven deep into human bodies, causing torrents of blood to flow; women and children are raped and beaten in close-up; and Macbeth's head is, in close-up, severed at the end. More than one critic complained that the violence was not only intense but unremitting. A defense of Polanski's approach has to do with the then-current tenor of the times. Opening at theaters the same week as *Macbeth* was *Dirty Harry*; *Taxi Driver* and *Death Wish* would follow, and all were preceded by *The Wild Bunch*. The sweet dream of late-sixties's youth had soured; free love at Woodstock in 1969 gave way to cold-blooded killing at Altamont a year later. Sweet-spirited longhairs degenerated into drug-addicted figures of menace in the public imagination—and in the movies.

For the sake of social commentary, then, Polanski cast look-alikes of Zeffirelli's Romeo and Juliet as his leads. Had those nice kids survived, perhaps they wouldn't have forever exchanged flowers. Zeffirelli's film allowed Shakespeare's *Romeo and Juliet* to herald the emergence of a love-and-peace culture; Polanski's film employed Shakespeare's *Macbeth* as an epitaph for the age of Aquarius.

In at least one respect, Polanski was truer to Shakespeare than Welles. Shot entirely in color on English locations, the world of this filmed *Macbeth* is pictorially attractive despite squalor, including dirty peasants and squealing pigs. When Duncan talks about the "pleasant seat" of Macbeth's castle, we share his vision of the place's "appearance." But Polanski effectively undercuts this pretty surface by suggesting the bleaker "reality" via ominous dark clouds rolling in and over Scotland's Inverness—actually England's Bamburgh Castle.

Despite obvious differences from the Welles film, numerous critics argued that Polanski's film ultimately failed for the same reasons. "The visual images are often gripping," Jay Cocks argued in *Time*, "but the poetry of the play—as well as its force—is missing." In fact, Shakespeare's words are mostly there, though the acting approach deemphasizes the beauty Maurice Evans insisted on. "The language is flattened into conversation," Cocks complained, "and some of the best lines simply tossed away. This may make *Macbeth* more contemporary, but it also makes it ordinary."

"Savage spectacle" (to quote Brutus) tends to overpower the story of a man torn apart by the twin poles of ambition and guilt. "Epic scenes bore me to death," Polanski pronounced to reporters halfway through the filming. "The real stuff is in the studio, where you can get into your characters." Ironically, most reviewers argued that, as spectacle, the film rated as a success but failed on the level of human drama. Although a competent actor, Finch projected an emotionless screen presence, and he failed to make the audience grasp the inner torture, which is the greatness of Macbeth. Film historian Anthony Davies once argued that Shakespeare's Macbeth is a morally complex character, "human in his reflections and inhumane in his actions." There is no sense in Polanski's film, however, that Macbeth *deepens* as a result of all that happens to him; if he does not, then he is merely the counterpart of the simpler, static villain Richard III. This Macbeth never appears to gain wisdom even as he loses innocence, nor does he come to a greater, truly tragic understanding of his limited place in the universe.

Much in the film, however, is fascinating; in particular, Polanski's conception of Ross, who was left intriguingly ambiguous in the original. On the eve of Watergate, Polanski turned Ross into a minor Machiavelli, a political animal who remains uncommitted to any cause and survives by joining whichever side appears likely to win. Banquo is murdered by three men, two of whom are earlier seen receiving money from Macbeth. The third remains a mystery in the play. Polanski's third man is Ross, in league with Macbeth. As in Shakespeare, Ross later visits Lady Macduff, appearing to be a devoted family friend. In the play, Ross leaves her castle; moments later, the place is besieged by Macbeth's hired killers. Polanski's Ross leaves the castle, all smiles; then darkness passes over his face as he notices the killers approaching. He seemingly signals them to attack before slipping away, implying complicity. When the tide turns against Macbeth, Ross changes sides and heads for England, where he stands alongside righteous Macduff and feigns surprise when he hears what happened to Macduff's family.

Polanski's approach to the film's ending is problematic. The director goes out of his way to undermine the Bard's intent and, for that matter, Shakespeare's entire *oeuvre*. Will always provided a sense of closure, making clear that the play's "world" has survived a difficult catharsis that nonetheless banished chaos and restored order. In *Macbeth*, Malcolm returns from England and is crowned king. But

Polanski adds a wordless sequence in which Donalbain, Malcolm's younger brother, arrives from Ireland, hears the witches chanting, and stops. The implication is that he'll listen to prophecies similar to those spoken to Macbeth, then be corrupted by his own ambition, causing chaos to again overwhelm the land.

Shakespeare's plays are optimistic, sending audiences home with the positive attitude that good will eventually conquer evil. Polanski's films are pessimistic predictions of an ever more ugly universe, and our illusion that forces of darkness have been driven away is a temporary fantasy with which we delude ourselves. Certainly Polanski has as much a right to his vision as Shakespeare his; the issue, though, is whether Polanski had the right to corrupt Shakespeare's philosophy to present his own.

In this context, Macbeth's last lines take on a meaning altogether different from what Shakespeare intended. Life, Macbeth growls, "is a tale told by an idiot, full of sound and fury, signifying nothing." The phrase presages twentieth-century nihilism, but the Bard did *not* intend Macbeth as the author's spokesperson. Macbeth's philosophy represents a good man gone bad, projecting his own inner darkness onto the outer world. Macbeth is Shakespeare's foil for Hamlet, who emerges *from* darkness, deciding to do the right thing. "There's providence in the fall of a sparrow," Hamlet realizes before his final reckoning, at which point he acknowledges that "the rest is silence"—his life after death will be peaceful in a way Macbeth's will not.

Follow the example of Hamlet and you will be born again, even as he regains belief in the cosmos as a positive place. Go the route of Macbeth and you die perceiving the world as a sty. Not that it is but because one's individual peception is his reality, since "nothing's either good nor bad, thinking makes it so." Polanski perceives the world much as Macbeth does, making the character's frightful final pronouncement on life the central vision of his film; Shakespeare's play employed those words to teach his audience the necessity of *rejecting* such an outlook as well as an amoral mode of behavior that always leads to such a negative conclusion about existence.

## Variations on a Theme

*Macbeth* spin-offs have been popular since the birth of the cinema. In 1917, Italy's Enrico Guazzoni retold the tale from the wife's point of view in *Lady Macbeth of Minsk*, from a novel by Nikolay Leskov.

France's noted existential-absurdist author Jean Anouilh modernized the tale for *Le rideaurouge: Ce soir, on joue Macbeth*, starring Michel Simon and Pierre Brasseur, directed by Andre Barascq. In 1961, Andrjez Wajda directed a Yugoslavian remake of Leskov's novel, this time called *Siberian Lady Macbeth*.

In America, *Macbeth* has twice been turned into a crime film. Screenwriter Philip Yordan's *Joe Macbeth*, in the words of the *New York Times*'s Bosley Crowther, "paraphrased the plot with sophomoric precocity" and "labored the obvious," eliminating the glorious poetry, in 1955. At least director Ken Hughes provided the proper film-noir feel. Their *Joe Macbeth*, set in Chicago, had a mobster hero (Paul Douglas) goaded into knocking off his boss (Duncan the Duke) by his ambitious wife (Ruth Roman). The witches become a fortune-teller, precisely the device writer-director William Reilly opted for in his similar 1991 opus *Men of Respect*. In its favor, this film depicted Mafia rituals more accurately than any previous movie, including Francis Ford Coppola's *Godfather* and Martin Scorsese's *GoodFellas*; however, it lacked the cinematic storytelling skills those major film-makers provide. John Turturro, a competent character actor, did not possess the substantial presence Robert De Niro or Al Pacino would have brought to the role. Leonard Maltin found it "pretentious," even unintentionally comic when Lady Macbeth (Katherine Borowitz) sleepwalks with a flashlight.

By far the greatest variation on *Macbeth* is Akira Kurosawa's 1957 *Kumonosu-Jo*, alternately titled *Castle of the Spider's Web* or *Throne of Blood* in America. As with his previous classics *Rashomon* (1950) and *The Seven Samurai* (1954), Kurosawa combined the stark visual poetry of John Ford's westerns with the stylized tenets of his homeland's kabuki theater to present a samurai story. Although none of Will's dialogue remains, words have successfully been replaced by imagery, which is at once vivid for the viewer and functional for conveying information the Bard had expressed in words. *Ge-koku-jo* is how Kurosawa typed the story: a tale of politically motivated murder during Japan's civil wars that is informed and enriched by parallels to *Macbeth*.

Kurosawa directed Toshiro Mifune and the other actors to perform as if they were performing in ancient No theater. This explains the rigid expressions that resemble full-face masks. It also makes clear why the film does not work as a psychological drama, since Kurosawa's approach purposefully forces us to focus on the surface of people, objects, and events. His film is an entity all to itself and has more in common with Verdi's tragic opera *Otello* or Nicolai's musical comedy *Merry Wives of Windsor* than with filmed Shakespeare. Kurosawa's images of the visions of the wood witch, the cavalry crashing their way toward the castle, or Mifune becoming a human porcupine from a hail of arrows when the forest approaches make an impression on the memory as indelible as do Shakespeare's lines.

# 11

# A WOMAN OF INFINITE VARIETY
## Antony and Cleopatra

*Only Antony hath destroyed Antony.*
—Mark Antony

For his first foray into tragedy, young Will had presented Romeo and Juliet as wise beyond their years. Instinctively sensing that romantic love must be fused with friendship, they subordinate "bestial" longings to civilized order. At age fifty-four, the Bard offered a pair of middle-age people as compliments to those exemplary teenagers.

By 1607, Shakespeare was well aware that Cleopatra had been transformed from a historical personage into a literary symbol, the ultimate icon of female sensuality. So the author scuttled (at least, in his first three and one-half acts) Plutarch's rich depiction of the queen as a capable ruler and good-humored companion, reducing her to an aggressive seductress. Nevertheless, after Antony's death, Cleopatra changes from tantalizing betrayer to epic heroine, truly possessing "infinite variety." Charlton Heston, a lifelong devotee of the play, once observed: "The several women contained within her range from slut to schoolgirl, wise queen to willful tyrant, lost lover to vengeful virago, wily politician to, at the last, tragic heroine."

Antony single-mindedly pursues her sexuality, thereby reducing Cleopatra to a character of pure sex. Shakespeare has a broader view, however, which we are allowed to see only after Antony is temporarily out of the picture. This allows for a prefeminist element. The male's tragedy is that he too easily succumbs to lust and too late falls truly in love with her full personality. Still, he does do just that, moments before death, and she forgives him, which explains why their twin ends can move an audience to tears.

Conceived by the Bard as a living Colossus, Antony's flaw is an all-encompassing lust, which makes him forget social dedication, personal ambition, and marital responsibility (to Octavius's sister). He gives up *the* world to make one woman *his* world. The author probably projected lingering resentments concerning that early, self-destructive affair with Anne Hathaway onto a charismatic figure from antiquity. The sort of grievious error onetime friend Brutus committed for the body politic, Antony now likewise commits for the body female. The result is a tragedy of character, not fate. However much we resent his irresponsibility, we cannot help but admire the brutally self-critical honesty of a man who assumes full reponsibility for his actions.

If the vision is tragic, the narrative spans such vast terrains of time and space that the effect is epic. There's also humor, as ripe as anything in the comedies, plus poetry that puts the sonnets to shame. One possible way to perceive this work is as an apotheosis of Shakespere's *oeuvre* (i.e., poetry, comedy, history, tragedy, and didacticism), created with the knowledge that his triumphant career was fast coming to a close.

Yet the scene shifting is so rapid and constant and the challenge of Cleopatra's character so difficult that alone among the Bard's plays, *Antony and Cleopatra* was considered too theatrically complex to mount during his lifetime. During the following centuries, it has become the least performed of Shakespeare's plays due to the challenge of bringing both Rome and Egypt to vivid life on "an unworthy scaffold" as well as immense battles both on land and at sea. Ironically, many critics consider it the Bard's greatest work.

## Early Efforts

"The play," as Heston put it, "cries out for a camera." In 1899, Georges Melies filmed Cleopatra's death scene in his Paris studio. Four years later, America's Vitagraph produced a ten-minute encapsulation, which at least scratched the story's surface. Ferdinand Zecca offered an expanded Gallic *Antony and Cleopatra* in 1910, which was handsomely mounted in the *film d'art* style, though the approach was more Plutarch than Shakespeare. That was also the case with the hour-long American version of 1912, directed by Charles Gaskill and starring Helen Gardner. During the Italian period of spectacular silents, Enrico Guazzoni's 1913 *Marcantonio e Cleopatra* played more as opera minus music than a cinematic adaptation of the Bard.

Other early versions, including a 1912 vehicle for the prewar vamp star Theda Bara, played down Shakespearean elements to emphasize exploitive sex and violence.

## Variations on a Theme

Both major sound films to approach this subject failed due to a departure from Shakespeare's conception. The title, *Cleopatra*, of both Cecil B. DeMille's 1934 epic and Joseph L. Mankiewicz's 1963 film indicates the shift away from Antony as a tragic hero with Cleopatra as the catalyst to his fall. Both films focus instead on the woman. Since the central figure in a Hollywood-based film must be made emotionally appealing to an audience, her personality was reconceived.

In the postflapper 1930s, a kittenish child-woman was the ideal. She would be sexually liberated, but with no great ambitions in life. That's precisely the image of Cleopatra offered by Claudette Colbert, who seduces first Caesar and then Antony but willingly allows men to run the world while she stands by her man. For the 1960s, Elizabeth Taylor's Cleopatra was a modern feminist, the queen of the Nile employing sexual wiles to seduce men, only to replace each, in turn, as the wielder of power. To keep her sympathetic, though, this Cleopatra schemes to achieve world peace, not world domination, suggesting that a woman in charge may replace the male principle of war with love.

However intriguing, such notions lead to large-scale tableaus rather than intense tragedy, more impressive for elaborate sets than psychological depth. DeMille told the tale in an economical one hundred minutes; Mankiewicz stretched it out to a whopping 243. Both directors dazzled audiences with unforgettable imagery. DeMille's was created inside a studio, while Mankiewicz's was shot on location; but lacking poetry, neither touched the heart, or mind, as Shakespeare had.

## A Labor of Love
### *Antony and Cleopatra*
Rank, 1973; Charlton Heston

Dear as Shakespeare's entire *oeuvre* is to Charlton Heston, Mark Antony has always cast a special spell over the actor. When Heston read *Antony and Cleopatra* in high school, he fell in love with the play. His delivery of Antony's funeral address from *Julius Caesar* earned him a drama scholarship to Northwestern University. Heston made his Broadway debut in 1947 in a supporting role (Proculeius) to Katharine Cornell's Cleopatra, the only American staging to win acclaim in this century. For more than twenty years, Heston dreamed of doing a film. No sooner had he finished work on *Julius Caesar* than he began planning *Antony and Cleopatra* as a sequel. This was 1969, however, and the movie industry had changed drastically in the wake of *The Graduate, Bonnie and Clyde*, and *Easy Rider*. The superstars of the 1960s were suddenly scrambling to find work.

Still, Heston's dedication grew into a labor of love that consumed four years of his life. Peter Snell, a Canadian now based in London, agreed to produce; Heston himself edited the lengthy play down to a manageable script. That autumn, he met with Snell in London, where they set about trying to pick a leading lady. Among the possibilities were Anne Bancroft, Glenda Jackson, and Irene Pappas. Heston was influenced by the fact that Cleopatra was not Egyptian but Alexandrian Greek. He also remained insistent, due to the difficult dialogue, that the part be played by a woman who spoke English as her native tongue. This explains why he rejected his *El Cid* costar, Sophia Loren, although her combination of beauty and talent made her a natural, and her husband, producer Carlo Ponti, could easily have financed the project.

Commonwealth, which had backed *Julius Caesar*, indicated interest but was short on money; another company, Shaftel, might provide funds. "I'm tempted to break down and beg somebody to make *Antony*," Heston noted in his journal. In Hollywood, Richard Zanuck, who was a big Heston fan, recoiled in horror at the thought of Twentieth Century–Fox having anything to do with the name Cleopatra. His company's commercially disastrous 1963 film was still a potent nightmare. Warner Bros. appeared intrigued until *Julius Caesar* disappointed at the box office. Heston moved on to journeyman work (*The Hawaiians, The Omega Man*); meanwhile, he and

Snell—via endless cocktail parties with possible investors, which the star graciously hosted—attempted to raise enough money to shoot the film independently.

Too often, attendees were only interested in meeting a celebrity, then escaping with pocketbooks intact. Heston considered Susannah York and Barbara Jefford while flying back and forth to London for financial conferences that led nowhere. Meanwhile, there was some industry buzz about a new girl named Hildegard Neil. When Heston caught her in a B-grade thriller, he sensed problems, but also potential, particularly if she wore a Grecian wig. He also became convinced that his old friend Orson Welles should direct. Welles indicated interest but backed off after learning that an important actress was not booked for Cleopatra. "Believe me, dear boy," he insisted, "if you don't find a great Cleopatra, you can't do this."

Heston then decided to direct. "As it happens," he commented, "almost all the films made from Shakespeare's plays have been directed by the actors playing them." Plowing ahead, he oversaw the building of sets at Pinewood Studios, met with more possible backers, and shot test scenes with Neil. Famed American producer Walter Mirisch saw the tests and backed off due to strong reservations about Neil's lack of screen presence. At last Rank, the prestigious British company, agreed to distribute.

The plan was to shoot the film for a meager $1.5 million. Early in 1971 the banks insisted that Heston sign on the dotted line as guarantor of production costs. He now had his own money, as well as time and heart, involved. With regret he passed on the *Deliverance* role that then went to Burt Reynolds. Izaro, a Spanish company, would contribute one-half the budget if action scenes were shot in that country, with a Spanish cameraman, crew, and cast members, including the excellent Fernando Rey. Heston flew to Almería, to scout desert locales, then to Alcazaba, discovering an existing castle which rendered expensive sets unnecessary. Back in London, he caught Neil as Lady Macbeth and felt she was better than her scathing notices suggested. He was determined to use her despite the negative reaction of his wife, Lydia, when she watched the screen tests. Back in Los Angeles, he tried to convince Robert Shaw to play Pompeius. Though that never materialized, Shaw did give Heston the idea of having Pompeius impersonate Antony during the party on his galley.

Heston wanted to buy leftover action footage from *Ben-Hur*, including the galleys at sea, to embellish his movie without exceeding the minuscule production budget. M-G-M initially refused, insisting *Ben-Hur* was too special to treat as stock footage. Studio boss Kirk Kerkorian relented after realizing he might someday need Heston for a future project. That May, in London, Heston began a week of rehearsals at a dingy hall in Covent Garden, following coaching from his friend Laurence Olivier. By June 1971 the company was in Spain. The day before shooting commenced at Sevilla Studios, the roof caved in and rendered work impossible. The camerman arrived from Madrid a day after he was needed. When on-location shooting started, a sudden wind threatened to blow everyone and everything away. Carmen Sevilla (Octavia) had not arrived from Argentina, so her scenes had to be played with Heston speaking to a stand-in. Close-ups of the actress were shot and inserted later. The galley wasn't ready in time for its big moment. When it was finished, the boat rolled so badly, everyone became seasick. When Heston needed his armor, he learned that a costume man had carried it to a distant location.

Once on a soundstage, lighting expert Rafael Pacheco moved at a snail's pace, forcing Heston to sacrifice extra shots (and quality) on a daily basis. As everyone sat down to dinner before an evening of filming on the papyrus barge, the boat sank before their astonished eyes. A floor in the throne room, which Heston insisted must be sturdy enough to support a man on horseback, proved so slippery that the desired shot was impossible. The actor and his horse slithered across the floor rather than wildly thundering in.

Heston had picked Spain, despite hesitations, because it was supposedly cheap to shoot there. Myriad problems, leading to vast time overruns, caused *Antony and Cleopatra* to become more expensive than if filmed in London, where Heston could have exerted more control. The concept required at least ten weeks of shooting but was slated for only eight due to budget restrictions, turning what might have been an artistically rewarding experience into a daily bout with frustration. In midsummer, Snell arrived, growing horrified when he saw dailies of Neil's performance. The film was finished on August 7, and a month later, Heston viewed his rough cut back in Hollywood. He could come up with but one word: *"Terrible."*

He possessed sixty-eight cans filled with film, "with my picture in there somewhere. I've got to find it." Slowly but steadily, he and editor Eric Boyd-Perkins attempted to cut the monstrosity down to a releasable two hours and twenty minutes. In London, during sound editing, Richard Johnson, Heston's *Julius Caesar* costar, offered to dub in various voices, since the Spanish actors were incomprehensible. The world premiere was set for London, March 2, 1972. The event was a black-tie affair at the Odeon in Leicester Square. Critics were less than kind. George Melly of the London *Observer* claimed Neil "comes on like a tennis-club flirt," while Frank Kermode of the *New York Review of Books* tagged the film "a work of no imagination, tediously executed." Heston's performance was generally hailed, with *Films and Filming* noting that he "plays the part of Antony in the years of dissipation with a rugged charm that would be difficult to equal." Ironically, numerous reviewers cited the striking sea battle as the best sequence, unaware it had been borrowed from *Ben-Hur.*

"I'm not sure we have a good movie," Heston admitted. Shortly, he was back home, working on such bread-and-butter projects as *Skyjacked* and *Soylent Green.* Months went by, with no one willing to risk distributing *Antony and Cleopatra* in America. That summer, he and Snell tried to book a small art house in New York for one week, without luck. In the summer of 1973 the film was finally screened in a small Washington, D.C., theater. Heston cut the film to an even shorter length after critic Gordon Gow damned the original print as "protracted and sometimes plodding." He eliminated much of Neil's big finale, which was considered her weakest moment, when she must carry the film alone. "Cleopatra seems to have been bitten by the asp even before the messenger [travels] by ship and horse from Rome to Egypt," Rothwell and Melzer commented in *Shakespeare on Screen.* Only *Variety* praised Heston's direction: "an excellent distilation of Shakespeare's script"; the language was recited "stylish[ly] without being self-consciously reverential."

In fact, several of Heston's concepts were intriguing. One sequence features Antony, Octavius (now Augustus), and Lepidus dividing their world into three parts. Mostly, this scene is exposition. Less than scintillating onstage it could have been deadly on film. Rather than have the men sit around a table talking, Heston had them meet at the gladiator training arena, cutting back and forth between the brutal battles between men below and the casual dickering of the world leaders above for an exciting contrast. Heston later admitted his desire to parallel the ancient situation with politicians of today, discussing world policy while taking in the Super Bowl.

Heston transformed this visual action into a harbinger of what was to come, by having one gladiator spear another with a trident even as Antony begrudgingly agrees to a political marriage with Augustus's sister, Octavia. The words, intercut with the action, make it clear that the wedding will serve as a spear through the heart of Antony, who was already obsessed with Cleopatra. Stunt director Joe Canutt devised a fierce land battle Shakespeare could only allude to, doing so in the style of a grand-scale western. He then devised a "stairway of shields," allowing Proculeius (Julian Glover) to quickly ascend and thwart Cleopatra's suicide.

For the "age cannot wither her" speech of good soldier Enobarbus (Eric Porter), Heston chose to shoot the sequence at a Madrid villa. In this way, he could reveal his character growing frustrated with his unresponsive new wife, Octavia, then wander out into the garden in a state of despair. Thereby, Antony accidentally catches the discussion between Enobarbus and a fellow officer, all of which renders the scene cinematic rather than theatrical.

Cinematic also describes the transition Heston achieved between this scene and the next. Antony angrily throws his goblet at a wall as Enobarbus concludes; from the spilled drink, Heston cuts to Octavia, coldly sitting in her room, reacting fearfully to the noise. Next, we logically see Antony at his ship's bow, gazing forward with anticipation as he heads for Egypt. There is no need to tell us, in words, of his decision to leave; the montage says it all.

In 1975, Snell came up with a novel idea: to refilm all of Neil's scenes with another actress in her place, a concept never before attempted with a previously released movie. That did not happen. *Antony and Cleopatra* was eventually written off as a tax deduction for Heston, who did not direct again, later recalling how he "dragged *Antony and Cleopatria* kicking and screaming to the screen." Despite his unpleasant experience, Heston's filmmaking debut was impressive enough to make one wish he had drifted into directorial waters again. As for his Antony, this is something more than merely another in the impressive gallery of cinematic portraits Heston has offered. Clearly a case of personal expression, the part allowed an actor who ordinarily disappears in diverse roles to express his own deeply held belief in individual responsibility for one's actions. Mark Antony was, simply, the single part Charlton Heston always knew he was born to play, proving that in this film.

# 12

## SANS EVERYTHING
### *King Lear*

*I am a man more sinned against than sinning.*
—King Lear

Apporaching the end of his career Shakespeare sensed that the time had come to consider that final age of man: *sans everything*, as he had put it in *As You Like It*. True to his ongoing vision, Will would provide one more variation on issues which consistently captured his interest: the disaster of a divided country; the debacle of civil conflict; and the responsibilities, as well as the rights, of a prince. In the legend of Lear, the Bard could hardly help but recognize perfect material for this particular moment in his development as a citizen and a scribe. An earlier play by another author, *The True Chronicle History of King Leir* (1594), lacked artistry and appeal. Before he began his own retelling, Will reread the sources, Holinshed's *Chronicles* and its predecessor, *Historia Regum Britanniae* (1135), each a combination of history and folk fable.

Ultimately, though, Shakespeare again relied on his own imagination. Previous plays had concerned kings or ordinary men; here he fused the two, paralleling Lear's failure with that of a loyal subject. For this parallel plot, the Bard turned to Philip Sidney's *Arcadia*, which included the blinding of Paphlagonia, redubbed Gloucester for Shakespeare's play. Thereby, Will could make clear that parental insensitivity, like death, is a great equalizer with an impact on the humble and the lofty alike. However decent his intentions, Lear fails both as king and father; his mistake is at the same time political *and* personal.

Politically incorrect as ever, the Bard continued his portrayal of anything unnatural as symbolic of evil. Like Don John in *Much Ado About Nothing*, this play's bastard, Edmund, is drawn by bad blood to Machiavellian scheming against his righteous half brother, Edgar. Will may have added a Fool primarily to provide a suitable role for comic actor Robert Armin, beloved for his performances as Touchstone and Feste. Yet *Lear* would be drastically diminished without the man of motley, who is perceived as a silly fellow but forever proves himself sage. He is truly a "wise fool." The notion of playing this tale for tragedy was Will's, since earlier versions concluded with a happy ending. Shakespeare retained the initial fairy-tale tone of his sources, then slowly and steadily shifted the mood, edging toward a dark vision of failure as the natural conclusion not only to Lear's story but to all human endeavor.

As in past plays, good characters devoutly believe in their god(s). Now, though, such faith fails to save them because the unnaturals (bastards born of unholy union and ungrateful, if legitimate, daughters) create chaos. Still, despite the implied hand of Fate in the play's most quoted line—"We are to the gods as flies to children; they kill us for their sport"—Lear is doomed only by his own misguided decision to divide his kingdom. To add insult to injury, Lear dismisses Cordelia, his sole sincere daughter, when she refuses to flatter him for personal gain. His tragedy derives from a flaw of character, not fate. If Lear is Shakespeare's last great example of a good man who creates his own dark destiny by doing a bad thing, then the king's flaw is his inability to distinguish between appearance and reality, which had been a failing in Shakespeare's heroes since his earliest writings.

Lear's domain was initially healthy; the poison administered, ironically if unintentionally, by the "best," (Lear, Gloucester) who, as Yeats would phrase it in 1916's "The Second Coming," lack all conviction; the worst—Goneril, Regan, Edmund—are filled with passionate intensity. Although Shakespeare reached back into the distant past for his story, the vision he here provided was nothing if not modernist. His earliest tragedies glanced backward, offering a medieval view; his middle-period plays were works of the Renaissance in which he flourished; but his last are full of foresight, presaging our twentieth-century existential notion of man.

Perhaps this play does, as many literary scholars have argued, surpass even *Hamlet, Othello,* and *Macbeth* for full tragic impact. Lear is, as critic John Simon once put it, "redeemed and exalted by suffering and love." That is why we realize Lear is correct and not self-pitying when he shrieks in the storm, "I am a man more sinned against than sinning." With the possible exception only of Sophocles' Oedipus, there is no greater literary example of a unique, specific character who also serves as Everyman. This is due to his painful acquisition of a full understanding of himself as well as his (and mankind's) proper place in the universe.

## The Theatrical Tradition

Richard Burbage created the role of Lear in 1607, doubtless playing the king's oncoming madness at full throttle. The legendary Thomas Betterton (c. 1635–1710) played it following the reopening of theaters (closed by Cromwell in 1642 during the English Civil War and which remained so throughout his Protectorate), though with a happy ending of the sort that compromised most of Shakespeare's tragic *oeuvre* throughout the eighteenth century. In time, the great David Garrick (1717–79), and after him the indomitable Edmund Kean (1787–1833), saw to it that Shakespeare's vision was restored. When the first flickers were fashioned at the beginning of the twentieth century, *Lear* had been reestablished in the popular imagination as a tragedy.

## Early Efforts

*Lear* was first adapted for the emerging film medium in Germany, circa 1905, though this one-reeler is long lost. A print still exists, however, of Vitagraph's 1909 American version, produced by Stuart J. Blackton in New York. Despite its brief running time of eight-and-a-half minutes, this movie includes an abbreviated version of every key scene. It was shot in a studio against notably artificial backdrops of the type favored by France's Georges Melies. On the other hand, the film d'art version of 1910, despite a running time of more than thirty minutes, entirely eliminated the Gloucester subplot and, with it, the play's complex vision.

Still, this film's *mise en scène* was, in the period's emerging Italian style, constructed on location. Ermete Novelli played the king, under the direction of Gerolamo Lo Savio; that year, Guiseppe De Liguoro directed an alternative Italian version, also eliminating the Gloucester plot, in a film that ran five minutes. Louis Feuillade made the story contemporary for his 1911 French film *Le roi Lear au village*. In 1914 America's Ernest Warde expanded the narrative to an hour, adding spectacle and showmanship by staging a large-scale battle. He cut within each individual sequence to allow for close-up reaction shots from characters to events in long shot. Warde himself did double duty, playing the Fool to Frederick B. Warde's Lear. Frederick B. Warde portrayed the king in bombastic fashion worthy of Burbage.

The only filmed version during the 1930s was the *Yiddish King Lear*, an East Side modernization by Harry Thomashefsky. Although occasional televised *Lears* appeared on England's BBC and America's PBS, there would not be another version of *King Lear* of note until 1970, when a controversial Briton and an acclaimed Russian set to work on their notably different interpretations.

## Night of the Living Dead Cordelia
### King Lear

Filmways London, 1971; Peter Brook

Peter Brook's adaptation proved so controversial that critics evenly split as to whether the movie was a mess or a masterpiece. "I didn't just dislike this production," Pauline Kael announced in the *New Yorker*, "I hated it!" Robert Hatch, in the *Nation*, hailed what he perceived as "excellent a filming of the play as one can expect." The *New York Times* printed *two* reviews. "A catastrophe and a scandal," John Simon lamented; "an exalting *Lear*, full of exquisite terror," Vincent Canby countered. More than a movie, Brook's *King Lear* emerged as the litmus test by which reviewers as well as interested members of the moviegoing public finally had to decide what Shakespearean cinema ought to be. What right does a director have to impose his own vision on a classic? What responsibility burdens a filmmaker to present the Bard's original vision translated into cinematic language?

Brook was inspired by the controversial essays of Polish critic Jan Kott, who argued that *King Lear* serves as a precursor to bleak, modern theater of the absurd, including Samuel Beckett's *Endgame* and *Waiting for Godot*. Although there's an element of truth to this, the concept falls apart under close scrutiny. Lear is initially as all-powerful as an earthling can be but brings doom down upon himself. Beckett's Vladimir and Estragon are infinitely small men and are trapped in a universe they did not make and cannot comprehend, even at their game's end—that very point at which Lear transcends previous limitations and at last learns to see as clearly as his Fool.

Kott's observation only states the obvious. Certainly Shakespeare toward the close of his career inched toward a vision that can be considered contemporary. The problem is, Kott's approach limits rather than expands our experience with a masterwork. Likewise, Brook unthreaded this single line from a rich, multidimensional piece, needlepointing a reductive film which flattened the great play to fit Kott's simplistic notion. "Ideas in the theater are rare," Pauline Kael commented, "but to have a conception is not the same as having a *good* conception." The problem reaches even further than that. This "is not so much Shakespeare in the style of Beckett as Beckett in the style of Shakespeare," critic Charles Marowitz noted. Brook's approach implies that Beckett is more significant than Shakespeare, and that *Endgame* is a more important work than *King Lear*. To perceive the Bard as a forerunner of black comedy is to pay him one more compliment; to stage his work on the level of an absurdist sketch is to reduce rather than enhance.

No *King Lear* can work unless it initially reveals the seemingly impregnable nation and the high-spirited, if foolish, man who lords over it. Step by step the *mise en scène* must darken, the color gradually seeping out of the image as Lear's single, incalculable mistake leads him, and the entirety of his demi-monde, to disaster. Instead, Brook's opening image is of darkness: a frozen, colorless, already-dead world, filmed by cinematographer Henning Kristiansen with self-consciously grainy images in the northernmost reaches of Denmark's Jutland peninsula. A film of *King Lear* ought to rightly begin in autumn, corresponding to that period in the protagonist's life where his last moment of happiness is mirrored by fall foliage; midway through the film, winter sets in (literally and symbolically), until the final image is of T. S. Eliot's "Wasteland" on ice. By beginning so starkly, Brook leaves Lear, the land, and *us* with nowhere to go.

George Wakhevitch's production design offers pigsties in place of palaces as well as castles resembling primordial caves. Adele Anggard put everyone in savage costumes, bedecked in fur and leather like the futuristic barbarians in William Cameron Menzies's 1936 film of H. G. Wells's *Things to Come*. Such an approach in fact *is* historically accurate so far as what early England must have looked like. Yet it's all wrong aesthetically, as the film's own producer ironically made clear. Shortly before *King Lear*'s release, Lord Birkett stated: "The danger Brook and I wanted to avoid was 'authenticity.' . . . The only possible answer for filming Shakespeare is to *invent* a setting which has a period and flavor of its own, a setting dictated *not* by the particular moment in *history*, but by the *play*." His statement is astute, explaining why his approach was all wrong.

Though the "good" people here pray to primitive gods, they nonetheless symbolize Christian values, subscribing to the religious vision of their time and place. The villains, conversely, are godless forces of self-interest. Lear's court, if Shakespeare is to be properly represented, must suggest the height of civilization, since the Bard's theme is a degeneration *back* to barbarism—precisely what Brook's land appears to be from the opening.

Brook's visualization is inappropriate in other respects. Placing Lear, in the film's opening, on a throne that, as Vincent Canby put it, "encloses him like a canoeshaped coffin" offers an image of a trapped hero shut in by forces he is unaware of. Shakespeare's Lear, on the other hand, unwisely traps himself. A true understanding of the play and of film language would lead a director to initially portray Lear via open images, implying his freedom of choice; then, when the king utters his awful decision—"Know that we have divided in three our kingdom"—the filmmaker ought to cut away to a closed shot, showing Lear entrapped not by fate but by his own edict.

Likewise, directing Paul Scofield to say these words in a monotone sets up a performance style without soul. Rather than Will's happy, if self-satisfied, old fool, Brook gives us a Lear who approaches stasis. We might mistake Scofield's opening monologue for his death scene; that is how dehumanized Lear appears from the moment we meet him. An immediate intimacy between actor and audience is imperative for Shakespeare's intended impact, but Brook will not allow it. Instead, we watch this Lear clinically, and the experience becomes as cold and clammy as the performance.

The female members of the cast also interpret their characters in incongruous manners. Cordelia (Danish actress Annelise Gabold) seems coldly, harshly stoic, which undercuts our admiration for her honesty. She is nasty, willful, sharp-tongued, sullen, bitter, and moody rather than being Shakespeare's zesty, spirited woman of integrity. On the other hand, Goneril (Irene Worth) and Regan (Susan Engel) are transformed into glamorously sexy bitches and are given bits of business to humanize them; they appear no better or worse than most moderns, who always look out for number one. Gloucester, Kent, and Lear, by contrast, aren't noble victims but pathetic losers, lacking the skills necessary to survive in a corrupt universe. The acting is at the same time stylized and minimalist and keeps us distanced from the characters; Shakespeare, rather, thrusts us into the play's world, where we would discover ourselves.

Even Brook's montage "seems designed as an alienation device," Kael (who insisted that a more appropriate title would be *Night of the Living Dead*) noted, "but who wants to be alienated from Shakespeare?" The casual cutting of the exposition made it impossible to get a fix on the multitude of characters and their complex relationships. Much of what transpires is unintelligible to all but the diehard Shakespeare buff. Editing is necessary to reduce a four and one-half-hour play to a manageable running time of one hundred thirty-seven minutes. Yet the cutting appeared to be less arbitrary than purposefully perverse. It appears intended to reshape, even reverse, Shakespeare's aim for Brook's ambition. Words suggesting what Hemingway refered to as *nada* (a fear of nothingness in the universe) *do* fill the play: "Nothing shall come of nothing." Brook, however, eliminates the Bard's moral context while retaining such existential lines. The filmmaker emphasizes Lear's statement at the sight of his dead Cordelia, "Never, never, never, never, never!" The fivefold repetition does suggest encroaching nihilism, but Brook eliminates what the old king says next: "Pray you, undo this button." The line emphasizes Lear's belief that there's some force in the universe powerful enough to undo the mistakes of any man; as *Time* noted, the cut deprives "the act of tragic purgation."

Like Job, Shakespeare's Lear refuses to allow the slings and arrows of outrageous fortune to rob him of faith. Brook's Lear leaps into the muck and sinks therein, with the director and audience going under with him. Brook undermines Shakespeare and presents a world without decency, which is a far cry from Will's vision.

Though the attitude of Brook's stage play was retained, the director set out to make the movie as cinematic as possible, but in the worst sense. He employed zoom lenses, arty angles, handheld cameras, and close-ups at inappropriate moments. At one point, he even cuts within a great soliloquy for no apparent reason and draws us away from the power and beauty of Will's words without providing any clear commentary through the technique. Jump cuts and under-exposure of image techniques fail to facilitate the storytelling process. They exist on a pyrotechnic level and are cinematic effects as arty affectation rather than to facilitate communication of the narrative. Instead of developing his own cinematic style, Brook derivatively combines elements of Ingmar Bergman's medieval *mise en scène* from *The Seventh Seal* with Jean-Luc Godard's radical montage for *Breathless.*

The famed storm scene is presented as a combination of the then-fashionable Timothy Leary LSD trip with the atomic-holocaust denouement of Stanley Kubrick's *Dr. Strangelove.* In addition to the scene's embarrassing appearance (one critic suggested it may have been shot through Vaseline), Brook's storm could not thematically work due to a lack of any contrast. Shakespeare presented the immense natural world (macrocosm) reflecting man's little inanities (microcosm), but since Brook's *mise en scène* was barren from the beginning, his storm seems only one more aspect of the heightened ugliness—an arbitrary storm rather than the logical extension of Lear's inner torment.

There is one great performance: Jack MacGowran's Fool. He is subtly satiric toward the film's villains and wonderfully warm with his abused master. There is also one emotionally involving moment when Lear and Gloucester, meeting on the Dover coast, finally perceive each other as foils. This is when these fine, failed fellows at last realize that status and power have nothing to do with achieving happiness in this life. As Sophocles put it, "Count no man lucky until his death," and then only if he expires without experiencing the pain of betrayal that these men have known. Otherwise, Brook rates as one of those misguided artists who believe that to rub a viewer's nose in muck provides catharsis. Shakespeare did not recoil from the dirt of life; then again, even at his darkest, he never fails to notice that the sun occasionally does shine through the clouds.

## Monologue Without Words
### *Karol Lear*

Lenfilm, 1972; Grigori Kozintsev

Filmed in the Baltic region, mostly on the river Narwa in Estonia's village of Ivangorod between 1968 and 1969, then shown theatrically in the Soviet Union in 1970, the Russian *Karol Lear* did not appear on American screens until 1972. This was months after the release of Peter Brook's botched British version, and the Russian film was hailed as a breath of fresh air. Director Grigori Kozintsev and screenwriter-adapter Boris Pasternak revealed the same appreciation for this work's tragic grandeur as they had for *Hamlet* in 1964. *Karol Lear* is supremely true to the spirit, if not the letter, of the Shakespearean source.

Critic Anikst Alexander rightly hailed the collaborators' "serious, deeply thoughtful," even "philosphical approach." He also appreciated the fact that there were "no attempts at sensationalism, no efforts to 'modernize' Shakespeare by introducing Freudian themes, Existentialist ideas, eroticism, or sexual perversion. [Kozintsev] has simply made a film of Shakespeare's tragedy." Though Alexander was too polite to name names, there can be little doubt that his implied comparison was to Brook's nearly concurrent debacle, which suffered from all those elements.

At 140 minutes, *Karol Lear* is abbreviated in terms of text but complete in that the author's vision is communicated as fully as possible. Ionas Gritsus's striking black-and-white cinematography immediately sets the tone for a tragic outcome without being so frigid or off-putting that we feel this kingdom is frozen from the start. Wisely, Kozintsev edited in several shots of Siberia's white wasteland toward the movie's end, providing sharp contrast to the initially warmer establishing images shot by Dagestan near the Caspian sea. Thus, the artistic and philosophical world the filmmakers created out of diverse photographic materials were visually orchestrated to convey the big chill that gradually overcomes this play's ever-sadder little land.

Dmitri Shostakovich's stirring musical score suggests epic dimensions without drowning the action in a tidal wave of emotional bathos. Costumes by Simon Viraladze were authentic for the period, only with aesthetically conceived deviations to convey the filmmakers' attitude toward the work. The set design by Eugene Enie incorporates an existing fifteenth-century castle carefully ornamented with the play's ideas in mind. These design elements jointly created an image of a once-happy world helplessly witnessing the death of its golden age. The performance of Yuri Yarvet is dynamic. We see the old king arcing from vital if foolish ruler to humbled and powerless old fool as well as from embittered father and former king to, finally, forgiving and wise sage. Valentina Chendrikova's Cordelia is fittingly humble and honest but radical and unyielding in the righteousness of her idealism rather than (in Brook's interpretation) arrogant and unpleasantly self-possessed.

To convey that the Fool is far more sophisticated than the seemingly clever people around him, Kozintsev purposefully chose for that role a Moscow-based actor, Oleg Dal, whose diction communicated a sense of heightened intellectuality. All other cast members were recruited from the northern provinces so that their less cultivated voices would sound crude in contrast to Dal's foil.

In comments made to Neia Zorkaija (of Moscow's *Literary Gazette*) at the time of the film's release, Kosintsev made clear his understanding of this play in particular, its place in the Shakespeare *oeuvre*, and the reason why he had chosen to make this as a companion piece to his earlier *Hamlet*. If *Hamlet* is, arguably, the Bard's greatest play in which a single character dominates as the sun of the work's universe and all the other figures are mere planets revolving around him, then *King Lear* (despite the title and the king's commanding presence) is an ensemble piece in which all characters are fully developed, with Lear as the first among equals. *King Lear* concerns itself with a kingdom that has inadvertently been poisoned by the hero himself (much like Thebes at the hands of Oedipus of old), whereas *Hamlet's* microcosm has been spoiled by a villain and the hero sets things right. Lear's tragic situation derives from his inability to comprehend reality by looking at people and grasping what is beneath the surface, but this is Hamlet's greatest strength. In their *Hamlet*, Kozintsev and Pasternak had effectively designed a series of cinematic devices to convey that play's ideas; here they set out to accomplish the same task, but for a very different kind of work. This explains why *King Lear* provided a challenge rather than merely allowing them to go through the motions of something they had already mastered.

They did see a common thread (indeed, the through line that most socialists perceive in Shakespeare) running through these two plays: the ruler's gradual sense that he is at one with the people he governs. As with *Hamlet*, Kozintsev visually achieved this in *King Lear* by adding shots in which the camera moves from principal figures to the nearby town, filled with the proletariat that waits to see how royal decisions will affect their everyday lives. If this were accomplished by crosscutting, it would create an incorrect sense (in the context of Kozintev's political approach) of apartness. Instead, it is achieved by panning, conveying the proper sense of continuum at the heart of this interpretation. Even as Kozintsev emphasized Prince

Hamlet's growing reliance on common man Horatio, so does he here focus on the similarity of plights between King Lear and the more everyday Gloucester.

As to the unique situation of adapting this particular play, Kenneth S. Rothwell and Annabelle Henkin Melzer, in their *Shakespeare on Screen*, note that Kozintsev employs cinematic technique not for its own sake (as is the case with Brook) but to convey Shakespeare's themes, thereby fusing elements of film and dramatic poetry in a manner that proves equally satisfying to buffs of the Bard and to fans of film. One instance fittingly serves as a representative of Kozintsev's near-perfect approach. "Give me the map there," Lear shouts early in the play; the implication in the original is that this simple physical object represents the kingdom about to be divided as well as the dire consequences to come. Onstage it isn't easy to draw attention to that map, though a single beam of light, directed at it, can suggest Shakespeare's symbolism.

Cinema, however, with its natural ability for cutting to the close-up, can visually emphasize what can only be hinted at in live theater. The map, as Rothwell and Melzer note, is first glimpsed through the flames of the hearth, neatly suggesting the fire (political, social, and moral) about to engulf the entire kingdom. The map is thus:

> privileged [by careful camera placement] to underscore its powerful potential. It then becomes the locus for all of the king's movements and gestures during the division of two-thirds of the kingdom to Goneril and Regan. At the end of the sequence, however, Kozintsev shows how to use the map most effectively. The king punctuates his denunciation of Cordelia . . . by waving it, ripping it, tearing it. The map becomes what [the early Russian theorist and filmmaker] V. I. Pudovkin calls "an expressive object," which . . . can create "a filmic monologue without words."

Or, in more poplar terms, the map becomes a MacGuffin of the type Hitchcock employed: a seemingly insignificant object, introduced early on, that contains the key to all strange events, intellectually unlocking the story's "situation." Whether it is the necklace in *Vertigo* or the handkerchief in *Othello*, the MacGuffin works well in the Elizabethan theater of contemporary cinema. The cinema, at its best, can serve Shakespeare when, and if, a director understands both his contemporary medium and the classic material, then bridges the gap between the two. This must occur without merely servicing Shakespeare's plays in the canned-theater sense or, on the other hand, abandoning any responsibility to those plays to create filmic effects with no relationship to the original. As always in the finest art, function dictates form. That includes the unique developing art of the Shakespearean cinema in which the function is an adaptation of Will's work via the formal devices of filmmaking.

## Cinéma-Vérité Shakespeare
### *King Lear*
Cannon Releasing, 1988; Jean-Luc Godard

Israeli-born, American-bred Menahem Golan, with his partner Yoram Globus, was known for producing the violent, déclassé *Death Wish* flicks starring Charles Bronson. These films made Golan a laughingstock (if a wealthy one) among serious filmmakers. At the 1987 Cannes Film Festival, Golan cornered France's ever-controversial New Wave director Jean-Luc Godard. Golan, embarrassed at existing at the low end of capitalist cinema, somehow talked the avant-garde socialist auteur into signing a contract, written on a restaurant's napkin, to fashion a modern-dress, cinéma-vérité *King Lear*.

The film would be written by and star the Jewish Hemingway, Norman Mailer, with his daughter Kate as Cordelia; Woody Allen was set to appear as the Fool, a role he had offered an appealing variation on in his own earlier *Everything You Always Wanted to Know About Sex (But Were Afraid to Ask)*. Though the concept sounded intriguing, the results bordered on the grotesque.

Mailer, who in the late sixties had attempted some Godard-inspired alternative cinema of his own (*Beyond the Law; Maidstone*), became incensed during the first day of filming. Arriving at Nyon, Switzerland's Beau Rivage hotel, he grasped that Godard intended to burlesque Mailer's deadly serious Lear-as-mafia-don script; daughter in hand, Mailer stormed off. The eventual film in fact opened with brief images of Norman and Kate arriving and departing.

Burgess Meredith was rushed to the location and assumed the role of "Don Learo," with fading Brat Packer Molly Ringwald as Cordelia. Puckish theater gadfly Peter Sellars appeared as William Shakespeare Jr. the Fifth, attempting to reconstruct his ancestor's original. Godard showed up in punk drag with Rastafarian dreadlocks as the Professor, who explains the relationship of classic theater to today's cinema and sounds more crazed than Lear at his maddest. New York footage of Allen, as a film editor called "Mr. Alien," served as an epilogue. Allen is observed trying (with little luck) to fashion a film from the frenetic footage we had just witnessed. As with many other Godard ventures, the film is about the experience of making the film.

This *King Lear* is filled with endless *homages* to literature, painting, and cinema, as well as title cards serving as deconstruction devices. It was tagged by *Time*'s Richard Corliss "a cynical, pun-laden, nonlinear meditation on virtue vs. power," ultimately "Godard's most infuriating, entertaining pastiche in two decades." Vincent Canby of the *New York Times* wrote: "(It is) a late Godardian practical joke, sometimes spiteful and mean, sometimes beautiful, sometimes teetering on the edge of coherence and brilliance, often amateurish and, finally, as sad and embarrassing as the spectacle of a great, dignified man wearing a fishbowl over his head to get a laugh." Meredith, a fine actor, did get to speak several Shakespearean lines and delivered them so effectively that one could only wish serious filmmakers had starred him in a legitimate version. Otherwise, the supposedly clever dialogue can be summarized by a single exchange: "Are you trying to make a 'play' for my daughter?" Learo questions Shakespeare V.

## Variations on a Theme

As was the case with previous tragedies, *King Lear* had been so transformed from folk legend to universal myth by the Bard that its plot has regularly been readjusted to varied times and places. Six years before resetting *Macbeth* in a Chicago-gangster milieu, screenwriter Philip Yordan retold the *King Lear* tale in New York's Little Italy with *House of Strangers* (1949). Joseph Mankiewicz, who would mount the 1953 *Julius Caesar*, directed Edward G. Robinson as Gino Monetti, strong-arm aging father of an Italian banking family. Gino makes the mistake of dividing his financial empire between surly sons Luther Adler and Efrem Zimbalist Jr. when his youngest and best-loved boy (Richard Conte) goes down the river in his place after government officials discover discrepancies in the old man's books.

An oddly engaging and atmospheric postwar film noir until its unbelievable happy ending, *House of Strangers* was remade five years later by Edward Dmytryk as an eerily atmospheric western entitled

*Broken Lance.* Spencer Tracy portrayed an old cattle baron whose beloved half-breed son (Robert Wagner) is mistreated by his half brothers (Richard Widmark and Hugh O'Brian). Here again daughters are replaced by boys for the Americanized versions. *King Lear* has, in fact, indirectly influenced portraits of aging ranchers in numerous westerns, ranging from lead roles (John Wayne's Dunson in Howard Hawks's *Red River*) to supporting parts (Emile Meyer's Ryker in George Stevens's *Shane*). Sadly, though, what may have been the most memorable of all Hollywood Shakespeare variations never saw the light of day. For more than a decade, filmmaker Anthony Mann, who is rightly famed for brutally realistic westerns, tried to launch *King of the Cowboys*, starring either of his favorite stars, Gary Cooper (*Man of the West*) or James Stewart (*The Man From Laramie*). Unaccountably, the film never saw the light of day.

*Lear* was, however, transformed into a circus drama in *The Big Show* (1961), which featured Nehemiah Persoff as Bruno, the tyrannical head of a touring European circus. Through arrogant and arbitrary decisions, Bruno loses the love of gentle young Joe (Cliff Robertson), only to have the boy's manipulative brothers (Robert Vaughn and David Nelson) wrestle the show away from him. The Fool, incidentally, was here recast as a circus dwarf. Daughters were also transformed into sons for Akira Kurosawa's *Ran* (1985), the greatest of all *King Lear* variations thus far. Completing the trilogy that earlier resulted in Eastern versions of *Macbeth* and *Hamlet*, Kurosawa spent five years preparing the script for what he planned as his masterpiece. Then, employing a $11.5 million budget (the largest ever for a Japanese film up to that time), the seventy-five-year-old director mounted his story, set during the feudal wars of sixteenth-century Japan.

The title translates to "Chaos," precisely what Shakespeare believed would result from a divided kingdom. Tatsuya Nakadai played Hidetora, an aging warlord who unwisely splits his land between two unworthy sons, betraying the only decent youth. Kurosawa chose to keep his camera far removed from characters and action and to emotionally distance the audience from events. Richard Schickel of *Time* spoke for many critics when he noted: "The very word 'adaptation' distorts and diminishes both intention and accomplishment. For what Akira Kurosawa has done is to reimagine *Lear* in terms of his own philosophy, which blends strains of Western existentialism with a sort of elegaic Buddhism, and the imperatives of the movies."

*King Lear* has also influenced modern American movies. In *Harry and Tonto*, writer-director Paul Mazursky told the story of an aging English teacher (Art Carney) evicted from his apartment and forced out into the storm of modern life. Harry quotes *King Lear* every inch of the way. His children try to take him in, but the situation becomes unpleasant, until Ellen Burstyn appears as a contemporary Cordelia. Harry's cat Tonto is his Fool. "Informed" by Shakespeare's play, the project allowed a serious-minded filmmaker to comment on today's abuse of the elderly. Novelist Jane Smiley had a feminist agenda firmly in place for her novel *A Thousand Acres*, winner of the Pulitzer Prize more for its political correctness than any literary merits. *A Thousand Acres* was filmed in 1997 with Jason Robards as an aging Iowa farmer, the Lear-like character reduced to a supporting role, automatically eliminating any chance for a tragic dimension.

Here the children are once again daughters, and the story is told from their point of view. Goneril (Jessica Lange as Ginny) and Regan (Michelle Pfeiffer as Rose) are legitimized when we learn they mistreat their elderly father because he sexually abused them; apparently Cordelia (Jennifer Jason Leigh as Caroline) escaped such cruelty and remains unflinchingly loyal. When the old man divides his farm among them for the purpose of tax deductions, the contrived parallels between this story and its classic source become obvious, forced, and unintentionally comic.

# 13

## YOU CAN'T GO HOME AGAIN
### *The Winter's Tale* and *The Tempest*

> *A sad tale's best for winter.*
> —Mamillius

The time had come to close the twin curtains of theater and life; as a literary antidote to the growing gloom in his final tragedies, Will provided bittersweet bookends, two mature comedies of melancholia. As Thomas Wolfe would note four centuries later: You can't go home again; likewise, the Bard provided no happy return to simple roots. Gone were the bawdy revelry of *The Taming of the Shrew*, the lyric pastoralism of *As You Like It*, the courtly sophistication of *Twelfth Night*, and the sweet-spirited social satire of *Much Ado About Nothing*. In their place was a sense of weary reconciliation. It was the guarded optimism of an author who had lived his last years on the edge of moral, philosophical, and intellectual darkness. It appears that he desperately desired, while there was still time, to once again embrace the light, however tenuously.

### The Triumph of Time
### *The Winter's Tale*
Peter Snell Productions/Hurst Park, 1968; Frank Dunlop

Will began work on *The Winter's Tale* in early August 1610. Improvising freely from *Pandosto*, a novel by Robert Greene, he continued to experiment artistically. The shepherds in the source were mere romantic stereotypes, but Shakespeare transformed them into realistic, believable characters; in puckishly perverse contrast, he incongruously made improbable plot devices appear even more outrageously artificial than in the original. It was as if Shakespeare self-consciously set out to create a play that, in modern terminology, *deconstructs* pastoral playwrighting in particular and the very theatrical experience in general.

Even at this late point, Shakespeare continued to retell old tales in such a way that he artistically exorcised personal demons while he entertained an audience. Once again, he focused on a jealous male, Leontes, who convinces himself that his gracious wife, Hermione, is guilty of an indecent flirtation with Lord Antigonus. Complicating (and dramatically enriching) matters here are two children, Princess Perdita and Prince Mamillius. Othello and Iago combined, Leontes subjects himself to the horrific mindgames a villain once played on an unsuspecting Moor. On the edge of jealous insanity, Leontes accosts his children as to their ancestry: "How now, you wanton. Are you my calf?" Yet Shakespeare is older—and more forgiving. The woman, we ultimately learn, is innocent; the questionable children are indeed his own; and the play provides a happy ending in which seemingly deceased Hermione (who does die in the source) reappears as an idealized statue of a wife who comes as close to the ideal as any mortal woman can.

*The Winter's Tale* is too bizarre (dramatically intense but theatrically operatic) to easily lend itself to cinematic treatment, explaining why adaptation has rarely been attempted. Mr. and Mrs. Edwin Thanhouser mounted a one-reeler in 1910, directed by Barry O'Neil with Anna Rosemond as Hermione and Martin Faust as Leontes, but no prints survive. Baldassare Negroni's 1913 rendition, starring Pina Fabbri and V. Cocchi, runs two reels, liberally combining elements from Greene with Shakespeare for a fuller study of what the Bard tagged "the triumph of time." This illustrates his reassuring (and antinihilistic) theme that time does indeed heal all wounds or all's well that ends well. Even today, this film is enchanting due to the effective playing in an Italian operatic style. Unfortunately, the 1914 German version, *Das Wintermärchen*, starring Senta Soneland and Albert Paulig, under the direction of Belle Alliance, remains lost.

Another filmed version was not attempted until 1966, when a celluloid recording was made of a hippie-era production by the Edinborough Festival's Pop Theatre group, and augmented by Shakespearean-actor-turned-movie-star Laurence Harvey. Moira Redmond was Hermione, and miniskirted starlet June Asher played their daughter, Perdita. The film (if one charitably chooses to call it that) runs 151 minutes. Originally intended for broadcast on British TV, it is composed largely of close shots. Nonetheless, it was released to the American art-house circuit in a vain attempt to cash in on the popularity of Zeffirelli's *Romeo and Juliet*. The film was produced by Canadian Peter Snell, who would shortly mount *Julius Caesar* and *Antony and Cleopatra*. The *Winter's Tale* experiment, Snell's first stab at cinematic Shakespeare, is best written off as a dry run for more ambitious work to come.

Frank Dunlop's direction of the stage production was more mannered than inspired and the subsequent film cannot be classed even with the Olivier *Othello* or the Gielgud-Burton *Hamlet*, which were brilliant stagings that suffered when transferred to film. This *Winter's Tale* left critics wondering how anyone in his right mind could believe that the botched approach merited an initial staging, much less the tribute of cinematic immortalization. Uninspired acting was grotesquely exaggerated when blown up several times life-size, while the sets were unimpressive and unimaginative. Worse still, the filmmakers didn't bother to adjust lighting for the cinema's notably different demands. Dunlop arbitrarily, rather than functionally, cut back and forth between occasional long and oppressively overdone closer ranges. The kindest comment one can muster is that Snell's *Winter's Tale* is somewhat easier to watch on TV than the larger theatrical screen, a backhanded compliment at best.

> *O brave new world, That has such people in't!*
> —Miranda

## The Tempest

Shakespeare wrote his final comedy late in 1610 for a court performance before James I. He had recently read a pamphlet recounting the misadventures of Sir Thomas Gates and his crew aboard the ship *Sea Adventure*, headed for the Virginia colonies but wrecked in a storm on July 28, 1609; survivors washed ashore on the enchanted island of Bermuda, nicknamed Isle of Divels. Other than published records of that event, *The Tempest* is a rare Shakespearean creation in that no previous literary source can be found. Yet elements that constitute the play's business abound in Renaissance literature.

Prototypes for Prospero, the banished magician, and his beautiful daughter Miranda can be discovered in Italian history and German plays.

Here the Bard bids final farewell to an audience that for so long had been loyal while (as always) masking his message in the cloak of easily accessible entertainment. Theater historians have noted that the closing of Prospero's books and the laying aside of his magic mantle foreshadow Shakespeare's own subsequent retirement as author-enchanter. Prospero's last great speech ("We are the stuff that dreams are made on; our little life rounded by sleep") summarizes Gentle Will's vision of individuals sleepwalking their way through existence toward eternity.

With its Utopian vision of a perfect world achieved, *The Tempest* stands as Shakespeare's end vision of what might yet be, if only everyone—princes and paupers alike—would try a little harder. This is his final comedy of forgiveness, filled with foreboding but ending on a hopeful note. As to the maturity of its conception in comparison to an earlier Green World comedy, critic Edward Dowden wrote: "In *A Midsummer Night's Dream*, the 'human mortals' wander to and fro in a maze of error, misled by the mischievious Puck . . . here, the spirits are brought under subjection to the human will of Prospero." Indeed, "Prospero *is* a harmonious and fully developed *will*," which (to borrow from Leni Reifenstahl) triumphs. Shakespeare reverses his earlier vision of men at the mercy of anything otherworldly; man, as the ancient Greeks put it, is the measure of all things if only he, like Prospero, can learn to balance intelligence and emotion.

Prospero has, in the words of literary scholar Hardin Craig, "also reached an altitude [moral, intellectual, and emotional] from which he can survey the whole of human life [and] see how small yet how great we are." This, of course, could serve as an apt description of the Bard at forty-six (a considerably more advanced age than today). *The Tempest* serves as an apotheosis of everything Shakespeare wrote, all the poems and plays wrapped up in one dazzling final show: Young love, brotherly betrayal, rulers and fathers—all find perfect expression in this piece. There could be no better bookends to conclude the *oeuvre* than Ariel, symbol of man's longing to fly like an angel, and Caliban, the representation of man's bestial origins. They are, essentially, the Bard's Jekyll and Hyde, his last and greatest images of what we try to be at our best and what we fear we are at our worst.

Ironically, it is Caliban—that living embodiment of man's dark side—that great actors have been attracted to. Similarly, Shakespeare's predecessors noted that when staging crude morality plays, the Devil's role always went to the most accomplished cast member. However upsetting the idea may be, there is something frightfully attractive about absolute evil. Whether you call him Mephistopheles, Hyde, Dracula, Iago, or Caliban, such roles demand any era's heavyweight actor. Perhaps it is because such parts allow them and us, the audience, to understand that aspect of ourselves which still connects us, however we might deny it, to those fabled creatures with split toes and forked tongues from mankind's prehistory.

## Early Efforts

Stage directors of the late nineteenth and early twentieth centuries chose to play *The Tempest* as an elaborate fairy tale for adults, emphasizing the spectacular elements of the Green World conception. One such rendition was Sir Herbert Beerbohm Tree's adaptation at His Majesty's Theatre in London in 1905. Filmmaker Charles Urban recorded the opulent storm sequence for a brief flicker. To convey the proper sense of enchantment, Urban had his craftspeople tint individual frames of this two and one-half-minute film by hand, creating a color motion picture long before the advent of color film stock. Three years later, producer Percy Stowe mounted a one-reeler more than ten minutes long. Intriguingly, he chose to focus on the "back story" of Prospero and Miranda arriving on the enchanted isle, when they first encounter Caliban and Ariel. By the advent of the title sea storm, charmingly conveyed through miniatures, Stowe was all but out of time.

In America, director Edwin Thanhouser mounted a one-reeler, which has been lost; also unavailable is the French 1912 version by Eclair. Despite the play's continued popularity as a stage vehicle, there would be no further film versions of Shakespeare's text during the silent era—or, for that matter, since. All motion-picture versions are, in fact, variations on a theme, and the only legitimate *Tempest* in existence is a *Hallmark Hall of Fame* television production (NBC; February 3, 1960) that stretched as far in the direction of cinema as was possible at that time. George Schaefer, the director responsible for so many of Hallmark's ventures into Shakespearean waters, here outdid himself. He created (within the budgetary limitations of live TV) a consistent Green World, thanks to Rouben Arutanian's sumptuously suggestive set design and various technical tricks that could change Ariel's shape and size in seconds. The impressive cast included *Hallmark* veteran Maurice Evans as Prospero, Lee Remick as Miranda, Roddy McDowall as Ariel, and Richard Burton as Caliban. Critic Virginia Vaughan proclaimed that "in capturing the joy of the original, the production remains faithful to the spirit of Shakespeare's text. . . . Schaefer's *Tempest* may be light as a soufflé, but it is substantial enough for the main course." What a shame that Schaefer was not given the opportunity to later remount this production for the motion-picture camera, as had been the case with his *Macbeth*. At least a videotape of the impressive production has been intermittently available for purchase and rental; its availability is all the more important, considering the fact that there is no legitimate film of *The Tempest*.

## Shakespeare Conquers the Universe
## *Forbidden Planet*

M-G-M, 1956; Fred McLeod Wilcox

*Forbidden Planet* has the same kind of relationship to *The Tempest* that *Castle of the Spider's Web* does to *Macbeth*. This is a totally original work, containing none of Shakespeare's poetry, yet inspired and informed by one of the Bard's great plays. Best of all, it is supremely true to the spirit of that literary work. Released by M-G-M in 1956, the science-fiction film boasted a considerable budget, considering how déclassé this genre was at the time. The cast was also composed of A-list actors (Walter Pidgeon, Anne Francis, Leslie Nielsen). This film once more made clear that Will's mythic vision is truly universal (no pun intended), and that his vision is transferable to various times and places, including the future.

The Green World has now become a distant planet, Altair-4. Prospero (Pidgeon) is a banished scientist living there with his Miranda-like daughter Altaira (Francis) and their Ariel, a robot named Robby. Also dormant on the planet, however, is a Caliban-like brute force, all the more dangerous because it remains invisible. When a spaceship from earth (substituting for one of Shakespeare's seabound ships) beams down, the handsome Commander Adams (Nielsen) falls under Altaira's innocent spell, though he and his men are soon menaced by the unseen monstrous force.

It turns out to be the dark side of Morbius, unleashed while he sleeps. These "monsters from the Id" are a ploy popular in films of all genres during the fifties, when Freudian psychology arrived on the motion-picture screen. Though *Forbidden Planet* can hardly be dissected as a Shakespearean adaptation, director Wilcox deserves praise for capturing the essence of Will's concept. He created a believable alternative universe composed, in equal measures, of sensuous dream and foreboding nightmare.

## Sand in the Shakespearean Spinach

### The Tempest: by William Shakespeare, as Seen Through the Eyes of Derek Jarman

World Northal Films, 1980; Derek Jarman

Instead of a pre–James Barrie never-never land, here was a film offering what one critic tagged "a gloomy Northumbrian seacoast." Jarman's motion picture (the title indicates its admitted ambiguity of authorship) was never released on the art-house circuit in America, much less to mainstream movie houses. It did receive a public screening during the "British Film Now" series at the New York Film Festival in September 1980, followed by a mercifully brief run at Manhattan's Cinema 3 before disappearing from sight.

Kinder than most critics, Rothwell and Melzer praised this as "a daring and creative appropriation of the subtext of *The Tempest*, not a film for those who prefer that the text on screen literally capture [what was] on the page." However, one need not be a literalist to despise Jarman's *Tempest*. It even offended those viewers who appreciate the distinction between film and theater and are comfortable when a filmmaker (like Olivier, Welles, Zeffirelli, or Branagh) takes liberties with the precise text while visually conveying Shakespeare's intent. The problem is not that the director dared cut, rearrange, and even change the original; rather, that Jarman employed Will's plot, characters, even his enduring, endearing name to indulge in the avant-garde posturing that characterizes Jarman's work. He purposefully distorted the play's tone and the temperament of its admittedly conventional author.

The most notable case in point is when Sycorax, mother of Caliban, who is played as a sow, breast-feeds her fully grown monster of a son (Jack Birkett). This is a sequence that sent numerous movie-goers, who had come expecting Shakespeare's most delightful play, dashing for the exits on opening night. Like Ken Russell, for whom Jarman had earlier served as production designer on *The Devils* and *Savage Messiah*, he attempts to bridge the gap between a surrealist style of alternative cinema and more mainstream movies. Employing an antinarrative technique that hails back to the surrealist-inspired *Un Chien Andalou* (1929) by Luis Buñuel and Salvador Dali, such filmmakers (including, more recently, Kenneth Anger and Yoko Ono) self-consciously set out to shock the bourgeois audience out of its complacency. Whatever one thinks of such ambitions, it is worth noting that Buñuel and Dali concoct their own nonstories rather than making mincemeat of a great (if conservative) writer of narratives.

The less offensive, if no less outrageous, staging of the final wedding pageant featured a black American blues singer, Elizabeth Welch, belting out "Stormy Weather." "You can barely see through the production to Shakespeare," Vincent Canby wrote in his *New York Times* review, noting that the film "would be funny if it weren't nearly unbearable. It's a fingernail scratched along a blackboard, sand in spinach, a 33-r.p.m. recording of 'Don Giovanni' played at 78 r.p.m. Watching it is like driving a car whose windshield has shattered but not broken." Will, as evidenced by the plays themselves, appears to have embraced heterosexuality wholeheartedly, charmingly portraying his young lovers from the early *Romeo and Juliet* to Ferdinand and Miranda here. Jarman nastily undercuts such scenes. This is not surprising, since his best-known film, 1978's *Sebastiane*, was in Canby's words, "a ridiculous, sadomasochistic homoerotic film about St. Sebastian."

Jarman's film certainly lives up to its title. He bitterly undercuts everything Shakespeare set out to say and do in his gentle, forgiving, stylistically frothy yet philosophically formidable play. Taken as a vicious absurdist attack on the Bard and all the old-fashioned story-telling technique and middle-class moral values inherent not only in *The Tempest* but the entire *oeuvre*, the film does have a certain semicrazed validity. Critics who appreciate the cynical politics of contemptuous cinema understandably praised the work: "Jarman's film of *The Tempest* comes as a breath of fresh air in contrast to the stale, safe atmosphere [of] the BBC's series of INSTITUTIONAL SHAKESPEARES," Samuel Crowd insisted. Yet one can likewise recoil from an overly reverential approach and still despise what

Jarman attempts. No question that Welles, Olivier, Zeffirelli, and Branagh have all taken daring risks as cinematic Shakespearean interpreters. Their often wonderful, if always debatable, movies truly do offer an effective alternative to "stale, safe" examples of canned theater.

Nonetheless, there were several interesting elements in Jarman's piece. As in *Forbidden Planet*, evil is released when Prospero (Heathcote Williams) dreams, the dark side of a decent man released. Here the storm that sinks Sebastian's ship first exists subjectively, in Prospero's nightmare, then extends to the wider world outside his mind, even as the invisible "monster from the ID" stalked Leslie Nielsen's spacecraft in the M-G-M classic. Jarman instructed costume designer Nicholas Ede to pull costumes from varied eras to, in Jarman's words, symbolize "the timelessness of the play." Rather than a contemporary equivalent of Shakespeare's anachronistic costuming, the result was more on the order of an inelegant collage, with Ariel (Karl Johnson) incongruously dancing about in a white jumpsuit. There's a distinction, apparently lost on Jarman, between offering an original approach to an old play and reducing the work to what Susan Sontag would have considered low camp. As Vincent Canby concluded: "No poetry, no ideas, no characterizations, no narrative—no fun."

## You Can't Run Away From It

### *Tempest*

Columbia Pictures, 1982; Paul Mazursky

If not poetry, there were certainly ideas, characterizations, narrative, and fun to be found in *Tempest*, which is director-coscreenwriter (with Leon Capetanos) Paul Mazursky's contemporary version of the original. Mazursky has been acclaimed as a social observer who punctures modern pretensions with a perceptive wit that avoids cruelty and condescension. The best of Mazursky's films include *Bob & Carol & Ted & Alice*, *Blume in Love*, and *An Unmarried Woman*. Writing about his work in *McLean's*, critic Lawrence O'Toole commended Mazursky as "a satirist with a broad forgiving streak, a wry humanist with large reserves of sentiment." He might have employed the same words to describe Shakespeare; not surprisingly, the meeting of these two artists resulted in an agreeable, if uneven, film.

Arriving on screens in the early stages of what would shortly be tagged the Me Decade, *Tempest* offered the first cinematic attack on the selfishness which came to characterize those years. But Mazursky went further; his *Tempest* can be viewed as a rejection of our cumulative contemporary worldview that began forming in the mid-sixties, the very moment when Mazursky moved from obscure screen actor to behind the camera. Prospero here becomes Phil (John Cassavetes), a successful Manhattan architect who suffers from midlife crisis and grows weary of the cynicism with which he approaches assignments to design garish Atlantic City casinos. With his fourteen-year-old daughter Miranda (Molly Ringwald) in hand, Phil heads off for the Aegean. En route, they pick up Ariel/Aretha (Susan Sarandon), an aging hippie who hopefully brings her faded free-love dreams along when she decides to keep the two company.

Unfortunately, Phil wants something other than to be the guru for a commune. Practicing celibacy while trying to get back to the basics, he keeps Aretha at arm's length, even as goatherd Kalibanos (Raul Julia) sets out to seduce Miranda in his cave. There Kalibanos keeps the forbidden fruit, which is a TV that has been rejected by Phil along with all the junk culture of our time. Morbius-like, Phil emotionally reaches into the depth of his psyche, bringing forth a storm that sends the yacht of his archenemy (a Mafia boss instead of a duke, played by Vittorio Gassman) and his entourage smashing down onto the beach. Phil comes to realize the truth to the old adage You truly cannot run away from it. Real life follows him to the place where he has attempted to make a separate peace; in time, he follows the yachting party back to New York.

Mazursky's most memorable moments include some spontaneous dance sequences, including one classic moment during which Kalibanos plays his ancient, pre-Christian pipes of Pan while goats dance about to the tune of "New York, New York." The film ends with the characters, all finally at ease with one another and themselves, dancing an elegant tango. Gentle Will would end comedies with a festive jig, symbolizing the dance of life that comedy celebrates, even while criticizing our foibles. Then, as if to acknowledge his piece's theatrical origins, Mazursky has the entire cast come forward for a curtain call.

Despite joyous moments, *Tempest*'s parts are superior to the whole. Too often the script meanders aimlessly, including an unnecessary subplot concerning Phil's actress-wife (Gena Rowlands, Cassavetes's real-life wife) and her ambitions to return to the stage. It is as if Mazursky were influenced by Cassavetes, who, as a director, always emphasizes the improvisational in his films. At 140 minutes, *Tempest* is overlong and rambling and fails to allow us to understand the characters' motivations, often the case in a Cassavetes film but seldom in a work by Mazursky. There's a tonal problem resulting from an indecisiveness as to whether this should be played as a modern fairy tale or a realistic reenactment of the Bard. At one point, Phil decides to sacrifice one of Kalibanos's goats to ancient gods; in close-up, we see the animal struggle, then watch as its neck is cut and all-too-real blood flows. The sequence is gruesome enough to negate any charm generated earlier.

## The Sound and the Fury
## *Prospero's Books*

Palace/Allarts/Cinea/Camera One/Penta/Elsevier Vendex/Film Four/VPRO/Canal Plus/NHK, 1991; Peter Greenaway

If a single director qualifies as more self-consciously determined to outrage a middlebrow audience than Derek Jarman, it is Peter Greenaway. Utterly contemptuous of every contemporary filmmaker other than himself, Greenaway fashions the most unpleasant offerings imaginable; for instance, in *The Cook, The Thief, His Wife, & Her Lover*, he depicted a person being roasted and eaten. Greenaway's unappealingly iconoclastic films present the lowbrow material one would expect from drive-in explotation flicks in the high-minded style of art-house divertissements. All of which disqualifies him to fashion a film from Shakespeare's swan song, one of the most sweet-spirited concoctions ever created. With *Prospero's Books*, however, that's precisely what Greenaway attempted.

*The Tempest* ought to be brought to the screen by someone like George Lucas, Robert Zemeckis, or Steven Spielberg—each, in his own way, a contemporary Shakespeare. They are superb craftsmen within their medium of choice, crowd pleasers who slip elements of self-expression into easily accessible entertainment. Indeed, Peter Pan's island in Spielberg's *Hook* appeared suspiciously like some Shakespearean Green World. Sadly, though, none of the great Hollywood directors has ever brought this extremely cinematic play to the screen despite endless efforts by John Gielgud to find backers for a film version.

Gielgud has been universally heralded as our century's greatest stage Prospero. During the late 1980s, he mounted a major campaign, hoping to talk some A-list filmmaker into mounting a full-fledged movie or, at the very least, setting up a camera and recording for posterity a production of the play. Incredibly, there were no takers, so the project was eventually passed on (down?) to Greenaway. He immediately set about changing the concept even more radically than Jarman had a decade earlier. Whereas Shakespeare, in his own theatrical endgame, provided answers that more or less explained the meaning of life, which is that the secret to happiness is maintaining a perpetual, if guarded, sense of optimism despite endless disappointments. Greenaway only wanted to transform this glorious piece into another of what critics refer to as his "cinematic conundrums," which are puzzles without any answers waiting at the end and are less truly complex than simply confusing.

Seizing on the long-held notion that Prospero is indeed Shakespeare's disguised image of himself while grasping at a single line indicating the old enchanter will afterward put away his magic books, Greenaway freely invented a new scenario. Here Prospero's magical books (mostly pornographic) number twenty-four and their various titles serve as chapter headings for a like number of sequences in Greenaway's movie. Prospero/Shakespeare (Gielgud) sits down to exact revenge on those who have betrayed him throughout his long life by writing a play that puts them in their place—a play named, of course, *The Tempest*. This, at least in Greenaway's mind, legitimizes his approach for the one hundred twenty-nine minute film, shot over an eight-week period in an Amsterdam studio. Gielgud (oftentimes offscreen) reads every line, not only Prospero's dialogue but that of Miranda and the others as well, while performers play out the scenes as grotesque tableaus and bizarre ballets, photographed in eccentric traveling shots, bathed in a golden light apparently intended as the art cinema's equivalent to a porn film's golden shower.

Lovers of Shakespearean cinema were as furious at the outrageous imagery as they were seduced by the sound of Gielgud's eloquent voice. "Nothing like an elocutionist," the *New Republic* noted, Gielgud *"realizes* the lines," bringing each sentence to life with a meticulous understanding of the Bard's basic meaning, bolstered by the beauty of his vocal instrument. The accompanying music is a radical-rock redux of Renaissance melodies. For the sake of state-of-the-art experimentation, Greenaway and his equally avant garde cinematographer, Sacha Vierny (in the 1960s, Vierny shot *Hiroshima Mon Amour* and *Last Year at Marienbad* for Alain Resnais), employed not only film but also video technology, relying on a new contraption called the digital-electronic Quantel Paintbox.

This allowed the collaborators to overlap various images (some via the hard-edged quality of celluloid film; others with the softer semblance of video) into what the director later referred to as his "complex visual cascade." Others had less kind words for his concoction. "A self-preening postmodernist who couldn't articulate the simplest story to save his life" is how *Commonweal* dismissed the man and his movie; in fact, Greenaway isn't so much a storyteller as he is a philosphical enemy of the very storytelling process that Shakespeare perfected. Perhaps that explains why he and Jarman, as antinarrative artists, so relish any opportunity to adapt the Bard. Rather than merely making a nonstory film, they can puckishly poke fun at the greatest storyteller who ever lived, undermining rather than servicing his key aim.

If Jarman is an incoherent radical, Greenaway is an out-of-control extremist. He insisted on a great deal of nudity, although it was in no way appealingly erotic. His film is antipornographic and caused most audiences to collectively turn their eyes away rather than stare. Even Sir John, eighty-seven years old at the time of filming, was persuaded to strip down and bare all for a series of embarrassing shots. The young men and women, playing denizens of the island, were painted up in such a grotesque manner that the director managed to make them appear repulsive, in part through the maddeningly hideous decorations he attaches to the men's private parts.

In large part, Greenaway opts for such an approach due to his orientation, which puts an emphasis on cinema's connection to painting and graphic arts rather than (as with most moviemakers) its relationship to drama and literature. "Greenaway's insistent corporeality—his penchant for ruddy flesh, lumpy bodies, coarse faces, and such creaturely actions as spitting or pissing, recall the roistering, visceral art of Jacob Jordaens," Bradley and Amy Fine Collins noted in *Art in America*. Still, the filmmaker's self-congratulatory reveling in self-consideration rather than communication, and his unpleasant excessiveness ultimately turned off even the most charitable critics, the Collinses notwithstanding:

> Greenaway proves capable of translating the art historical into the cinematic, but many of the film's scenes are hardly more than clunky tableaux vivants of the paintings that fascinate

him. There is something kitschy about his cinematic variations of Botticelli's *Birth of Venus*. . . . The dominant note of *Prospero's Books* is that of a gratuitous assault on the spectator's sensibilities, evident in the director's puerile urge to violate the viewer.

There are four Ariels, though why, Greenaway never makes clear. That, of course, defines his values: Nothing is explained in a Greenaway film. Fans insist this self-conscious obscurity is intellectually stimulating, challenging the viewer as more conventional moviemakers do not. By providing an "open" rather than "closed" viewing experience, each member of the audience is free to find his or her own film. The majority of moviegoers, however, would agree with critic John Simon's assessment: "contemptible and pretentious." For such observers, those who tolerate Greenaway are like the crowds cheering their duped ruler's nonexistent outfit in Hans Christian Andersen's *The Emperor's New Clothes*. They convince themselves that anything they cannot comprehend must be deep indeed and that to rebel against what, in fact, is an incoherent atrocity would give them away as fools—never realizing that the true fool joins the pseudosophisticated herd in praising an empty exercise in style.

## The Bard and the Gray
### *The Tempest*
NBC Motion Pictures, 1998; Jack Bender, director

When NBC executives initially announced that their 1998 season would include a version of *The Tempest*, Shakespeare buffs held their collective breath: Perhaps at last we might see a fully realized filmization of this bittersweet play, on the order of ambitiously middlebrow *Hallmark Hall of Fame* presentations from yesteryear. Instead, Jack Bender's film emerged as yet another offbeat variation on Will's theme, but with the Bard's immortal poetry entirely excised. The original script by James Henerson reset the tale in the Deep South during the War Between the States. Peter Fonda was effectively cast as an enlightened plantation owner who tolerates (for practical reasons) but despises (owing to personal morality) the institution of slavery. His evil brother (Julian Glover) seizes the plantation, banishing Gideon Prosper to the back-bayou country. Gideon survives, in a makeshift fort, with his onetime belle-daughter. Their Ariel is the ghost of a murdered slave, and Caliban is a scurrilous swamp rat. Prospero's magic is the voodoo Gideon learned from African Americans he once owned but loved and learned from. When the Union Army invades, a sudden storm tosses several soldiers, along with Gideon's sibling, into their midst. The only major disappointment here is the lack of any glorious language; numerous stage directors have reset various works in a wide assortment of time periods, so there is ample precedent for the Civil War milieu to coexist with iambic pentameter. That aside, this *Tempest* is an intriguing, if less than significant, addition to the long list of Shakespearean derivatives. As to a definitive film of *The Tempest*: The Bard's buffs are still eagerly, if ever less patiently, waiting.

## One Fascinating Footnote

By far the most faithful representation of *The Tempest* presented on film was a cocreation of Moscow's Christmas Films and the Dave Edwards Studio in Cardiff. Originally produced for Channel 4, Wales, this puppet animation featurette, directed by Vladimir Naslov, was included by HBO as part of their "Shakespeare: The Animated Tales" series of six such pieces during the early 1990s. Most others were produced as traditional cell animation, abbreviated if fascinating renderings of *Macbeth*, *Hamlet*, and the like, and intended to make such plays user-friendly for young viewers. At a mere twenty-nine minutes, the great limitation of this *Tempest* (and the reason it hasn't received theatrical distribution) is its Reader's Digest Condensed Books quality—the shooting script merely a sampler of memorable lines contained in a bare-bones suggestion of plot. Otherwise, the production is thoroughly captivating, beautifully rendering the fairy-tale quality of Shakespeare's penultimate play. Each character comes vividly to life, much as in the masterful Czech version of *A Midsummer Night's Dream*, though that had been a full-length film. Nevertheless, this lovely little gem makes abundantly clear what Jiri Trinka long ago proposed: Animation—in particular, puppet animation—is a wonderful way to approach the Green World comedies.

# 14

## PLAYING SHAKESPEARE

A unique subgenre of Shakespearean cinema is those films which address the issue of acting the plays in various situations. In addition to movies already covered in the text (*Looking For Richard* under "Richard III"; *A Double Life* under "Othello," etc.), what follows are the most memorable of such works in the order they appeared on-screen.

### If Hamlet Were a Woman
### *Morning Glory*

RKO-Radio Pictures, 1933; Lowell Sherman

Judith Anderson played the tortured male Hamlet onstage, Sarah Bernhardt did so onstage and then on film, and Asta Nielsen offered a cinematic performance which insisted that Hamlet had been a woman all along. Mention should be made of Katharine Hepburn, whose gaminlike sensuality nicely qualified her for female leads in Shakespearean comedies. The great Kate essayed the role of Hamlet, albeit briefly, in *Morning Glory*, the film that resulted in her first Oscar. As Eva Lovelace, a small-town girl who yearns to light up Broadway, she dares to recite the "To be or not to be . . ." speech at a chichi cocktail party and manages to wow everyone with the depth and sensitivity of her delivery. The very notion of a well-brought-up young lady who chooses a life in the theater was at that time controversial. Daring to assume a man's role when only a short while earlier men had to play the women's roles was doubly daring. A 1958 remake, entitled *Stage Struck* and starring Susan Strasberg, failed to reignite the spark; Zoe Atkins's script was never anything more than an excuse to let Kate be Kate.

## Shakespeare Versus Hitler
### *To Be or Not to Be*
Alexander Korda Productions, 1942; Ernst Lubitsch

In the early 1930s, Berlin-born Lubitsch was famed for the sophisticated touch with which he mounted Hollywood's high comedies, like *Trouble in Paradise*; the horrific advent of World War II caused him to create a darker style for this precursor to contemporary black humor. *To Be or Not to Be* stunned critics and audiences of the time by alternating realistic footage of Poland under the Nazi occupation with ripe belly laughs. As the ostensible star of Warsaw's Teatr Polski, Joseph Tura (Jack Benny) loves to slowly recite Hamlet's famed soliloquy; in happier times, this allowed his wife (Carole Lombard, in her final role) to entertain male admirers backstage. Art becomes inextricably tied to life, however, when the company employs various plays to communicate with Poland's underground resistance. They even kill a despised informer (Stanley Ridges) during all the roaring thunder of a grand tragedy. As to the quality of Tura's acting, one Gestapo member admits: "What he did to Shakespeare, we are now doing to Poland." The film was remade, with modest success, by Mel Brooks in 1983 and costarred Brooks and his wife, Anne Bancroft.

## Will Goes West
### *My Darling Clementine*
Twentieth Century–Fox, 1946; John Ford

As had been the case with the work of his predecessor and inspiration, D. W. Griffith, the films of John Ford were profoundly influenced by his love for and understanding of the Bard. In *My Darling Clementine*, first of the brooding postwar Westerns, Ford modeled his American heroes on Shakespearean archetypes: Henry Fonda's

Wyatt Earp is Henry V, a simple, straightforward man of action who brings peace to the troubled land; and Victor Mature's Doc Holliday is the frontier's Hamlet. A darkly aristocratic man of thought, consumed with self-loathing and a near-nihilistic vision of life, Holliday nonetheless rises to heroic proportions only moments before his date with destiny and death at the O.K. Corral—in this fictional version, at least, since the real Holliday survived the legendary gunfight. Midway through the movie, culture comes west in the insubstantial personage of a drunken actor (Alan Mowbray), modeled on the legendary Booth. Unable to perform the "To be or not to be . . ." soliloquy at Tombstone's Birdcage Theatre, Doc does it for him, speaking for himself as well as the literary character.

## Taming of the Show
### *Kiss Me Kate*

M-G-M, 1953; George Sidney

Padua's Petruchio and Kate reached Broadway in the early fifties by way of Cole Porter, whose champagne music ("Always True to You in My Fashion"; "So In Love") enhanced Samuel and Bela Spewack's thin tale of a contemporary husband-wife acting team who vent their love-hate relationship by playing the Bard's battling couple. Howard Keel and Kathryn Grayson were cast in M-G-M's watered-down version, with the studio excising all double entendres (mild by today's standards) so that the movie could play in Peoria. Still, the "Brush Up Your Shakespeare" number (featuring Keenan Wynn and James Whitmore as Runyonesque gangsters) benefited from cinematic expansiveness, while art director Cedric Gibbons provided a breathtakingly stylized northern Italian landscape. One number, "I Am Ashamed That Women Are So Simple," was excised, though "From This Moment On," newly written to showcase young talents Bob Fosse and Carol Haney, became a pop standard. The film was framed by actor Ron Randell playing Porter, who was adapting Shakespeare's material for the modern stage. *Kiss Me Kate* was released in 3-D and flat versions, because Radio City Music Hall insisted on the latter.

## The Mad Booths
### *Prince of Players*
Twentieth Century–Fox, 1955; Philip Dunne

During the nineteenth century, the Booths (father Junius and sons Edwin and John Wilkes) became America's first family of Shakespearean actors, plying their craft from Colorado gold towns to the London boards. Their lives were as truly tragic as anything found in the Bard's canon. Playwright Moss Hart freely adapted Eleanor Ruggle's best-selling biography for the screen. Raymond Massey played the insane alcoholic father, with Richard Burton and John Derek as his sons, the latter more famous for assassinating President Abraham Lincoln. Integrating scenes from Shakespeare into the drama much as a musical regularly breaks spoken words for songs, director Dunne allowed his actors, playing those actors, to rage against the encroaching moral and philosophical night in appropriate scenes. It is far more significant for its accurate re-creations of the romantic theatrical style of the 1800s than the hackneyed story, which is historical melodrama. The recently perfected wide-screen CinemaScope process allowed for a live-theater presentation to be properly conveyed for the first time in a film.

## An End to Empire
### *Shakespeare Wallah*
Merchant-Ivory Productions, 1966; James Ivory

In this, their second of many collaborations, producer Ismail Merchant (Indian), director James Ivory (American), and screenwriter Ruth Prawer Jhabvala (Polish-German) forwarded the notion of internationalized cinema—as a team and in choice of subject. The then-contemporary story concerned a troupe of English actors who for years eked out a living by performing the Bard's plays from one end of India to another. This went well enough as long as Anglos were in charge of India, since upwardly aspiring natives sensed the need to learn English culture. But with the British in withdrawal and movies replacing live theater even in provincial areas, the anachronistic company plays to dwindling audiences. Real-life husband and wife Geoffrey Kendal and Laura Liddell portrayed the leading couple of the troupe. Their daughter Felicity is cast as the team's teenage off-spring who falls into a doomed *Romeo and Juliet* love affair with a young Indian playboy (Shashi Kapoor). The most esteemed of all Indian directors, Satyajit Ray, composed the musical score for this leisurely, bittersweet visual ballad of anachronistic actors who have outlived their era and can't adjust to the changing times.

## He Put the "Ham" in "Hamlet"
### *Theatre of Blood*
United Artists, 1973; Douglas Hickox

The plight of a bad Shakespearean actor plotting a cunningly the-atrical revenge against reviewers who blasted his efforts was the sub-ject of the one-of-a-kind film *Theater of Blood*. Aided by a Cordelia-like loyal daughter (Diana Rigg), Edward Lionheart (Vincent Price) kills off the London critical establishment (Harry Andrews, Coral Browne, Robert Coote, Jack Hawkins, Michael Hordern, Arthur Lowe, Robert Morley, and Dennis Price) via living-theater renderings of death scenes by the Bard. He adds insult to injury by dreadfully reciting Will's words at the terminal moment. This uneasy, if irresistible, blend of dark humor (supplied by screenwriter Anthony Greville-Bell) and grotesquely overdone gore (courtesy of director Hickox) resulted in camp, but it was too highbrow for the drive-in and too vulgar for the art-house. Vincent Price (who himself set out to be a serious Shakespearean actor but settled for the less demanding, more commercial route of horror-flick stardom) was both the best and worst thing about the movie. Price was appropri-ately outrageous as the hammy actor, though he lacked distance from his character—merely being, rather than truly playing, the part.

## Right Performance, Wrong Richard
### *The Goodbye Girl*
Rastar/Warners, 1977; Herb Ross

Neil Simon's social comedies are as crowd-pleasingly popular in our age as Shakespeare's were in his—and for that matter still are. Not surprisingly, Simon tipped his hat to the Bard in *The Goodbye Girl*, his humorous paean to the legitimate-theater boards and the people obsessed with stepping out on them. Richard Dreyfuss, in his Oscar-winning role, played Elliot Garfield, a bearded and intense Chicago actor who arrives in New York to find sometime dancer Paula McFadden (Marsha Mason, then Simon's real-life wife) and her daughter (Quinn Cummings) residing in the apartment he has rented. After their awkward but cute meeting, she must stand beside him when Elliot lands the lead in a flamboyant production of *Richard III*. The insipid avant-garde director (Paul Benedict) who hired Elliot insists that the king be played with limp wrists and a pronounced lisp. The inner torture of an actor forced by a misguided and pretentious director to perform the role of a lifetime in a manner he knows is all wrong has never been more touchingly portrayed. In fact, such an approach might have worked quite well for *Richard II*; right performance, wrong Richard.

## To Sir, With Love
### *The Dresser*
Goldcrest/Columbia Pictures, 1983; Peter Yates

Sir (Albert Finney, modeling his characterization on noted actor Donald Wolfit) is an aging stage star who, in his senile years, sometimes dresses for *Othello*, only to walk out onstage and start reciting lines from *King Lear*. Norman (Tom Courtenay) is his dresser and verbal whipping boy. Seemingly servile to Sir, Norman is always in control of the old-timer, whose work veers between outright mugging and moments of sheer genius. They are, without knowing it, a twentieth-century Lear-and-Fool duo. Set during World War II, Peter Yates's movie does a commendable job of capturing, as only a film can, the vivid atmosphere of a frayed touring company during that unique period. Excellent as the production is in all respects, it cannot (by its very nature as a movie) deliver the aura of excitement that Ronald Harwood's two-character stage play delivered. That work exists as a delicate theater piece about the very nature of the theatrical experience. Still, a happier film version could not have been produced. Finney's delivery of the Bard's dialogue is exquisite, even if his costumes don't always match the play he is supposed to be performing.

## "Hamlet Is Bosnia!"
## *A Midwinter's Tale/In the Bleak Midwinter*
Rank/Midwinter, 1995; Kenneth Branagh

Branagh wrote and directed (but did not star in) this highly personal black-and-white fable about a London stage actor-director, Joe Harper (Michael Maloney). One Christmas, Joe mounts a provincial performance of *Hamlet* in a drafty church, all the while weighing offers for lucrative movie deals, and in the process discovers something about his own values as a dedicated theater person. Joe's performers range from charming amateurs to the impossibly pretentious. ("Hamlet is Bosnia," one actor [Nicholas Farrell] insists.) Marvelous moments are supplied by John Sessions's drag-queen Gertrude. Sadly, though, what begins as a tidy and perceptive essay on the meaning of Shakespeare in particular and the theater in general degenerates into an embarrassingly maudlin soap opera. Satire and slapstick take a backseat as each character reaches the most obvious epiphany before the final curtain comes down on such sloppy sentimentality. It is fascinating, though, as a prelude to Branagh's next film, the full-length *Hamlet*. Peter makes the play work for his simple audience by jazzing it up as an action tale, foreshadowing (and justifying?) Branagh's own approach.

## A Literate Crowd Pleaser
## *Shakespeare in Love*
Miramax, 1998; John Madden

Other than the brief, if rightly praised, prologue to Olivier's *Henry V*, the performance of a Shakespearean play, as staged in the Bard's lifetime, has remained notably absent from popular cinema. Until, that is, the advent of *Shakespeare in Love*, director John Madden's enjoyably intelligent rendering of the Elizabethan theater, circa 1593. The script, by Marc Norman and Tom Stoppard, offers speculative fiction that remains scrupulously true to what little is known about Will and his early life and times. Introduced here as an alternately gleeful and despondent would-be writer (enacted with warmth and energy by Joseph Fiennes, younger brother of film star and Shakespearean stage actor Ralph Fiennes), the author-in-embryo labors to complete a nonsensical bit of romantic comedy called *Romeo and Ethel*, which concerns a shipwrecked swain in love with a pirate's daughter. Until, that is, Will meets Viola (Gwyneth Paltrow), a physically breathtaking, intellectually enlightened member of the gentility. Will pursues the spirited girl (already promised in marriage to a high-born cad). As he does, the spirit of their love infuses the play Will simultaneously writes. When the affair soon appears doomed, Shakespeare darkens his work's ending, thereby moving from superficial comedy to substantive tragedy for the first time in his career.

The result is that idiotic artifice gives way to important art as contrivance is displaced by inspiration. In the process, Shakespeare himself transforms from clever entertainer to profound poet-philosopher. Along the way, the filmmakers educate their audience as to the peculiarities of that era's theater conventions while managing to keep such material entertaining. That women's roles were played by boys causes Viola, desperate to become part of the exciting show-staging process, to disguise herself as a boy to eventually win a role as a woman. This delightful bit of business offers a viable explanation as to why cross-dressing would become so significant a part of Shakespeare's later high comedies; and having him fall for a woman named Viola allows us to understand why he would bless the most irresistible of his heroines, in *Twelfth Night*, with that name. The film's sly sense of humor allows for engaging postmodern anachronisms, as when Will, who is rushing after his beloved, tells an oarsman waiting to water-taxi people across the Thames, "Follow that boat!" The Elizabethan world is vividly, accurately, and gloriously brought to full-bodied life, with Oscar–winner Dame Judi Dench supplying just the right touch of mercurial nobility as Queen Bess. *Entertainment Weekly*'s Owen Gleiberman spoke for most critics when he tagged *Shakespeare in Love* as "that rare thing, a literate crowd pleaser."

Which, of course, puts this film about Shakespeare in the same league as his own literate, crowd-pleasing plays. That is also true, as this tome set out to prove, of the very best movies made from his work during the twentieth century and doubtless into the next.

# AS WE GO TO PRESS

In its Oscar show in 1997, the Motion Picture Academy presented a ten-minute salute to movies based on the Bard's work—past, present, and future. On March 21, 1999, *Shakespeare in Love* won seven of its thirteen Academy Award nominations, including best picture of the year, and the emerging renaissance of Shakespearean cinema became obvious to everyone. While popular motion pictures based on Shakespeare's works seem unlikely candidates for a commercial trend in an era when wild teenage comedies and expensive special-effects extravaganzas dominate the studio's offerings, that's exactly what happened. The professionals and the public simultaneously rediscovered this enduring body of work, and, with Hollywood's help, Shakespeare is being rescued from the academics and returned to the masses, who have established Gentle Will as the most beloved author of all time.

Among the first pictures of the new crop to appear on screen will be *William Shakespeare's a Midsummer Night's Dream*. The film was written and directed by Michael Hoffman, who has been acclaimed for his work on *Restoration*. The film stars Michelle Pfeiffer as Titania, Calista Flockhart (Golden Globe–Winner for TV's *Ally McBeal*) as Helena, Kevin Kline as Bottom, Stanley Tucci as Puck, Christian Bale as Demetrius, Rupert Everett as Oberon, and David Strathairn as Theseus. Other filmmakers are moving into production with Shakespeare-inspired works. As Jessica Shaw noted in *Entertainment Weekly*: "Producers have discovered that not only is the play the thing, but the play starring nubile young actors can be cauldron-bubbling hot." *The Taming of the Shrew* has been given a contemporary, nonpoetic treatment in *10 Things I Hate About You*, starring Andrew Keegan (from TV's *Party of Five*), Julia Stiles (*The Sixties* miniseries), and newcomer Heath Ledger. Kenneth Branagh is working on a version of *Love's Labour Lost* with *Clueless* star Alicia Sliverstone opposite *Scream* sensation Matthew Lillard. Branagh will approach the film in the vein of a 1930s Busby Berkeley musical.

Two more films on the way are contemporary, nonpoetic interpretations of *Othello* and *Macbeth*. The first, titled *O*, is from first-time screenwriter Brad Kaaya and transforms Othello (Mekhi Phifer) into a modern young black man who is accepted into an all-white prep school due to his basketball skills. *Near in Blood*, which is directed by David Dobkin, transports *Macbeth* from the battlefield to the football field. The Bard's words, however, are retained in an updated version of *Hamlet*, starring Ethan Hawke, Sam Shepard, Bill Murray, and Julia Stiles. This production is set in present-day New York, yet still adheres to Shakespeare's poetry.

Doubtless, if these films are even moderately successful, Tinseltown will add more to the list. Apparently, William Shakespeare, once hailed by Orson Welles as the original screenwriter, is alive and well and living in Hollywood.

# INDEX

Abbott, George, 15
*Adam's Rib*, 24
Adler, Luther, 215
*Adventures of Robin Hood*, 48
Alexander, Anikst, 211
Alexander Korda Productions, 234
*Alexander Nevsky*, 129, 180
Algren, Nelson, 49
*All About Eve*, 104
*All Night Long*, 173
Allen, Woody, 70, 214–15
Alleva, Richard, 37, 56, 98–99
Alliance, Belle, 219
Alpert, Hollis, 162
Ambrosio, Arturo, 153
Amyot, Jacques, 100
Anderson, Judith, 185–87, 233
Andrews, Harry, 237
Andrews, Nigel, 94
Anger, Kenneth, 225
Anggard, Adele, 207
Animal imagery, 92, 118–19
Annis, Francesca, 187, 189
Anouilh, Jean, 193
*Antony and Cleopatra*, 108,
    196–202, 220
  variations on theme, 197
Appearance vs. reality motif, 95,
    121, 131, 151–52, 181, 190,
    204
*Arabian Nights*, 17
*Arcadia*, 90, 203
Armin, Robert, 204
Arnheim, Rudolf, 9, 162
Art-Film Germany, 118
Arturo, Ambrosio, 19
Arutanian, Rouben, 222–23

*As You Like It*, 89–94, 95, 203, 218
Asher, June, 220
Atkins, Zoe, 234
Avon Productions, 102
Azeglio, Lamberto, 19
Azzuri, Paulo, 62

Bacall, Lauren, 109
*Bad Sleep Well, The*, 149
Baldwin, Alec, 39
Baldwin, James, 165
Bale, Christian, 241
Ball, Robert Hamilton, 153
Bancroft, Anne, 198, 234
Bandello, Matteo, 41, 86
Banks, Leslie, 83
Bara, Theda, 43, 197
Barascq, Andre, 193
Barber, C. L., 75
Barker, William George, 29, 117
Barrie, Sir James, 91
Barrier, Edgar, 181
*Barry Lyndon*, 157
Barrymore, John, 44, 47, 132
Barton, Anne, 89
Bavaria Attelier, 123
Baxter, Keith, 75
Bayley, Hilda, 172
Bazin, Andre, 155
Beatty, Warren, 59
Beauman, Sally, 83
Beckett, Samuel, 206–207
Begg, Gordon, 24
Belleforest, 116
*Ben-Hur*, 199–201
Bender, Jack, 231–32
Benedict, Paul, 238

Benny, Jack, 234
Benson, F. R., 19, 29,
Benson, Frank, 102
Bentley, Eric, 7
Bergman, Ingmar, 70, 115, 210
Bergner, Elisabeth, 91
Bernhardt, Sarah, 117, 118, 233
Bernstein, Leonard, 59
Betterton, Thomas, 205
*Beyond the Law*, 214
Bierce, Ambrose, 25
*Big Show, The*, 216
*Birds, The*, 158
Birkett, Jack, 225
Birkett, Lord Michael, 10, 208
*Birth of a Nation, The*, 29, 118, 177
Bishop, Henry, 61
*Black Cat, The*, 147
*Black Commando*, 174
Blackton, J. Stuart, 42, 96, 101, 152, 205
Blair, Thomas A., 178
Blom, August, 117, 172
Bloom, Claire, 33, 39
*Blue Angel, The*, 153
*Blue City*, 150
*Blume in Love*, 226
*Bob & Carol & Ted & Alice*, 226
Boiastuau, 41
Bondarchuk, Sergei, 159
*Bonnie and Clyde*, 22, 59, 187, 198
Booth, Edwin, 30, 117, 236
Booth, John Wilkes, 236
Booth, Junius, 236
Borgnine, Ernest, 173
Borowitz, Katherine, 193
Bouchier, Dorothy, 172
Boulois, Max H., 174
Boyd, Stephen, 21
Boyd-Perkins, Eric, 200
*Boys from Syracuse, The*, 15
Bradley, Mrs. A. Ballard, 179
Bradley, David, 102–103, 178–79
Braham, Lionel, 92, 182
Bramlett, Bonnie and Delaney, 174

Branagh, Kenneth, 3, 79–84, 86–88, 97–98, 140–47, 167–70, 224, 226, 239, 241
Brando, Marlon, 104–106, 112–13
Brasseur, Pierre, 193
*Breathless*, 210
Breen, Joseph, 65
*Bride of Frankenstein*, 121
*Brigham Young*, 40
*Broken Lance*, 216
Bronson, Charles, 214
Brook, Peter, 206–210, 211, 212, 213
Brooke, Arthur, 41
Brooks, Mel, 234
Brown, Coral, 237
Brown, Joe E., 63, 65
Brown, John Mason, 122–23
Brown, Pamela, 33
Browning, Todd, 121
Brubeck, Dave, 174
Brusati, Franco, 52
Buchowetzki, Dimitri, 153
Bunuel, Luis, 225
Burbage, Richard, 5, 26–28, 34, 83, 89, 116, 152, 205, 206
Burge, Stuart, 9, 108–113, 161–66
Burnel, Adrian, 24
Burrough, Tony, 35
Burstyn, Ellen, 217
Burton, Richard, 21–24, 67, 105, 108, 125–26, 128–29, 131, 223, 236
Burton, Tim, 7
Bushman, Francis X., 43

*Cabinet of Dr. Caligari, The*, 153
*Cabiria*, 102
Cagney, James, 63, 65
Calhern, Louis, 105–106, 110
Calmette, Andre, 29
Camus, Albert, 115
Canby, Vincent, 206, 208, 215, 225, 226
Canineberg, Hans, 125
Cannon Releasing, 214

Canutt, Joe, 113, 202
Canutt, Yakima, 113
Capetanos, Leon, 226
Capra, Frank, 181
Cardiff, Jack, 92
Carney, Art, 217
*Carnival*, 172
*Carnival in Flanders*, 92
Carter, Helena Bonham, 98, 137
Caserini, Mario, 152
Cassavetes, John, 227–28
Castellani, Renato, 48–51, 53–55
Castellari, Enzo G., 150
*Castle of the Spider's Web*, 193, 223
Castle Rock, 167
*Catch My Soul*, 174
Cerf, Bennet, 105
Cerval, Claude, 148
Ceskoslovensky Film, 66
Chabrol, Claude, 148
Chamberlain, Richard, 109, 111,
    132–35
Chaplin, Charlie, 20
Chendrikova, Valentina, 211
Cheshire, Godfrey, 36
*Chimes at Midnight, The* (a.k.a.
    *Falstaff*), 74–78
Christie, Julie, 141–42
*Chronicles of England, Scotland,
    and Ireland*, 16
Churchill, Winston, 79–80
Cinthio, Giraldi, 151
*Citizen Kane*, 5–6, 76, 120, 154,
    156, 180
Cleopatra, 195
*Cleopatra*, 21–22, 197
Clift, Montgomery, 105
Close, Glenn, 136–37
Cloutier, Suzanne, 154
Cocchi, V., 219
Cocks, Jay, 190
Coe, Richard L., 127
Coffey, Warren, 171
Colbert, Claudette, 197
Coleridge, Samuel Taylor, 162
Colleran, Bill, 125–26

Collins, Amy Fine, 230
Collins, Bradley, 230
Colman, Ronald, 173
Color noir, 32
Columbia Pictures, 130, 167, 187,
    226
*Comedy of Errors, The*, 15
Comedy of forgiveness, 221
Comerio, Luca, 117
Commonwealth United, 108, 198
*Confessions of an Actor*, 122
*Cook, the Thief, His Wife, & Her
    Lover, The*, 228
Cooper, Gary, 216
Coote, Robert, 237
Coppola, Francis Ford, 193
Corbucci, Sergio, 150
Corliss, Richard, 88, 140, 167, 215
Corman, Chip (a.k.a. Andrea
    Giordana), 150
Corman, Roger, 40, 134
Cornell, Katharine, 198
Costello, Dolores, 62
Costello, Helene, 62
Courtenay, Tom, 238
Craig, Hardin, 17–18, 221
Croft, Emma, 94
Crowd, Samuel, 225
Crowther, Bosley, 102, 129, 193
Crutwell, Hugh, 87
Crystal, Billy, 141
Cukor, George, 44–48, 49, 91, 173
Cullen, R. J., 91
Cummings, Quinn, 238
Curran, William, 18
Curtis, Tony, 174
Curtiz, Michael, 48
Czinner, Paul, 91–93

D'Amico, Masolino, 52
*Daemonologie*, 175
Dal, Oleg, 212
Dali, Salvador, 225
Danes, Claire, 56–59
Daniel, Samuel, 71
*Das Wintermarchen*, 219

Daves, Delmer, 173
*David Copperfield*, 63
Davies, Anthony, 191
*Day in the Country*, 70
deGraft, Joe, 148
de Havilland, Olivia, 63
De Liguoro, Guiseppe, 205
de Mille, Agnes, 44
De Niro, Robert, 193
de Winter, Max, 120
Dean, James, 48–49, 51, 58, 147
*Death of a Salesman*, 115
*Death Wish*, 190
Dee, Sandra, 59
del Giudice, Filippo, 73
*Deliverance*, 199
Demicheli, Tullio, 25
DeMille, Cecil B., 5, 29, 80, 108, 141, 159, 197
Denby, David, 88–89, 140, 142, 167, 168
Dench, Judi, 69, 80, 86, 240
Dent, Alan, 120
Derek, John, 236
*Desdemona*, 172
Desfontaines, Henry, 19
*Devils, The*, 225
Devine, Andy, 44
Dews, Peter, 132
Dexter, John, 161, 163
DiCaprio, Leonardo, 56, 57, 59
Dieterle, William, 64
*Dirty Harry*, 190
Dixon, Audrey, 166
Dixon, Richard, 166
Dmytryk, Edward, 124, 215–16
Dobkin, David, 242
*Dog Day Afternoon*, 7
Domestic tragedy, 152
Donaldson, Prof. Peter, 122, 127
Donen, Stanley, 7
*Double Life, A*, 173, 233
Douglas, Paul, 193
Dowden, Edward, 221
Doyle, Pat, 82
*Dr. Kildare*, 132

*Dr. Faustus*, 41
*Dr. Strangelove*, 37, 210
*Dr. Zhivago*, 128
*Dracula*, 121
*Dresser, The*, 238
Dreyfuss, Richard, 238
*Drugstore Cowboy*, 78
Dual nature of man, 12
Dudley, M. B., 30
Duff, Mrs. Frances Robinson, 44
Duffy, Prof. Robert A., 121
Dunaway, Faye, 59
Dunlop, Frank, 218, 220
Dunne, Philip, 236
*Dvenadtsataia noch*, 96

Eagle Films Ltd., 161
*East of Eden*, 48, 58
*Easy Rider*, 198
Ede, Nicholas, 226
Edison, Thomas, 42
Edward IV, 27
*Edward Scissorhands*, 7
Edzard, Christine, 94
Eilers, Sally, 147
*Ein Sommernachtstraum*, 62
Eisenstein, Sergei, 129, 141, 157, 159, 180, 183
*El Cid*, 110, 198
Electronovision, 126
Eliot, T. S., 207
Elizabeth I, Queen, 13, 16, 26, 175
*Elstree Calling*, 24
Emerson, John, 177
*Emperor's Nightingale, The*, 66
*Endgame*, 206–207
Engel, Susan, 208
Enie, Eugene, 211
Evans, Joan, 58
Evans, Maurice, 73, 96, 185–87, 190, 223
Evans, Stephen, 80
Everett, Rupert, 241
*Everything You Always Wanted to Know About Sex*, 214
Eyre, Richard, 36

Fabbri, Pina, 219
*Faerie Queene, The*, 86
Fairbanks Sr., Douglas, 19, 20
*Fairy Queen, The*, 61
Faithful, Marianne, 130–31
*Falstaff* (a.k.a. *The Chimes at Midnight*), 74–78
Farrell, Nicholas, 239
Faust, Martin, 219
Fawkes, Guy, 175
Ferguson, Otis, 45
Feuillade, Louis, 205
Fiennes, Joseph, 239
Fiennes, Ralph, 239
Film noir, 119–20, 147, 150, 180, 215
Filmways, 130, 206
Finch, Jon, 187, 191
Fine Line, 97
Finlay, Frank, 165
Finney, Sir Albert, 238
*Firm, The*, 57
Fishburne, Laurence, 166, 168
*Five Kings*, 74
*Flash Gordon's Trip to Mars*, 180
Flockhart, Calista, 241
Flynn, Errol, 48
Fonda, Henry, 234–35
Fonda, Peter, 134, 231
Fontanne, Lynne, 21
*Forbidden Planet*, 223–24
Ford, Glenn, 173
Ford, John, 24–25, 32, 123, 156, 181, 193, 234
Forrest, Edwin, 152
*Fortunes of Falstaff, The*, 75
Fosse, Bob, 235
Fox, James, 94
Francis, Anne, 223
*Frankenstein*, 145
Free will vs. fate, 106, 160
Freindlich, b., 96
French, Valerie, 173
*Frenzy*, 163
Freres, Pathe, 152
Freud, Sigmund, 135–36

Fried, Yakow, 96
Furse, Roger, 122
*Future Shock*, 9

Gabold, Annelise, 208
Gade, Svend, 118–19
*Gamlet*, 127–29, 141, 145
Gardner, Helen, 197
Garrick, David, 117, 205
Garson, Greer, 105, 107
Gascoigne, George, 17
Gaskill, Charles, 197
Gassman, Vittorio, 227
Gavin, John, 59
Gemp, Robert, 30
Gender bending, 98, 118
Giaconda, Lisa Gherardini, 88
Giannetti, Louis, 4
Gibbons, Cedric, 44, 235
Gibson, Mel, 124, 135–40, 144
Gielgud, John, 7, 38, 75, 77, 105–106, 108, 110–11, 125, 127, 128–30, 134, 228–30
Gilbert, John, 43
Gill, Brendan, 162
Giordana, Andrea (a.k.a. Chip Corman), 150
Gleiberman, Owen, 240
Glen, Iain, 150
Glenesk, William, 123–24
Glenn, Grosvenor, 103
Globus, Yoram, 214
Glover, Julian, 202, 231
Godard, Jean-Luc, 210, 214–15
*Godfather*, 193
Godfrey, Derek, 69
Goethe, 117
Golan, Menahem, 214
*Good, the Bad, and the Ugly, The*, 150
*Goodbye Girl, The*, 237–38
*GoodFellas*, 57, 193
Goodman, Walter, 49
Gordon, Ruth, 173
Gould, Jack, 73
Gow, Gordon, 201

*Graduate, The,* 22, 59, 198
Grammaticus, Saxo, 116
Grand Prize Films, 185
Granger, Farley, 58
Grant, Richard E., 97
Grayson, Kathryn, 235
Green World comedy, 61, 64, 70, 86, 95, 221–23, 228, 232
Greenaway, Peter, 228–31
Greene, Robert, 41, 218
Greville-Bell, Anthony, 237
Gribbon, Eddie, 18
Griffin, Alice, 186
Griffith, D. W., 18, 20, 24–25, 29, 118–19, 122, 177, 234
Gritsus, Ionas, 211
Guazzoni, Enrico, 102, 192, 197
Guernsey Jr., Otis L., 102–103
Gunpowder Plot of 1605, 175

HBO, 232
Halberstadt, Ilona, 94
Halio, Jay, 134
Hall, Peter, 3–5, 10, 68–70
Hall, Tudor, 62
Halliwell, Lawrence, 94
Hallmark Entertainment, 132
*Hallmark Hall of Fame,* 73, 96–97, 222, 231
*Hamile,* 148
Hamlet
  as Byronic hero, 132–33
  as external character, 128
  as indecisive and effeminate, 117
*Hamlet,* 33, 114–50, 168, 176, 211–212, 242
  Burton-Gielgud, 161, 220
  Kenneth Branagh's, 10, 140–47
  Olivier's, 7, 73, 119–24, 129, 137–40, 149
  public perception of, 126–27
  variations on theme, 147–50
  Zeffirelli-Gibson, 10, 135–40
*Hamlet: Prinz Von Danemark,* 123–25
Handley, Tommy, 24

Hardinge, H. C. M., 172
Haney, Carol, 235
Harris, Julie, 58
Harris, Leonard, 126
Harris, Paul, 173
Harris, Rosemary, 96
Harrison, George, 134
*Harry and Tonto,* 217
Hart, Lorenz, 15
Hart, Moss, 236
Hartung, Philip T., 34, 107, 122
Harvey, Laurence, 49, 51, 220
Harvey, Tim, 88
Harwood, Ronald, 238
Hasso, Signe, 173
Hatch, Robert, 33–34, 50, 53, 120, 157–58, 206
Hathaway, Anne, 12, 16, 42, 165, 196
Havelock-Allan, Anthony, 162
Havens, Richie, 174
*Hawaiians, The,* 198
Hawke, Ethan, 242
Hawkins, Jack, 237
Hawks, Howard, 119, 181, 216
Hawthorne, Nigel, 97
Hazlitt, William, 61–62
*Hecatommithi,* 151
*Hedda,* 97
Hefner, Hugh, 97, 189
Hemingway, Ernest, 115
Henerson, James, 231
Henry IV, 72
*Henry V,* 33, 79–84, 130
  Branagh's, 79–84
  Olivier's, 73, 79–84, 119, 239
Henry VII, 27
Hepburn, Katharine, 24, 87, 89, 91, 233
Hepworth, Cecil, 117
Herbert, Jocelyn, 161
Herve, Jean, 19
Hervey, Irene, 15
Heston, Charlton, 4, 102–103, 108–109, 111–113, 141, 145, 178–79, 195, 196, 198–202

Hickox, Douglas, 237
Hills, Walter, 150
*Hiroshima Mon Amour*, 230
*Histoires Tragiques*, 116
*Historia Danica*, 116
*Historia Regum Britanniea*, 203
*Historiae Anglicae Libri XXVI*, 27
Hitchcock, Alfred, 6, 12, 24, 32,
    34, 119, 120, 123, 158, 163,
    213
Hoffman, Dustin, 59
Hoffman, Michael, 241
Holm, Ian, 69, 80, 138
Homosexuality, 160, 165–66, 169
*Hook*, 228
Hopkins, Anthony, 131
Hopkins, Miriam, 163
Hordern, Michael, 237
*House of Strangers*, 215
*House of the Seven Gables, The*,
    40
*House of Usher*, 40
Houseman, John, 103–104,
    106–107
Howard, Leslie, 44
Howard University, 166
Hubley, Season, 174
Hughes, Ken, 193
Hunter, Ian, 65
Hurlie, Eileen, 127
Hurst Park, 218
Hussey, Olivia, 51–52

*In the Arena*, 111
Internacional films Espagnol, 74
*Intolerance*, 177
*Ivan the Terrible*, 157
Ivory, James, 236–37

Jackson, Glenda, 198
Jackson, Russell, 87
Jacobi, Derek, 83, 141, 143
James I, King, 175, 220
Jannings, Emil, 153
Jarman, Derek, 224–26, 228–30
Jayston, Michael, 69

*Jazz Singer, The*, 117
Jefford, Barbara, 199
Jennings, Talbot, 46
Jhabvala, Ruth Prawer, 236
Jocelyn, Andre, 148
*Joe Macbeth*, 193
*Johnny Hamlet*, 149–50
Johnson, Arthur, 18
Johnson, Brian D., 171
Johnson, Karl, 226
Johnson, Richard, 111, 133, 200
Jones, Allan, 15
Jones, Ernest, 120
Jones, G. W., 102
Jones, Gwangwa, 166
Jonson, Ben, 5
Jordaens, Jacob, 230
Jordan, Dorothy, 20
Jory, Victor, 63
Joube, Romuald, 19
*Jubal*, 173
Julia, Raul, 227
*Julius Caesar*, 7, 13, 14, 73, 100–
    113, 176, 178, 198, 215, 220
June, Mildred, 18
*Jungle Book, The*, 172

Kaaya, Brad, 242
Kael, Pauline, 206–207, 209
Kanin, Garson, 173
Kapoor, Shashi, 237
Karloff, Boris, 40
*Karol Lear*, 210–214
Kauffmann, Stanley, 8, 83, 89, 142,
    167, 188
Kautner, Helmut, 147
Kean, Edmund, 29, 117, 152, 205
Keane, James, 29–31
Keaton, Michael, 87, 89
Keegan, Andrew, 241
Keel, Howard, 235
Kelly, Gene, 7
Kemble, John Philip, 117
Kempo, Matty, 19
Kendal, Geoffrey, 236
Kenner, William, 161

Kent, Charles, 62
Kermode, Frank, 10, 201
Kerr, Deborah, 105, 107
*King Henry V*, 6
*King Lear*, 149, 187, 203–217
  variations on theme, 215–17
*King of the Cowboys*, 216
Kingsley, Ben, 97–98
*Kiss Me Kate*, 24, 235
Kline, Kevin, 241
*Knife in the Water*, 189
Knoles, Harley, 172
Koehler, Robert, 126
Korda, Alexander, 31–32, 172
Korngold, Erich Wolfgang, 64
Kott, Jan, 68, 206–207
Kotto, Yaphet, 166
Kowalski, Stanley, 104
Kozintsev, Grigori, 127–29,
  210–213
Krasker, Robert, 49
Krauss, Werner, 62, 153
Kristiansen, Henning, 207
Kroll, Jack, 11
Kronenberger, Louis, 5
Kruger, Hardy, 147
Kubrick, Stanley, 37, 157, 210
*Kumonosu-Jo*, 193
Kurosawa, Akira, 149, 193–94, 216
Kyd, Thomas, 41, 115–16

*La Bisbetica Domata*, 19
*Lady From Shanghai, The*, 6
*Lady Jane*, 97
*Lady Macbeth of Minsk*, 192
*Lamegre apprivoisee*, 25
Landmann, Ludwig, 177
Lane, Rosemary, 15
Lang, Matheson, 172
Lange, Jessica, 217
Larlonova, Anna, 96
*Last Laugh, The*, 153
*Last Year at Marienbad*, 230
*Laura*, 40
Lawrence, Florence, 18, 42
Lawrence, Gertrude, 173

Le Lion films, 62
*Le rideaurouge: Ce soir, on joue
  Macbeth*, 193
*Le roi Lear au village*, 205
Leary, Timothy, 210
Leavis, F. R., 162
Ledger, Heath, 241
Lee, Robert N., 39–40
Lee, Rowland V., 39–40
LeGault, Lance, 174
Leigh, Janet, 6
Leigh, Jennifer Jason, 217
Leighton, Margaret, 133
Lemmon, Jack, 145
Lenfilm, 127–28, 210
Leonard, Robert Sean, 87
Leone, Sergio, 150
Leskov, Nikolay, 192
*Lethal Weapon*, 136
Liddell, Laura, 236
*Life and Death of King Richard the
  Third, The*, 29–31
Lillard, Matthew, 241
*Lives of the Noble Grecians and
  Romans*, 100
Lo Savio, Gerolamo, 42, 205
Lodge, Thomas, 89, 90
Lombard, Carole, 234
Loncraine, Richard, 35–36
*Looking for Richard*, 38, 233
Lopert Productions, 31
Loren, Sophia, 198
LoSavio, Gerolamo, 152
*Love's Labour's Lost*, 15, 241
Lowe, Arthur, 237
Lubin, Sigmund, 101
Lubitsch, Ernst, 234
Lucas, George, 228
Luchko, Katya, 96
Luhrmann, Baz, 14, 55–58
Luis, Lucia, 96
Lumet, Sidney, 7
Lunt, Alfred, 21
Lydon, James, 147
Lynch, David, 7
Lyons, Donald, 142

M-G-M, 43–46, 73, 103–105, 108, 110–11, 200, 223, 226, 235
*Macbeth*, 11, 102, 149, 154, 175–94, 223, 242
variations on theme, 192–94, 215
Macbeth, 8–9
Macdonald, Ross, 150
MacGowran, Jack, 210
MacGuffin, 163, 213
Mack, Max, 153
Mack, Maynard, 14
MacLiammoir, Micheal, 154–55, 158
Madden, Claran, 134
Madden, John, 239
*Magnificent Andersons, The*, 6, 76
*Maidstone*, 214
Mailer, Kate, 214
Mailer, Norman, 214
Mallett, Richard, 7
Maloney, Michael, 239
Maltin, Leonard, 173, 193
*Man From Laramie, The*, 216
*Man of the West*, 216
Mankiewicz, Herman, 181
Mankiewicz, Joseph, 7, 103–107, 110–12, 197, 215
Mann, Anthony, 216
Manvell, Roger, 6, 70, 91, 156, 186
*Marcantonio e Cleopatra*, 197
Margolis, Miriam, 57
Marks, John, 93
Marlowe, Christopher, 5, 26–28, 41
Marowitz, Charles, 207
Mars-Jones, Adam, 94
*Marty*, 104
Marx, Groucho, 23
*Mas fuerte que el amor*, 25
Maslin, Janet, 146–47
Mason, James, 105–106
Mason, Marsha, 238
*Masque of the Red Death, The*, 40
Massey, Raymond, 236
Mature, Victor, 235
Mayer, Karl, 91
Mayer, Louis B., 43

Maynard, Rodney, 178
Mazursky, Paul, 217, 226–28
McBride, Joseph, 76
McCarthy, Todd, 31, 58
McCartney, John, 34
McDonald, Gerald D., 156
McDowall, Roddy, 182, 223
McEnery, John, 52
McGoohan, Patrick, 173–74
McKellen, Ian, 10, 35–39
McLaglen, Andrew V. 25
*McLintock!*, 25
McLuhan, Marshall, 17, 74
*Mean Streets*, 57
Meersom, Lazare, 92–93
Melies, George, 31, 42, 62, 101, 117, 196, 205
Melly, George, 201
Melzer, Annabelle, 65, 96, 155, 186, 201, 213, 224
*Men Are Not Gods*, 172
*Men of Respect*, 193
Mendelssohn, Felix, 64
Menzies, William Cameron, 207
Merchant, Ismail, 236
Merchant-Ivory Productions, 5, 236
Mercury Productions, 153, 180
Mercury Theater, 74, 103, 180
Meredith, Burgess, 214–15
Messel, Oliver, 44
Meyer, Emile, 216
Meyniel, Juliette, 149
Michell, Keith, 173
*Midsummer Night's Dream, A*, 10, 43, 60–70, 177, 221, 232, 241
variations on theme, 70
*Midsummer Night's Sex Comedy, A*, 70
*Midwinter's Tale, A / In the Bleak Midwinter*, 239
Mifune, Toshiro, 149, 193
Miller, Arthur, 115
Mirisch, Walter, 199
Mirren, Helen, 69
Mogador, 153
Mongiardino, Renzo, 22

Moorehead, Agnes, 154
Morality play, 101
Moranis, Rick, 150
Mori, Masayuki, 149
Morley, Robert, 237
*Morning Glory*, 233–34
Moro, Christopher, 151
Morris, Desmond, 189
Mosfilm, 159
Mowbray, Alan, 235
*Much Ado About Nothing*, 13,
    85–89, 90, 95, 97, 99, 204, 218
    review, 3
Murray, Bill, 242
Murray, Prof. John Tucker, 44
*My Darling Clementine*, 5, 234–35
*My Own Private Idaho*, 78
*Mystery of Hamlet, The*, 118

NBC Motion Pictures, 231
Nakadai, Tatsuya, 216
*Naked Ape, The*, 189
Napier, Alan, 181
Naremore, James, 76
Naslov, Vladimir, 232
*Near in Blood*, 242
Negroni, Baldassare, 219
Neil, Hildegard, 199
Nelson, David, 216
Nelson, Judd, 150
Neumann, Hans, 62
*New Babylon*, 128
Nielsen, Asta, 118, 233
Nielsen, Leslie, 223, 226
Nietzsche, 115
*Night at the Opera, A*, 23
*Noche de Reyes*, 96
Nolan, Jeannette, 182
Norman, Marc, 239
North, Sir Thomas, 60, 100
Norris, Frank, 18
Novelli, Ermete, 205
Novello, Ivor, 172
Nunn, Trevor, 97–98

O'Brian, Hugh, 216

O'Brien, Edmond, 105
O'Hara, Maureen, 25
O'Herlihy, Dan, 182
O'Kenner, Hugh, 165
O'Neil, Barry, 219
Oedipus complex, 127, 129, 135,
    137, 141
*Oedipus the King*, 115, 135, 176
Oldman, Gary, 150
Oliver, Edna May, 44
Olivier, Laurence, 7, 31–35, 39,
    79–84, 91, 119–24, 131, 134,
    144, 146, 161, 162–63, 181,
    183, 200, 224, 226
Oman, Julia Tevelyan, 110
*Omega Man, The*, 198
*On The Town*, 7
Ono, Yoko, 225
*Ophelia*, 148
*Otello*, 152, 194
*Othello*, 13, 151–74, 176, 213, 242
    Olivier's, 164–65, 171, 220
    variations on theme, 172–74
    Welles's, 184
Ottenhoff, John, 3, 8
*Our Contemporary William
    Shakespeare*, 128

Pacheco, Rafael, 200
Pacino, Al, 10, 38–39, 193
Padovani, Lea, 154
Paltrow, Gwyneth, 240
*Pandosto*, 218
Panter-Downes, Mollie, 34, 53
Pappas, Irene, 198
*Parallel Lives, The*, 100
Parfitt, David, 80, 97
Parfitt, Judy, 109, 131
Parker, Oliver, 166–72
Parrott, T. M., 152
Pasternak, Boris, 128, 159, 211,
    212
Pastrone, Giovanni, 102
Paulig, Albert, 219
*Peer Gynt*, 102, 178
Pembroke, Lord, 17

Penner, Joe, 15
Persoff, Nehemiah, 216
*Peter Pan*, 91
Peter Snell Productions, 218
Pettet, Joanna, 174
Pfeiffer, Michelle, 217, 241
Phifer, Mekhi, 242
Phoenix, River, 79
Pickford, Mary, 19, 20
Pidgeon, Walter, 223
Pinewood Studios, 199
*Pit and the Pendulum, The*, 40
*Platoon*, 82
Plutarch, 60, 100–101, 195
Polanski, Roman, 187–92
Ponti, Carlo, 198
Porten, Henny, 152
Porter, Cole, 235
Porter, Eric, 202
Postlethwaite, Pete, 57
Powell, Dick, 63
Price, Dennis, 237
Price, Vincent, 40, 237
*Prime of Miss Jean Brodie, The*, 52
*Prince, The*, 101
*Prince of Players*, 236
*Prisoner of Zenda, The*, 142
*Prospero's Books*, 228–31
*Psycho*, 6
Pudovkin, V. I., 4, 213
Purcell, Henry, 61
*Put Money in Thy Purse*, 155

Quartermaine, Leon, 91
*Quiet Man, The*, 25

Randell, Ron, 235
Rank, J. Arthur, 49, 119
Rank of England, 119, 198–99
Ranous, William, 29, 152
*Rape of Lucrece, The*, 41
Rapf, Maurice, 52
Rathbone, Basil, 39–40, 44, 47–48
Ray, Satyajit, 237
Raye, Martha, 15
*Rear Window*, 123

*Rebecca*, 34, 120, 186
*Rebel Without a Cause*, 48, 58–59
*Red River*, 119, 216
Redemption saga, 77–78
Redgrave, Michael, 134
Redgrave, Vanessa, 52
Redmond, Moira, 220
Reed, Carol, 32
Reeves, Keanu, 78
Reifenstahl, Leni, 221
Reilly, William, 193
Reinhardt, Max, 10, 43, 62–64
Reisch, Walter, 172
Remick, Lee, 223
Renoir, Jean, 70
Republic Pictures, 180
*Repulsion*, 189
Resnais, Alain, 230
*Rest Is Silence, The*, 147–48
*Restoration*, 241
Revenge tragedy, 115
Rey, Fernando, 96, 199
Reynolds, Burt, 199
Rich, Frank, 31
Richard II, 71–72
Richard III, 27–29, 34–37, 39
  as Everyman, 34–35
*Richard III*, 10, 26–40, 79
  variations on theme, 39–40
Richardson, Ian, 69
Richardson, Tony, 129–32
Ridges, Stanley, 234
Rigg, Diana, 10, 69, 109, 237
Ringwald, Molly, 214, 227
*Rio Grande*, 25
Robards, Jason, 109, 111, 217
Robbins, Jerome, 59
Robertson, Cliff, 216
Robinson, Edward G., 215
Rodgers, Richard, 15
Rodolfi, Eleuterio, 19, 117
Rogers, Roy, 180
Roland, Gilbert, 150
Roman, Antonio, 25
Roman, Ruth, 193
*Romanoff and Juliet*, 59

*Romeo and Juliet,* 14, 41–59, 78, 130, 134, 136, 138, 176, 177, 187, 190, 220
  as anti-romantic cautionary fable, 13
  religious elements, 57
  variations on theme, 58–59
Rooney, Mickey, 63, 65
*Rosalynde,* 89
*Roseanna McCoy,* 58
*Rosemary's Baby,* 189
Rosemond, Anna, 219
*Rosencrantz and Guildenstern Are Dead,* 150
Ross, Herb, 237–38
Ross, Katharine, 59
Rosson, Hal, 92
Rota, Nino, 54
Roth, Tim, 150
Rothwell, Kenneth, 65, 96, 155, 186, 201, 213, 224
Rowlands, Gena, 227
Rozsa, Miklos, 173
Ruggle, Eleanor, 236
Russell, Ken, 225
Ryder, Winona, 39
Rye, Stellan, 62

Sahu, Koshore, 148
*Sandpiper, The,* 21
*Santa Fe Satan,* 174
Sarandon, Susan, 227
Sarte, Jean, 115
*Savage Messiah,* 225
Schaefer, George, 185–86, 222–23
Schaffner, Franklin, 102
Schell, Maximilian, 123–25, 130
Scheuer, Philip K., 19
Schickel, Richard, 216
Schildkraut, Joseph, 172
Scofield, Paul, 80, 208
Scorsese, Martin, 57, 193
*Searchers,* 32
*Sebastiane,* 225
Sellars, Peter, 214
Selznick, David O., 32

*Sen Noci Svatojanske,* 66
Seneca, 28
Sennett, Mack, 18, 20
Sessions, John, 239
*Seven Samurai, The,* 193
Sevens, Marti, 173
*Seventh Seal, The,* 210
Sevilla, Carmen, 200
*Shadow of a Doubt,* 163
Shaftel, 198
*Shakespeare in Love,* 239–41
"Shakespeare: The Animated Tales," 232
Shakespeare, William
  and academia, 10–12
  and Anne Hathaway, 12, 16, 165, 196
  as playwright, 4–6, 11, 14, 16, 26–28, 41, 60, 71, 75, 79–80, 85, 89–90, 95, 100, 116, 151–52, 195–96, 203–204, 218
  as pre-Freudian psychologist, 61, 154–55
  and source materials, 27–28, 41–42, 60–61, 71, 86, 89, 95, 100, 116, 151, 175–76, 195–96, 203–204, 218–19, 220–21
*Shakespeare Wallah,* 236–37
Shakespearean
  cinema, 3–8, 10–11
  critics, 5
  plays as literary works, 3
  soliloquy, 7
  themes, 13
*Shane,* 216
Sharif, Omar, 109
Shaw, George Bernard, 13
Shaw, Jessica, 241
Shaw, Robert, 199
Shaw, Sebastian, 173
Shearer, Norma, 43–45, 48
Sheedy, Ally, 150
*Shekspir i Kino,* 159
Shelley, Mary, 145
Shentall, Susan, 49, 51
Shepard, Sam, 242

*Shepheard's Calender, The,* 90
*Shining, The,* 157
Shostakovich, Dmitri, 128, 211
*Siberian Lady Macbeth,* 193
Sidney, George, 235
Sidney, Sir Philip, 90, 203
Simmons, Jean, 121
Simon, John, 144, 206, 231
Simon, Michel, 193
Simon, Neil, 237–38
Sinatra, Frank, 7
*Skyjacked,* 201
Sliverstone, Alicia, 241
Smiley, Jane, 217
*Smiles of a Summer Night,* 70
Smith, Maggie, 165
Smith, Mel, 97
Smoktunovsky, Innokenti, 128
Snell, Peter, 108, 198–202, 220
Social comedy, 86, 95, 99
*Son of Frankenstein,* 40
Sondheim, Stephen, 59
Soneland, Senta, 219
Sontag, Susan, 226
Sophocles, 115, 176, 210
Sorvino, Paul, 57
*Soylent Green,* 201
Spacey, Kevin, 39
*Spanish Tragedy,* 116
*Spellbound,* 119
Spenser, Edmund, 86, 90
Spewack, Samuel and Bela, 235
Spielberg, Steven, 5, 228
*Squaw Man,* 29
*Stage Struck,* 233
Staunton, Imelda, 97
Steiger, Rod, 173
Stevens, George, 216
Stewart, James, 32, 216
Stewart, Sophie, 92
Stiles, Julia, 241, 242
Stone, Oliver, 82
Stoppard, Tom, 150, 239
Stowe, Percy, 222
*Strange Brew,* 150
*Strange Illusion,* 147

*Strangers on a Train,* 163
Strasberg, Susan, 233
Strathairn, David, 241
*Streetcar Named Desire, A,* 104
*Strictly Ballroom,* 55
Strunk Jr., Prof. William, 44
Stubbs, Imogen, 98
*Summer and Smoke,* 49
*Supposes,* 17
Suschitzky, Peter, 69
*Suspicion,* 163
*Sylvia Scarlett,* 91

*Tale of Two Cities,* 63
*Tamburlaine the Great,* 26
*Taming of a Shrew, The,* 17
*Taming of the Shrew, The,* 11, 13,
    16–25, 51–52, 61, 85–86, 122,
    136, 218, 241
  silent film versions, 19
  variations on theme, 24–25
Tarkington, Booth, 181
Tasker, Harold, 103
Tate, Sharon, 189
Taubman, Howard, 127
*Taxi Driver,* 190
Taylor, Elizabeth, 21–24, 125, 197
Taylor, Joseph, 152
Taylor, Sam, 20, 24
Teasdale, Verree, 65
*Tempest, The,* 220–32
*Tempest, The: by William
    Shakespeare, as Seen Through
    the Eyes of Derek Jarman,*
    224–26
*Ten Days That Shook the World,*
    141
*10 Things I Hate About You,* 241
Thalberg, Irving, 43–46
Thanhouser, Edwin, 43, 219, 222
Thanhouser, Gertrude, 43, 219
*Theatre of Blood,* 237
*Thief of Baghdad, The,* 172
*Things to Come,* 207
Thomas, Bob, 126
Thomas, Dave, 150

Thomas, Kristin Scott, 37
Thomashefsky, Harry, 206
Thompson, Emma, 89
Thompson, Howard, 110
Thorp, Margaret F., 155
*Thousand Acres, A*, 217
*Three Faces of Eve, The*, 32
*Throne of Blood*, 193
*To Be or Not To Be*, 234
Toffler, Alvin, 9
*Tom Jones*, 131
*Tombstone*, 5
*Touch of Evil*, 108
*Tower of London*, 39–40
Tracy, Spencer, 24, 87, 216
Tragedy of character, 114, 176,
    196, 204
Tragedy of fate, 156, 176
*Tragedy of King Richard II, The*,
    71–74
Tragedy of middle age, 187
*Tragedy of Othello, the Moor of
    Venice, The*, 153–59
Travers, Peter, 56
Tree, Sir Herbert, 177, 222
*Trial*, 6
Trnka, Jiri, 66–68, 232
Trojan, Vaclav, 67
*Trouble in Paradise*, 234
*True Chronicle History of King
    Leir, The*, 203
Tucci, Stanley, 241
Turner, Florence, 96
Turturro, John, 193
*Twelfth Night*, 90, 95–99, 218
Twentieth Century–Fox, 198, 234,
    236
*Two Cents Worth of Hope*, 49
*Two Gentlemen of Verona, The*,
    15
*2001: A Space Odyssey*, 157
Tyler, Parker, 104, 105
Tynan, Kenneth, 188–89

Ulmer, Edgar G., 147
*Un Chien Andalou*, 225

United Artists (U.A.), 19, 20, 35,
    237
Universal Pictures, 15, 39
*Unmarried Woman, An*, 226
Urban, Charles, 102, 222
Ustinov, Peter, 59

Valli, Alida, 148
Van Doren, Mark, 9
Van Eyck, Peter, 148
Van Horne, Harriet, 132
Van Sandt, Gus, 78
Vann, Mary Lois, 133
Vaughan, Virginia, 223
Vaughn, Robert, 110, 216
*Venetian Nights*, 172
*Venus and Adonis*, 41
Verdi, 67, 184, 194
Vergil, Polydore, 27
Verona Productions, 21, 48
*Vertigo*, 32, 213
Victoria, Queen, 29
Vierny, Sacha, 230
Vining, Edward, 118
Vipin, G., 96
Viraladze, Simon, 211
Virtue vs. power, 215
Vitagraph, 15, 29, 42, 62, 96, 152,
    196, 205

Wagner, Robert, 216
*Waiting for Godot*, 206
Wajda, Andrjez, 193
Wakhevitch, George, 207
*Walk on the Wild Side*, 49
Walsh, Moira, 21, 50, 104
Walsh, Raoul, 119
Walton, William, 82
*War and Peace*, 159
Warde, Ernest, 205–206
Warde, Frederick, 30–31, 206
Warner, David, 69
Warner, Jack, 43, 63, 65
Warner Bros., 63–64, 125, 135, 161,
    198
Washington, Denzel, 87

Wayne, John, 25, 32, 216
Webster, Margaret, 4, 73
Weiler, A. H., 96, 159
Weill, Kurt, 14, 115
Welch, Elizabeth, 225
Welles, Orson, 3–6, 9, 32, 74–78,
    103, 108–109, 120, 178,
    180–85, 186, 188, 190, 199,
    224, 226, 242
  as Falstaff, 75–76
  and Othello, 153–59, 165
Wellman, Paul I., 173
Wells, H. G., 207
West, Anthony, 53
*West Side Story*, 53, 59, 78
Whale, James, 121
White, Liz, 166
White, Tony Joe, 174
*White Heat*, 119
Whiting, Lenny, 51–52
Whitmore, James, 235
*Who's Afraid of Virginia Woolf?*, 21
Widmark, Richard, 216
Wilcox, Fred McLeod, 223–24
*Wild at Heart*, 7
*Wild Bunch, The*, 190
Wilds, Prof. Lillian, 125
Wilimovsky, Jain, 179
Will, Barker, 19
William, Warren, 147
Williams, Heathcote, 226
Williams, Robin, 141
Williams, Tennessee, 49
Williamson, Nicol, 130–32
Willow Productions, 178
Winslet, Kate, 142–43

*Winter's Tale, The*, 218–20
Winters, Shelley, 173
Wirth, Franz Peter, 123–25
Wolfe, Thomas, 218
Wolfit, Donald, 238
Wong, Anna May, 24
Wood, Natalie, 58
Wood, Peter, 132–34
Woodfall Productions, 129
Woodward, Joanne, 32
World Northal Films, 224
Worner Film, 153
Worth, Irene, 208
Wright, Frank Lloyd, 182
Wyler, William, 5, 108
Wynn, Keenan, 235

Yanshin, M., 96
Yarvet, Yuri, 211
*Yiddish King Lear*, 206
Yordan, Philip, 193, 215
York, Michael, 52
York, Susannah, 199
*Young Lions, The*, 124
Yutkevich, Sergei, 159–61

Zanuck, Richard, 198
Zecca, Ferdinand, 196
Zeffirelli, Franco, 8, 14, 21, 22–24,
    51–56, 59, 69, 124, 130, 134,
    135–40, 146, 167, 187, 190,
    220, 224, 226
Zemeckis, Robert, 228
Zimbalist Jr., Efrem, 215
Zimmerman, Paul D., 189
Zorkaija, Neia, 212